D1742988

—1866—

THE UNITED STATES DURING THE WAR

TRAVELS IN AMERICA

Auguste Laugel

Volume 166

APPLEWOOD BOOKS

Carlisle, Massachusetts

Thank you for purchasing an Applewood book. Applewood reprints America's lively classics—books from the past that are still of interest to modern readers. This facsimile was printed from digital files prepared by the Library of Congress. Applewood's facsimile edition of this work may include library stamps, scribbles, and margin notes as they exist in the original book at the Library of Congress. These interesting historical artifacts celebrate the place of the book in the library's collection. In addition to these artifacts, the work may have additional errors that were either in the original, in the scans prepared by the Library of Congress, or introduced as we prepared the books for printing. If you believe the work has such errors, please let us know by writing to us at the address below.

First Edition

ISBN: 1-4290-0405-3 (Paperback)

For a free copy of our current print catalog, write to:
Applewood Books
PO Box 365
Bedford, MA 01730

For more complete listings,
visit us on the web at:
awb.com

THE

UNITED STATES

DURING

THE WAR.

LONDON

PRINTED BY SPOTTISWOODE AND CO

NEW-STREET SQUARE

THE

UNITED STATES

DURING

THE WAR.

BY

AUGUSTE LAUGEL.

LONDON:

H. BAILLIÈRE, 219 REGENT STREET.

NEW YORK:
BAILLIÈRE BROTHERS, BROADWAY.

MELBOURNE:
F. F. BAILLIÈRE, COLLINS STREET EAST.

PARIS: GERMER BAILLIÈRE, RUE DE L'ÉCOLE DE MÉDECINE.

MADRID: C. BAILLY BAILLIÈRE, PLAZA DEL PRINCIPE D'ALFONSO.

1866.

E167
L37

INTRODUCTION.

———◆———

THE CIVIL WAR in the UNITED STATES will one day be numbered among the greatest events of history in the nineteenth century. The principles it has called into action, the future of a whole continent dependent on its issue, the sacrifices it has entailed on one of the first nations of the world, everything raises it above those miserable conflicts where mean ambitions and bygone interests wear themselves away.

I shall always consider myself fortunate to have been able to visit the United States during this period of their history, and to have known the principal actors in this great drama, that for several years has held the world in expectation. Perhaps I did not escape the influence of the passions by which I felt myself surrounded, and I shall not seek to deny that I yielded with a certain complacency to the emotions which came upon me. I heard those great, those beautiful words—liberty, equality, emancipation—that in my country the men of my generation have as yet but murmured, resounding in their full depth. I found myself in a living world, where action was sister to thought, where the pen could change into a sword, where principles were at the head of armies, where glory had a reward, and eloquence an object!

My youth no longer felt itself prematurely old ; a soft, a hidden ardour, penetrated slowly and dissolved, as by enchantment, the learned doubts, the ironical reserves, the selfish discouragements that we almost all carry with us in our chilled consciences.

I also felt a singular pleasure in finding myself in a real democracy. I am not one of those who accept democracy only with a sort of melancholy resignation, as a fact, as a social necessity, against which all resistance would be vain ; I like it from taste ; I admire it from preference, when it puts equality under the ægis of liberty, and not under that of despotism. It suits me better to find equals among men, rather than inferiors. '*Nihil humani a me alienum puto.*' But this upright, healthy, vital feeling, that draws man towards man, that has no need of dress, fictions, rules, formalities, is hardly to be found pure and unalloyed in old societies. Too much envy and hatred are mixed with equality, when it comes after too long a servitude. I find a kind of baseness in its ever anxious pride, in its tacit or avowed intention to sacrifice to its own interests the sacred interests of liberty, in its hackneyed flatteries of the multitude, in its instinctive respect for force, in its cruel and unjust suspicions, in its envious fear of any solitary greatness. Habits of thought are slow to be changed.

In the United States, liberty and equality are closely mingled in equal proportions to make up the democratic spirit. Everything has favoured this happy marriage: the immense territories that offer independence to any industrious man, the respect necessarily accorded to labour in a new society, the uncertainty and instability of destinies, the narrow circumscription of the functions of the state, the absence of all historic and traditional guidance, the necessity under which the citizens lie of constantly defending their rights and interests, the complete separation of Church and State, which makes the consciences of all familiar with the exercise of the highest and most delicate of liberties.

Democratic theorists have expressed three fears: they have thought that the excessive development of individualism would be fatal to the disinterested passion to which is given the name of patriotism; that the dominion of uncontrolled and unbridled majorities in the midst of every liberty would destroy the sense of liberty itself; lastly, they have thought that a general and uniform cultivation would gradually reduce all intelligences to the level of a common mediocrity.

I do not believe that the United States have thus far justified any of these fears: their patriotism has been striking enough to all the world. What have they not sacrificed for that Union which Europe was pleased to call chimerical; to that Constitution, which is not only the charter of their liberties, but the security of their national grandeur? On this first point it seems to me there is really nothing to be said, and all commentary would be vain.

Will it be said that liberty is dying out in a country which, in the midst of a frightful war, has exercised all its great political functions as quietly as in the past;

which has asked no other weapons but the law to defend itself from the savage fury of treason? Whatever the calumniators of the United States may have said, liberty has not received any severe wound in the midst of so many convulsions and catastrophes. Never has the nation uttered cowardly shrieks to invoke a Cæsar; never has she dreamed of buying victory by her own servitude.

Lastly, is it true that democracy is the enemy of all greatness and all originality, that it destroys independence of mind, that its manners are coarse, common, and tyrannical, that it respects nothing but wealth and success? More than one foreigner, thrown into the eddies of American democracy, like a buoy tossed by every wave, has perhaps received these impressions. From habit you no longer see a ground-work of common places and vulgarities, that is familiar to you from childhood, in your own country. It is this ground-work that first strikes the eye in a new country, and for a long time you see nothing else. American coarseness has besides something sharper, more aggressive, more living, and, for that very reason, more unpleasant than that humble, resigned, almost bovine coarseness of European multitudes. But in no country have you the right to judge a nation by the chance pictures of the public squares and streets. Nothing is, I think, more difficult than to justly appreciate the American character; to distinguish what is essential from that which is merely accidental; what belongs to the soil from that which is only an impure and temporary alloy. Americans sometimes say that no one can understand them but themselves; and I have heard so many ridiculous judgments passed upon them, that I am not far from thinking they are right.

At once ardent and cold, irritable and patient, vindictive and generous, communicative and reserved, grasping and prodigal, the American seems at first a tissue of contradictions. You are astonished to find so much cunning with so much frankness, such deep-laid plans under such easy indifference, such simple habits in the midst of wealth, such great refinement in obscure situations, so much diplomacy in the village, so much rusticity in the city. The American is not systematic; he always subordinates the means to the end; he can profit by circumstances, by men, even by chance. What he cannot carry by force he gains by patience, but he does not wear out his patience when audacity will succeed. There are no illusions for him: he has deep feelings, but no sentimentality. He is never imposed upon: in the statesman, the priest, the orator, he looks only for the man.

Also, I believe him to surpass all nations and all races in the knowledge of the human heart. That is his great, his one, his insatiable curiosity; art, abstract ideas, nature, philosophy, come very far behind. His memory seems able to contain all names, all genealogies, all anecdotes, all dates: if he studies a doctrine, the sectary interests him as much as the sect. He loves the poet as much as the poem. Longfellow, Bryant, Lowell, are personal friends for all Americans; they can sit by every hearth, all belongs to them; they are the real kings of this democracy, said to be so vulgar and rapacious, and that is represented on its knees before the almighty dollar. If an American travels, it is to meet men; like Poussin, he always requires figures in a picture; what surprises him the most in any place is that he should be there; he has not yet reached the point of flying from himself, and seeking the half-sleep of sad contemplations; he is eminently sociable, but his sociability is not that common-place amiability that goes through empty forms: it is more exacting, it asks the new-comer, the unknown : Who are you? what do you bring me? what can you teach me? are you better than I am? are you a man? do you excel in anything? do you know how to cut down this tree, or can you translate Homer? He casts the line into all consciences, and, above all, despises useless people, folly, stupidity, and mental idleness.

No matter how much he may be imbued with the spirit of equality, he is always looking for superiors; but he can recognise a superior in a log-house in Maine as quickly as in a palace in the Fifth Avenue; under a farmer's coat as well as a pastor's gown.

In the very depths of his religion, I still find the same social instinct: he needs a doctrine that penetrates deeply into the abysses and windings of the human soul, that analyses its contradictions, its fantastic tendencies, its strangeness, with an almost cruel curiosity; or a religion that brings God down to man—a human, reforming, fraternal Jesus; he loves poetry, for poetry is nothing if not personal, if it does not touch the most vibrating chords of the soul. History could not be neglected by so political a people, and one so fond of

living realities. Bancroft, Prescott, Motley, Hildreth,
testify sufficiently to the natural aptitude of the American mind for historical studies. It seems to me, on the
other hand, ill-adapted to metaphysical speculation : in
Emerson, an exquisite, poetical, active mind, at once firm
and supple, I find on the whole a moralist rather than
a philosopher, a sort of Montaigne—like him, fleeting,
capricious, with less wit and more depth, less grace
and more faith, but above all, profoundly human.

The sagacity, the finesse, and the art of moral diag-
nostic which are the privilege of the American character,
are not incompatible with profound ignorance and great
simplicity. Minds are not cast in uniform moulds.
They are moulded from early youth by the acci-
dents of life. There is always a certain proportion
between aptitudes and wishes. There are no dream-
ing, unclassified, misunderstood people. Hopes are
never fixed on too far-distant objects. An American
is not fond of complaining ; he is too proud, and
at the same time too clever ; he knows that complaints are the cry of weakness ; he is always contented
with his house, his wife, his children, his horses, his
fields ; with the school-master he pays ; with the
member of Congress for whom he has voted ; the President to whom he gave his support. If he receives
an insult he says nothing to any one : he will treat his
enemy as long as he can with an outside politeness, in
order not to give him the pleasure of a noisy outbreak
and insults. He is a sure and faithful friend, though he
does not expect too much from friendship for himself.
He has few illusions, but he is happier than we are, for

he has never had any, and we suffer in losing ours. From childhood he has looked at the realistic sharp side of things, without deceitful prisms or false colours; the education given to him does not throw him into life a stranger to everything, and everywhere deceived. The Americans are unacquainted with those agonies of fine minds, nurtured on chaste thoughts, cradled in sweet dreams, and suddenly brought in contact with a living, cold, crowded world : they never pursue the impossible, and ask nothing but from will and intelligence. Those are the weapons that are early sharpened: they believe that intelligence leads to virtue, and that will alone can attain to it. Their morality has been dipped in the muddy river of life, but it only comes out the more invulnerable.

There is perhaps something severe in this way of looking at life, in this submission to hard realities, and this divorce from all chimeras : woman fortunately appears in the midst of all this, like a ray and sunbeam of poetry; so hard to himself, the American always preserves for her a delicate and subtile tenderness. She is his equal, his joy, his true companion, the pride of his hearth. They sought each other, and chose freely. She did not come with downcast eyes, mute and timid, but with open hand and raised head; she is his ally and counsellor, the consoler and inspirer : beautiful, smiling, adorned, you think her frivolous; she smiles on the earth, as says the Persian poet, but a virile education has implanted in her heart a sentiment of duty proud and almost heroic. With her, alone perhaps in the world, the conjugal is stronger than the maternal love.

Her children have the future, her husband has only her. Both ask from the latter affection rather than respect. They think they have done enough when they have fitted them to live as they have lived themselves, and have taught them to value independence above all things.

When I see the light arrows that the old world throws at the new fly past, *telum imbelle sine ictu*, I always remember three things : the United States have shown that men can found a Government on reason, where equality does not stifle liberty, and democracy does not yield to despotism ; they have shown that a people can be religious when the State neither pays the Church nor regulates belief; they have given to woman the place that is her due in a Christian and civilised society. Nothing can take from them these three claims to glory.

A. L.

CONTENTS.

———◆———

.

THE UNITED STATES

DURING THE WAR.

CHAPTER I.

THE CAUSE OF THE WAR.

UNTIL the year 1860 the United States had escaped all the dangers which threaten democracies. The great republic had struck on none of the rocks signalised by Montesquieu, and foreseen, it is said, by the austere patriotism of Washington. She proudly entitled herself the 'model republic.' With no standing army, almost without a police, protected against political revolutions by the remembrance of her first President and by the constitution of the central power, strong against foreign enemies, uniting the advantages of political unity to those of decentralisation, she proved to the world that the spirit of liberty and the spirit of equality could go hand in hand, and that democracies do not perforce descend the path which leads to servitude.

But what was the result of the election of Mr. Lincoln? In a few months that grand body which seemed so full of life and strength fell into decomposition; the equilibrium so nicely established by the authors of the constitution between the federal government and separate States was violently broken; two armies disputed for the capital; the explosions of hatred and anger which burst forth on the other side of the Atlantic equalled in violence all that we might expect from two peoples inspired by historical and secular enmity. Europe watched with astonishment the unbridled passions of civil war, and waited for events to resolve her doubts.

This war was, however, but the last and bloody episode of a moral and political struggle which began long years before, and left its traces throughout the history of the United States. Two fundamental questions agitated the combatants—a constitutional question, and the question of slavery—but in the origin the first alone was stated; on one banner we read *Secession*, and on the other *Union*. One side claimed the right for any State to retire at will from the federation, and the other asserted that the sovereignty was vested in the federal power alone, and that no State could free itself from its obligations to the Union. What was at first this right of secession? Did it rest upon an exact interpretation of the American constitution? or was it contrary to that constitution, in opposition to the ideas of those who had founded, interpreted, and applied it until this time? The very principles of the federation were involved in this grave question. ' There is,' says Montesquieu, ' a strong probability that all men would have been obliged to live always under the government of one, if they had not imagined a sort of constitution which has all the interior advantages of a republican government, and the exterior strength of a monarchical one —I speak of the federative republic. This form of government is a convention by which several bodies politic consent to become citizens of a state larger than they wish to form. It is a society of societies which forms a new one, capable of enlarging itself by new associates who join themselves to it. Any one who should attempt a usurpation could not be equally accredited to all the confederate States. If he became too powerful in one, he would alarm all the rest; if he subjugated a part, the one which still remained could yet resist him with an independent force from that which he had usurped, and overwhelm him before he had finally established himself. If some sedition should occur with one of its members, the others could quell it. Should there be some abuse in one quarter the healthy States would correct it. This State may perish on one side and remain strong on the other. The confederation may be dissolved, and the confederates remain sovereign.'

It is impossible to express more forcibly the necessity in which the several members of the confederation are placed, of abandoning a part of the sovereignty in favour of a central power, and the right that this power possesses of quelling rebellions and repressing the abuses and usurpations of the confederates. Montesquieu admits, it is true, the possibility of a dissolution; but if we scrutinize narrowly the sense of his concise

formulæ, we shall find that he considers it as an acci-
dent, as the result of the decay of one of the limbs
of the social body. The voice of a single confederate
can alone provoke a dissolution by reclaiming the
integrity of his sovereignty; and this sovereignty,
according to Montesquieu, can only be restored by
the dissolution of the Union itself. But let us leave
political theories; the American constitution is too
recent, the traditions of American politics have passed
through too few generations to obliterate its sense.
When the representatives of the divers English colonies
having become later as many independent States, sealed
their union, and adopted a common constitution, did
they pretend to only construct a momentary political
alliance, or to found a durable republic? Were they
bargaining with time, or did they desire to transmit this
work to the farthest generations? Did they reserve
the principle of separate States? or did they ask of all
the States the eternal sacrifice of that portion of sovereignty necessary to the federal power? Whoever is
familiar with the history of the American revolution,
can, it would seem, reply without hesitation to these
questions. Democracies, although they must in their
commencements struggle against royalties, so called
legitimate, have also need of a certain legitimacy—that
is, there are some things they must protect from the
attacks of time, the fluctuations of human wishes; or
else let themselves drift into anarchy. No man builds
on the sand. At the end of the last century, we see
at first the thirteen rebel colonies of America bound
during the revolutionary war by a simple alliance,

and not yet forming a Confederation. England had then for adversary a league; the Congress was a diet composed of sovereign States, or States struggling to obtain sovereignty. Motley, the American historian, has compared it to the States-general of the old Dutch republic, or to the present Germanic Diet. After the war, the league fell rapidly into decomposition; the inglorious remembrances of this time have been swallowed up in the grandeur and power since attained by the republic, but it is not without instruction to recall what Americans gained by the Union.

'At the end of the war,' writes Motley, 'when our independence was recognised in 1783, we were rapidly falling into a state of complete impotence, imbecility, and anarchy. We had assured our independence, but we had not founded a nation, we were not a body politic. It was impossible to apply the laws, repress insurrections, or obtain the payment of debts; there was no security for person or property. Great Britain had concluded a treaty of peace with us, but scornfully refused to accord us a treaty of commerce and amity, not because we had been rebels, but because we were not a State—because we were but the half-dissolved league of quarrelsome provinces, incapable to guarantee the stipulations of a treaty of commerce; we were even unable to fulfil the conditions of the treaty of peace, and obtain conformably to the stipulations the payment of debts due to British subjects, and Great Britain refused in consequence to abandon the military posts which she occupied outside our frontiers. Twelve years after the recog-

nition of our independence, we were humiliated by
the sight of foreign soldiers occupying a long chain
of fortresses south of the great lakes, and on our own
soil.   We were a confederation : we were sovereign
States, and such were the fruits of that confederation
and that sovereignty!   It was up to the present day
the darkest hour of our history.   'The constitution
of the United States put an end to this situation ; it
marked the triumph of the *federal* or *national* party
over the party which even then struggled to give the
greatest possible extension to State rights.   Let us
listen on this point to the testimony of contempo-
raries.   The convention assembled to prepare the constitution, thus express themselves in recommending
its adoption to the people.'   In all our deliberations
we have constantly kept in view what seemed to us
the greatest interest of every true American, the
consolidation of our Union, with which is connected
our prosperity, our security, perhaps our national
existence.'   What says Henry, one of the adversaries
of the project?   'That the government is a consolidated government is perfectly evident.'   The constitution says, 'we the people' instead of 'we the
States,' thus it is the consolidated national government of the people of all the States.   The Supreme
Court, the constitutional authority par excellence,
speaks still more distinctly.   The new government
once established, the court expresses itself thus : ' It
has been said that the States were sovereign, that they
were completely independent, and were united together
by a league.   This is true ; but when these allied sove-

reignties have converted their league into a government; when they have converted their congress of ambassadors into a legislature charged with the promulgation of laws, the character in which the States appear to us has undergone a change.'

The political form which the United States have given themselves does not, then, consist in the superposition of one sovereignty upon other sovereignties; nowhere in the constitution is the sovereignties of States mentioned; this constitution is the charta of a great people. 'We, the people of the United States, to ensure a more perfect union, and to ensure the benefits of liberty to ourselves and to our posterity, we ordain and establish this constitution.' The States, in fact, do not possess one of the ordinary attributes of sovereignty. They can neither coin money, nor emit bank notes, nor maintain an army and navy, nor give letters of marque, nor make treaties with foreign powers, nor hold diplomatic relations with them, nor confer titles of noblesse. That which, until the civil war of the few last years, most struck Europeans in the political order of the United States, was the degree of self-government practised in the private affairs of the States, the absence of all those hindrances which in the old monarchical States hampered individual action and the liberty of associations, whatever their nature and object. Many minds had come to the conclusion that the founders of the American constitution had left the sovereignty to the States; whereas, they have vested it entirely in the president, in the supreme court, and in the congress. If we compare the attributes of the President of the United States to those of the constitutional sovereign of Great Britain, we are forced to confess that it is the President who has the most power.

The President alone is, by the constitution, the Commander-in-chief, not only of the army and navy of the United States, but also of the militia of the different States, when he sees fit to call it to the service of the United States. The President has the pardoning power in case of a crime against the United States; he has the power, with the advice and consent of the Senate, to make treaties; he names, with the advice and consent of Congress, ambassadors, consuls, judges of the supreme court, and all the officers of the United States; he chooses his ministers; he can take them and keep them even when they have not, or no longer possess the sympathy of congress, the responsibility of the President counterbalancing the ministerial irresponsibility. Each State represents in reality in the American Union only an administrative subdivision; they are what would be a department in France, if by a magic wand the prefect could be changed to a governor named by the inhabitants, the councils general to deliberative chambers legislating on departmental affairs. Administratively, we may say the State is all, politically it is nothing. A simple citizen can, as a citizen of the United States, hold in check the whole power of a State, for there is a supreme court specially invested with the power of settling 'all the disputes between two or several States, between one State and the *citizens* of another State.' The President knows nothing of States, he only knows individuals. He takes oath to the constitution, and that 'is and will be the supreme law of the country, notwithstanding all that might be contrary to it in the constitution or the laws of a State.'

All who have studied with care the American constitution have never interpreted it otherwise than as the expression of a national consolidated government, resting on the direct and exclusive sovereignty of the people. No democracy recognises any other sovereignty than its own; it cannot do so and be logical; for, does there exist a people of Maryland, a people of Massachusetts, a people of Virginia? The constitution was adopted by the whole American people. It was ratified, not by the States, but by the nation. If the vote took place in the different States, it was only because of a purely geographical necessity. 'The electors,' says Judge Story, one of the great constitutional authorities, 'of America met in their different States; but where else could they meet?' We observe nevertheless two tendencies among American statesmen. Some are most inclined to strengthen the central power, and the others more disposed to seek guarantees for the independence of the States. The federalists aimed at what we call to-day centralisation; the democrats were for decentralisation; but it would have never entered into the thoughts of Jefferson to encourage the conflict between the attributions of the Union and those of the States to the extent of an armed revolution. His supreme law was the Constitution. Whenever it contained upon a given point no formal and explicit limitation of the rights of the States, he pronounced against the intervention of the central power; but in acting thus his only end was to protect the people against the excesses of the central power. He had no wish to take from it its legitimate attributions. In Calhoun we see democratic opinion, led away by the remarkable talent of this statesman, take a direction which carried it fatally to the last extremities. His posthumous work, 'Disquisition on the Government,' gives us the key of his system. It continued to be for a long time the arsenal from whence the democrats took their arms. Calhoun succeeded in giving a generous colouring to doctrines whose sole aim was to assure the oligarchy of slaveholders the supreme direction of the affairs of the Union. His work may thus be resumed. A government is necessary to protect society against the egotism of individual interests, but individuals also need protection from the abuses of government. A free and absolute suffrage does not defend them against oppression and injustice, for it delivers them up to the caprices, the tendencies, and the passions, of the majority. The Press leans always on the side of the strongest interest, and liberty teaches it neither magnanimity nor justice. We must, then, find something to counterbalance the majority and give to the oppressed interests the right to detach themselves from those who embarrass them.

As in the Roman republic the power of the patricians was bounded by the *veto* of the tribunes, as in Poland the power of the assemblies was held in check by the *veto* of a single member, so in the United States each State must have the right to annul any act which tends to violate or diminish its rights.'

Calhoun's doctrine had been applied for the first time in its extremest consequences by South Carolina, who was the first, in 1861, to raise the flag of revolt. To go back to the Presidency of General Jackson, she proclaimed, respecting a new tariff, an act of nullification which was to have been a prelude to a complete renunciation of federal rights; but the President announced his determination to quell the revolt, and South Carolina was forced to retract at once. None the less did the Democratic theories gain ground, and soon they achieved a series of brilliant triumphs on a question which engaged the very future of the republic, inasmuch as it related to the developement of slavery. This question of territories became the battle-field of parties, the centre of all the internal and external policy to the Union. We read in the Constitution. ' The Congress shall have power to dispose of and make all needful rules and regulations respecting the territory or other property belonging to the United States; and nothing in this Constitution shall be so construed as to prejudice any claims of the United States, or of any particular state.'

This sovereignty over the territories assigned to Congress by the federal compact is absolute; it is limited by no stipulation; the territory is considered as State property in common with the vessels of the federal fleet, the arsenals, the forts, &c. Invested by the Constitution with absolute power over the territory, Congress has on the one hand the faculty of admitting new States, and, consequently, the right to refuse their admission. This double power gave to the American

Legislature an easy means of limiting the domain of slavery, by permitting Congress, first, to exclude it from the territories under its immediate jurisdiction, and secondly to refuse the admission of new States who should inscribe slavery in their State constitution. Consequently the South turned all her strength against these protective clauses of liberty, and by a series of attacks, more and more bold, she succeeded in wholly annulling their effect.

In 1787 the whole national territory had been without opposition wrested from slavery. The founders of the republic, who had not the courage to abolish it in the old States, desired at least to prevent the extension of an institution which they were unanimous in condemning. The Missouri compromise took away from free labour all that portion of the territories ceded by France situate south of the thirtieth degree of latitude. The annexation of Texas, the Mexican war, augmented still more the domain of slave labour. By the compromises of 1850, the choice between the *régimes* of liberty or slavery in the territories of New Mexico and Texas was left to the first occupants of these territories. The American people, represented by Congress, ceased to be considered the natural arbiters in regions destined to aggrandise their empire, and the fate of future States was abandoned to the caprice and cupidity of the most unscrupulous colonists.

The right of legislative intervention in the territories could not stand before the sovereignty of the territories themselves. The South was not long in triumphing over this contradiction, and, throwing aside the mask, denounced the Missouri compromise as an attempt on popular rights. The Nebraska bill was forced from Congress, and all geographical limits between the domains of slave and free labour were thenceforward effaced. From this time sagacious observers might well despair of the future of the Union. Never had the Constitution received a severer blow; never before had individual rights obtained so decided a victory over the public right; never had a nation so imprudently refused to protect itself against factious enterprise. Mistress of the Government, thanks to her electoral privilege and to the multiplication of slave States, the oligarchy of the South had found too easy accomplices in the Northern States. Intoxicated by their prosperity, the people had closed their eyes to the dangers of slavery.

The abolitionists alone, who recalled to the nation her moral obligations, were paid with public contempt and persecution. After the robust generation of statesmen who had founded the republic, and who were guided by the noble principles of liberalism and humanity inscribed on their constitution, we saw a generation of lawyers and sophists, who smothered the spirit of this great work with miserable quibbles, and reduced American politics to a struggle of parties, without fixed principles, broken as soon as formed, the more and more easy instruments of the slaveholding interest. The United States thus prepared for themselves the dreadful ordeal. The growth of public wealth, peace, and outside calm, cannot recompense a people for the loss of moral grandeur. Those who sleep in forgetfulness of their duties must expect a terrible awakening.

American politics became more and more concentrated upon the question of the territories, and upon that of slavery : the political authority of the South was so firmly established that the enemies of the democratic party, abandoning this hope of the abolition of slavery, only attempted to shut it out of the territories. Then, slowly, painfully, we saw formed a party which under different names—first, that of *liberty party*, *third party*, *free soil party*, and finally under that of republican party—took for its object the prevention of the extension of slavery, and gave all its strength to that article of the constitution which gives congress power over the territories. When the republican party nominated its first candidate, Fremont, for President, it is important to recall here its programme, or *platform*, to use the American expression :—Adhesion to the constitution of the United States, prohibition of slavery in the territories, (as well as polygamy, alluding to the Mormons,) re-establishment of law and order in Kansas, then ravaged by civil war, and the immediate admission of Kansas as a free State. The comparative success of the candidature of Mr. Fremont, proved to the statesmen of the South that the North was beginning to rebel against their constant usurpations and to look forward with dread to seeing the whole continent of America delivered up to slavery. The oligarchy of the South felt itself menaced, and foreseeing that the political direction of the Union was about to escape them, they consumed the four years of Mr. Buchanan's presidency in frantic attempts to keep the power or to render abortive the victory of their adversaries. At this moment, the cord which bound the constitutional question to that of slavery became more and more apparent. After having wrested from the North in the name of the Union the most numerous and the most shameful sacrifices, the Missouri compromise, the compromise of 1850, the fugitive slave law, and the Nebraska bill, the states-men of the South prepared to quit the Union the very first day the political balance ceased to incline on their side. The republicans had, however, added nothing to their programme ; they had only announced the *intention* of limiting the power of slavery in the territories. That sufficed for the South : the arsenals were emptied in all the free States, the ships of the federal fleet dispersed all over the universe, and had it not been for the honesty of Mr. Holt, one of Buchanan's secretaries of state, and that of General Scott, it is doubtful if Mr. Lincoln's first inauguration could have taken place at Washington. The rebellion was pre-pared at leisure : it was not the unanimous revolt of a people against a tyrannical government, it was the premeditated attempt of an aristocracy of slaveholders determined to leave the republic rather than lose its direction, the *coup d'état* of a minority against the majority, against the laws and against the constitution, the orders for secession were voted in such regular form and with a rapidity that sufficiently indicated that the leaders were resolved to stifle the protesta-tions of honest and peaceable citizens : they were promulgated by conventions, and were not submitted to the direct ratification of the people of each State. The first feeling in the North was surprise. She could not believe in the rupture of the Union. She had never considered the threats of separation of the *fire eaters* in a serious light. The new administration endeavoured to bring back the rebels; again she muttered the word compromise, but the day when Fort Sumter fell under rebel cannon, conciliation was impossible, and war became the first duty of the Government.

CHAPTER II.

THREE YEARS OF THE WAR.

THE 12th of April 1861, the first cannon was fired against Fort Sumter. Major Anderson, who commanded the Federal troops at Charleston when South Carolina separated from the Confederation, had reinforced Fort Sumter from the garrison of Fort Moultrie, another fortification of the harbour. This precaution was looked upon by the rebels as an act of hostility. They went so far as to ask President Buchanan to abandon Fort Sumter. He was not so shameless as to obey this injunction, and recalling a remnant of honour and courage, he even announced that he would send reinforcements to Fort Sumter. Jefferson Davis considered this reply a declaration of war, and sent General Beauregard, but yesterday an officer in the regular army, to direct the operations of a siege against the fort of Charleston. The 11th of April Beauregard asks Anderson to yield : he refuses. Some Federal vessels are seen at sea; the senseless anger of the rebels is at its height, and the first shells fall on the fortress. What would not a prophetic eye have seen behind their track of flame and their impious smoke ! What blood, ruins, fields of carnage, a whole world

c

overturned, proud Charleston herself given over to the flames, pillaged by her meanest inhabitants ; the star-spangled banner raised at the end of four years on the ruins of Fort Sumter, in presence of Garrison, the old abolitionist, and during the applause of negro regi-ments. Beauregard saw nothing of this, neither did Anderson, who, after a resistance of thirty-six hours, and with his ammunition exhausted, yielded with all the honours of war. There was, however, not a man killed on one side or the other—a singular début for a war which was to cause rivers of blood to flow.

The emotion that spread over the Northern States at the news of the taking of Sumter can be more easily imagined than described. By their anger, and by their sorrow, the American people felt they were a people, and not an arithmetical total. The same vibra-tion stirred as one soul all these millions of souls. Before the President called out 75,000 of the militia, every one was hastening to get under arms. Country people, hearing the news, started at once to be enrolled in the next town, without even saying good-bye to their wives or children. You recognised the sons of the farmers who ran to Bunker Hill in the last century. These spasms do not last in nations more than in indi-viduals. The slow and painful effort of the will must succeed the flash of passion. It is necessary that the regimental level should pass heavily over martial ardour. Once in the ranks, the soldier is no longer any-thing but an infinitesimal fraction.

While regiments are being raised in the North, the South is raising hers also. Virginia, Arkansas, North

Carolina, Tennnessee, hesitating until that moment, follow the impulse. Kentucky, between the hammer and the anvil, vainly proclaims her neutrality. Missouri is divided. Maryland fires on the Massachusetts soldiers in the streets of Baltimore, who are hastening to Washington with Butler. Earth is thrown up round the capital, and on Arlington heights; and the smiling hill sides of the Potomac are laid bare by the axe.

The war begins in Virginia. M'Clellan is spoken of for the first time, clearing the rebels out of the high valleys of Western Virginia. The star of 'Little Napoleon' rises. The Press has put the war trumpet to its lips; a battle is called for, a great battle. Who talks of organising the army; of teaching the drill and manœuvres to the soldiers; of forming brigades, divisions, corps, reserves, a military administration? What need is there of these old things, good enough for Europe? On to Richmond! Everything will fall back before the flood of the volunteers! M'Dowell follows rather than directs this flood. On the 21st of July 1861, he meets Beauregard on the banks of a torrent called Bull Run. He has a few regiments of regulars; all his other soldiers are recruits who have never smelt powder. The Confederates are drawn up on the southern bank of the stream. Behind, they extend to the railway, that serves for their communications. M'Dowell makes a false attack on the right, to divert attention, while a division is to turn their left flank. The Federal recruits cross the valley; fight bravely, and drive the enemy's left back to great pine woods. Johnston, hastening from the valley of the Shenandoah, and Beauregard, show themselves in vain on the battle-field; their troops continue to lose ground and fall back. M'Dowell can believe he is the victor. But now, at the decisive moment, Kirby-Smith arrives with fresh troops. All the Confederate line begins to move again; the oscillation is in the other direction. The Federals are worn out with so many hours of marching and fighting. Their ranks are disordered, and disorder in an armed multitude degenerates into panic; arms are thrown away, waggons, cannon, wounded are abandoned. The tide which should have flowed to Richmond recedes to Washington. Beauregard, astonished at his victory, never dreams of pursuing the fugitives.

The moral effects of this disaster were already great enough. For a moment the North doubted of itself, and from that day Europe never ceased to doubt of the North. After that there were twenty, there were a hundred battles, bloodier than that of Bull Run. But Bull Run was the first; it was thought to show the hand of God. The very next day Mr. Lincoln calls 500,000 volunteers to arms, the first challenge to the fate that insulted the stars and stripes. Volunteers came crowding in. There was no longer question of punishing the arrogance of the South, but of saving the capital of the United States; more than that, the honour of the nation. A general was needed; who should he be? Scott, the hero of the Mexican war, was too old. M'Dowell was not to be thought of. M'Clellan was chosen, it was difficult to say why. He was known to be young, he had been at Sebastopol during the Crimean war, he had seen armies. He is named at once Commander-in-chief of the armies of the United States; he organises the raw recruits, slowly and laboriously, as if he were preparing a war of seven—thirty years; reviewing the army again and again, deceiving the impatience of Congress by great military spectacles, intoxicating himself with the applause of his soldiers, which the enemies of the administration already began to echo. The autumn of 1861 was lost. A movement, begun in Virginia, terminated disastrously for the Federals at Ball's Bluff. M'Clellan is discouraged; he has no confidence in his army. Boiling with patriotism and passion, he shuts it into winter quarters. During this long expectation he makes plans—shall he go to Richmond by land or by water? Alas! he will go neither one way nor the other.

Now we come to 1862. M'Clellan at last makes up his mind to try his fortune. His first idea is to move on Annapolis and the Rapahannock, in order to post himself behind Manassas, where the enemy had been encamped all the winter. His plan is hardly adopted in a great council of war when the enemy evacuates Manassas. What is to be done? Follow him through the mud of Virginia, with so many large rivers, impassable forests, broken bridges, and bad roads in front; action is begun again by water. Fortress Monroe is situated on the point of the Virginian peninsula, a great tongue of land stretching between the James and the York rivers; this point, which has always remained in the hands of the Federals, is chosen for the disembarcation. 120,000 men come down Chesapeake Bay on board the transports, and reunite under the cannon of the forts.

The entrance to the James River was closed by the Merrimac, an iron-plated Confederate ship, which had sunk the Cumberland, thrown terror into all the harbour of Hampton Roads, and had only retreated before the Monitor, with injuries the nature of which were not very well known. It is necessary to follow the peninsula by land, by the York River and the Pamunkey, where the transports can come up as high as White House. From there the army can be thrown across the Chickahominy on Richmond.

But first comes Yorktown, with its old fortifications hardly altered since the times of Rochambeau, Cornwallis, and Clinton : can it be attempted by force? M'Clellan is too prudent to try. He wishes to turn Yorktown by water, but now they refuse to send him M'Dowell's corps from Washington, which he had intended to send on the left bank of the river. It never comes into his head to detach one of the corps that he has close at hand to operate this diversion. He commences a regular siege ; the cannon—100 and 200-pounders—the mortars, come heavily and slowly to their places. When all is ready the enemy has disappeared, and a month has been wasted without profit or glory to the army. They go in pursuit of the enemy. At last they come up with him at Williamsburg. Johnston, who commanded the retreat, held his ground two days, and fought furiously in the rain, in order to give the chief of his army and baggage the time to pass over the narrow roads of the peninsula.

After a little rest they are again on the road. They advance slowly, with enormous trains of waggons, following the Pamunkey as far as White House, which becomes the great depôt of the army. During this time, Jefferson Davis, in alarm, had evacuated Norfolk, the great arsenal of Virginia. There being no longer a port for the Merrimac, she was destroyed. The James River was again free, but it had been decided to march on Richmond from the north, following the line of the railway from White House to Richmond.

There was nothing, however, to hinder a movement, like that which Grant made later, on the James River, from this time freely navigated by the Federal gun-boats. The evil star of M'Clellan detained him in the swamps the Chickahominy. M'Dowell remained with his corps at Fredericksburg, and M'Clellan still hoped he would come to the help of his right wing. Nothing was more easy than to get into communication with him. Unfortunately the Confederate General Jackson had thrown himself into the valley of the Shenandoah; he had beaten in detail the troops under Fremont, Banks, and Sigel, who defended it. Washington was alarmed, and M'Dowell recalled. The army of the Potomac could no longer count on any reinforcement. Its time, its strength, and its courage were worn out on the banks of the Chickahominy. A bloody, confused, and useless battle at Fair Oaks, on the 31st of May; a battle the next day, in which Johnston, the Confederate commander, is wounded; a battle the 23rd of

June, on the road to Richmond, where Jackson's troops, returned already from their successful expedition in the Shenandoah, are in front.

It is impossible to advance or recede. Jackson already threatens the railway that supplies the army. M'Clellan at last decides to direct his decimated army by a flank movement on the James River. The retreat begins the 27th of June, by the great battle of Gaines' Hill, a desperate struggle that ends, in the mists of evening, in frightful disorder; 35,000 Federals had detained 60,000 Confederates for a whole day. The bridges across the Chickahominy are destroyed. The slow waggon trains, the cattle, begin to move; they fight as they march, before, behind, on all sides; in this way, under a horrible heat, they cross interminable swamps. At last they come to the Malvern Hills that overlook the James River: the army preserved its siege artillery, found its transports, and was again under shelter. This was plainly to be seen when, on the 11th of June, the Confederates tried to storm the positions of Malvern; a formidable artillery drives them back, and the seven days' retreat terminates with a victory. But the army of the Potomac was no longer in a condition to make an aggressive movement. It was shut up behind trenches, harassed, irritated, under a torrid heat, regretting so many lost hopes, so near and yet so far from Richmond. Lee, who henceforward commands the Confederate army, sends Jackson to make a diversion in the north of Virginia. This latter meets the army of General Pope on the very battle-field of Bull Run; this time there is no panic, but a dreadful effusion of blood that lasts two days. M'Clellan, recalled from the James River, returns slowly and sorrowfully to Alexandria. Profiting by the scattering of his adversaries, and by their distrust, which is betrayed by incoherent movements, Lee decides to invade Maryland. Jackson invests Harper's Ferry, while the main body of the Confederate army throws itself boldly across the Potomac. In the midst of general confusion M'Clellan assumes the command-in-chief, and adds to his army all the troops he can collect. On the 14th of September Hooker attacks and puts to flight the advanced guard of the Confederates at South Mountain. The next day comes the news that the commander of Harper's Ferry has yielded with a garrison of 11,000 men, after a wretched defence : this shameful capitulation permits Jackson to rejoin Lee. M'Clellan has therefore before him the whole Confederate army. Nevertheless, he gives battle on the 17th of September, on the borders of the Antietam, a little tributary of the Potomac.

All day long the left and the right of the two armies looked for and came against one another; the centres remained almost inactive. In the evening the two armies slept on the field of battle, in the midst of 20,000 killed and wounded. The next day Lee retreated, and ordered the evacuation of Harper's Ferry. M'Clellan let him go without hindrance, fearing, doubtless, to ask too much of fortune, which had at last accorded him a great victory.

A long pause followed. Opinion is again impatient. M'Clellan takes up the time in reconnaisances, fatigues the government with complaints, demands, reclamations. The command is taken from him and given to Burnside; the star of 'the little Napoleon' falls from the zenith, never to rise again. Burnside marches on the Rapahannock; the 11th of December he bombards Fredericksburg, and the 12th, favoured by a fog, he crosses the river. The next day he advances against the wooded heights occupied by Lee, Longstreet, and Jackson. There is no stratagem. The soldiers throw themselves vainly against insurmountable obstacles. Six times the Irish brigade advances to the assault of Lee's entrenchments. The enemy's artillery mows down the Federals like ripe corn. Hooker succeeds no better. The great butchery only stops with the night, and the army, discouraged, recrosses the river without having been able to break in on the Confederate position.

Burnside nobly takes upon himself the whole responsibility of this disaster, and yields the command to Hooker, the favourite of the army, known by the name of 'Fighting Joe.' But deep calls unto deep, and Hooker was not to be more successful than his predecessor. Very sad was the ending of the year '62, much sadder than that of '61. Then there was the amusement of counting the regiments of the increasing army of the Potomac. What had become of this army and the budding glory of M'Clellan, and the hope of crushing the rebellion? How was a ring of iron to be formed round it? How get a hold on that fatal Virginia, the soul and the shield of the Confederation? Nothing could console the North for the defeats of the peninsula and Fredericksburg; neither the defensive victory of Antietam, nor the brilliant combat of the Monitor, nor even the bold capture of New Orleans, where the Federal flag had once more floated since April, nor the victory of Rosencranz at Corinth in the State of Mississippi, nor the defeat of Bragg, who, beaten at Perryville, had been obliged to fly, after having for a moment overrun Tennessee and Southern Kentucky in triumph, and dared to threaten Northern Kentucky and even Cincinnati. The last day of the year, the 31st of December, Bragg attacked Rosencranz afresh at Murfreesborough in Tennessee, broke his lines and took from him twenty-eight cannon. The 1st of January 1863, Rosencranz, drawing his army together, had slowly regained the advantage; the next day he passed from the defensive to the offensive, and forced his adversary to retreat.

With 1863 opens the third year of the war. The army of the Potomac waits till April before it moves again. Lee had remained all winter on the heights of Fredericksburg. Hooker comes up with most of the army of the Rapahannock, crosses the river above Fredericksburg, and, appearing suddenly on Lee's left, menaces his communications with Richmond. As soon as Lee, terrified, should abandon Fredericksburg, Sedgwick, left behind, was to throw himself into it: then the cavalry of Stoneman was to dart into the very heart of Virginia to cut the bridges on the road to Richmond. What was wanting in this plan? In appearance, nothing. Hooker felt sure of a victory. Lee, nevertheless, instead of allowing his flank to be turned, makes a change of front, and, on the 2nd of May, orders Jackson himself to turn the Federal right near Chancellorsville. Jackson's corps shows itself unexpectedly at this point, and throws several regiments into disorder. It is very difficult to set matters straight on that side. The next day Jackson recommences his attack. While Hooker thinks only of his threatened right, Lee throws himself on Sedgwick, who had come to occupy the heights of Fredericksburg, and pushes him into the river. Hooker could have continued the fight, though he had lost a great many men. The Confederates had suffered less, but they had lost Jackson, hit by mistake by a Confederate bullet. The army of the Potomac receives the order to recross the Rapahannock with sullen discontent. Puffed up with success, the rebels talk of only stopping at Washington. It must come to an end, and conditions be dictated from the White House. In the Shenandoah the Federals are surprised at Winchester. Lee is already in Maryland, and his cavalry are joyously overrunning the peaceful valleys of Pennsylvania. Hooker disappears in the confusion which follows this successful invasion. The army of the Potomac, hastening back to defend Washington, receives a new general, Meade—a modest soldier, hardly known to the nation. But the army knows him; it has always seen him firm, calm, patient, doing whatever he had to do noiselessly. This man, unknown the day before, is about to give the greatest battle of the war: for one day the fate of the Union will be in his hand. I saw him later, fallen from the first to the second rank, in his tent before Petersburg; but I could only speak to him of Gettysburg. Gettysburg has remained in my mind as the turning point of the war. The cause of the Union, which had resisted so many shocks, might have succumbed there. Meade encamped his army on the heights of this village, and was attacked there by the whole Confederate army on the 2nd of July. Lee tried successively the left, the centre, and the right of the Federal lines, stationed, not in a straight line, but like the two forks of a V, the point of the V forming the centre. From the middle of his triangle Meade rapidly reinforced the points most furiously attacked. The first day was without result : the Federal right alone, had wavered a little. The next day Meade re-established his position. A great calm followed, soon broken by the thunder of a formidable artillery. Lee calls out all his cannon and sends Longstreet to the assault of the centre. For one moment the rebel columns crown the heights, then they give way and are obliged to bend. Three times they return to the charge, and three times they are driven back. Pickett makes a vain and last effort : he retreats also. The desperate struggle only ends with the night. The Federal army proudly remains in all its positions. Lee, who has lost the flower of his army, gives the signal to retreat, and returns slowly to the Potomac, still redoubtable, and capable of repulsing a few weak attempts to hinder him from passing the river.

What, however, was going on in the West during 1863, the critical year of the war ? There were great triumphs there, and fruitful victories, that restored to the Union not only a few towns or the line of a river, but whole States or immense territories. Farragut had reopened the mouth of the Mississippi, but, in the beginning of 1863, the fortifications of Vicksburg and Fort Hudson interrupted the navigation of the river. Between these two points the Mississippi receives the waters of Red River, and by this stream cattle, salt, and all the merchandise brought by land from Matamoras, reached the Confederates. The Red River was a sort of umbilical cord by which the rebel confederation could be nourished. Jefferson Davis attached so much importance to this means of communication, and to the possession of the lower Mississippi, that he declared that, if Vicksburg fell, the Confederation would fall with it. At the end of 1862 Sherman had already commenced operations against this strategical point, which commands one of the highest capes round which winds the Mississippi, but without success. Grant was convinced that Vicksburg could never be taken by assault from the north, and he resolved to try the attack from the south ; but how transport his army in that direction? The batteries of Vicksburg would have destroyed all the transports. A canal was begun on the right bank to allow a passage sheltered from the batteries. An inundation destroyed the unfinished canal. The winding and lazy affluents of the Mississippi were explored in all directions to see if, with the aid of art, a continuous route could not be made for light boats, to pass from one to the other, and thus reach to the south of Vicksburgh. Nothing succeeded. The engineers gave way to the sailors. Porter, who commanded the Federal flotilla above Vicksburg, lost two vessels in trying to pass the forts ; but Farragut, on the other side, was more fortunate. Braving the fire of the batteries, he sailed safely past the redoubtable forts, took Natchez, put to flight the Confederate fleet, and joined Porter. A body of cavalry, commanded by Grierson, starting from the frontiers of Tennessee, crosses the State of Mississippi, cuts all communication between Vicksburg and the East, and only rejoins the Federals near New Orleans, · preluding thus to the brilliant incursions to be made later by Sherman, in Georgia and the Carolinas. Grant, with the help of the fleet, transports the army to the south of Vicksburg, and takes the forts of Great Gulf, the key of this place. He tries vainly to penetrate by force, but this time he can at least completely invest it. Pemberton defends himself till the 4th of July, when he is obliged to capitulate with 30,000 men. Soon after Port Hudson yields to the army of Banks. The Confederates no longer hold a single military post on the river, and boats can go from New Orleans to St. Louis, with no fear but that of the bullets of a few guerillas. In the history of sieges there are, I think, few enterprises that can be compared to the siege of Vicksburg. Grant's army was detained for nearly a year in the *bayous* of the Mississippi, decimated by fevers, exposed towards the last to torrid heats. Grant showed what American tenacity is capable of. Disappointed daily, daily modifying his plans, always seeking for new means, using first *ruse*, then force, then again *ruse*, only retreating to return again ; determined, in short, to make everything—men, nature, chance even —bend before his indomitable will.

After the fall of Vicksburg the Confederates advanced into Tennessee, and Bragg was obliged to retreat to the frontiers of Georgia. Rosencranz seized Chattanooga, and pursued his enemy. Bragg, reinforced by Longstreet and Hood, turns round suddenly and gives battle to Rosencranz on the banks of the Chickamauga. On September 19th, the Federal division under Thomas, resists all assaults. The next day the Confederates, unable to break Thomas's line to the left, throw themselves on the right, overwhelm it, and finally put the centre to rout. Rosencranz's army begins to retreat, and retires as far as Chattanooga. Thomas, nevertheless keeps his place some time, and only retires slowly, still defying the enemy. Bragg takes up his post on Lookout Mountain and Missionary Ridge, in front of Chattanooga, where the Federals are entrenched. Grant takes the command ; Hooker is sent to his assistance with one of the corps that gained the victory at Gettysburg, and Sherman comes from Vicksburg just in time to be in the battle of November 25th. Besieged the day before, the Federals turn besiegers. A division climbs the heights of Lookout Mountain ; Hooker fights above the clouds, drives the Confederates into their highest entrenchments, and forces them into the valley on the other side of the mountain. Sherman, after bloody struggles, occupies Missionary Ridge. Bragg is forced to fly with his whole army. While he was being beaten, Longstreet, separated from his army, was making a raid into Western Tennessee, and vainly trying to take Knoxville.

Thus ended the year 1863 : Fortune, at its opening, which smiled on the rebels on every side, was everywhere against them. The Mississippi was free in all its length; the pride of Charleston had been humiliated. Though the Federal fleet had not been able to penetrate into the harbour, Fort Wagner at least had been taken, and the heavy cannon of Gillmore had half destroyed Fort Sumter. Meade had driven back the invasion of Lee, and the army of the Potomac had shown what it was capable of in a great battle. In the West the Federals took possession of the mountains that separate Tennessee from Georgia, and protected Kentucky definitively from Confederate incursions.

During the first months of 1864 the Confederates seemed to gain ground. Many little checks apparently interrupted the brilliant series of Federal victories —that of Sherman, who made a trial in Mississippi and Alabama of those long marches in which he was to excel later, but who did not receive the reinforcements of cavalry on which he counted; that in Florida, where an unfortunate general made a useless incursion; another in North Carolina, where the rebels retake Plymouth; another in Tennessee, where Forrest takes Fort Pillow by siege and puts all the black garrison to the sword; a more important check on the Red River, where Banks is beaten by Kirby Smith and comes near losing all his transports, saved only by an officer of artillery—Bailey—who throws a dam across the river, and lets the vessels down through a cutting, over improvised and impetuous rapids. But all eyes are turned towards Grant, who reorganizes the army of the Potomac. He starts in

D

May, and goes direct to the Rapidan, while Butler
ascends the James River towards Richmond. Lee and
Grant begin to fight on the 6th of May, in a valley
called the Wilderness, a happy name for such bloody
scenes. Two immense armies look for each other all
day in the woods, and are decimated without seeing
each other; in the thick under-brush the fight is
nothing but a fusillade, a continual cannonade, a
gigantic skirmish. The fight goes on the same on the
7th, the 8th, the 9th, the 10th, and the 11th. Grant
never retreats an inch, and advances slowly to the left,
unable to break the moving, but always solid, line of
his adversary. He advances thus obliquely, as far as
the Chickahominy. There he makes a circuit, quietly
crosses the river, reaches the James, and rejoins
Butler's army, established in front of Petersburg and
Richmond, at the confluence of the James River and
the Appomatox.

At the same time Sherman begins his campaign in
Georgia—the most astonishing of the war. What
others expect from the mass of battalions, the force of
artillery, he expects from their rapidity. The genius of
strategy is spontaneously and fully developed in this
ardent soldier, who is found capable of moving an
army as easily as others move a battalion. He first
forces Johnston, who is sent against him, to retreat
from Tunnel Hill to Dalton, and from there to Resaca.
Rome is the first reward of his efforts; he only stops
there for a moment, turns his adversary and makes
him retreat to Marietta, forces him to abandon the

Kenesaw Mountains, and at last to cross the Chatahoo-chee. At last he reaches Atlanta, the objective of his first campaign and the key of Georgia.

Such was the military situation of the United States when I embarked at Liverpool to visit them. Now I have to show what were the political consequences of these great events, what transformations opinions and parties had undergone during so long and so moving a drama.

CHAPTER III.

THREE YEARS OF POLITICAL AGITATION.

IF the civil war between the States is to be considered one of the greatest events of the nineteenth
century, it is because it was not only a war but
a revolution also. The political consequences of the
struggle, obscured for a long time by the smoke
of the battle-field, stood out more and more clearly.
Before the war the home politics of the United States
could be summed up in these three terms : the
triumph of the democratic party, the weakening of
the Federal power, and the indefinite extension of
slavery ;—the war begun, it could be summed up
in the three opposites : the triumph of republican
doctrines, the extension of the central authority, and
the destruction of slavery.

As doctors take advantage of sickness the better
to study the structure of the human body, the political philosopher could study on the living subject, so to .
speak, the American Constitution.   When De Tocqueville analysed it in a celebrated book, he threw an
anxious glance at the future.   In spite of the melancholy tendencies and pessimism of his mind, in spite

of his instinctive distrust of institutions to which
nevertheless he had raised so lasting a monument,
he certainly did not foresee that the hour of a great
crisis was so near.   That hour struck in 1861, and
from the day the civil war broke out, the press
and the statesmen of Europe had but one voice to
declare that the Constitution of the United States,
and with it the principles even of democratic institutions, were put to a dangerous trial.   There was some
truth as well as some error in this general feeling.
Certainly in no time and in no country have democratic
ideas been represented by so large and powerful a
society as that of the United States, in all their integrity, and unalloyed by the traditions of another age.
On the virgin soil of a new world, man has attempted
to begin history anew.

The dissolution therefore of the great republic founded
on democratic principles would have thrown the whole
world into a great moral trouble.   Then, again, it can
be denied that the crisis we have witnessed is the natural
result of the application of the ideas that triumphed
on the continent of America at the end of the last
century.   It can be loudly affirmed that the war would
never have broken out if privilege in its most unjust and
cruel shape had not been surreptitiously introduced into
the laws and customs of the Union ; into the laws, by
the constitutional protection afforded to slavery ; into
the customs, by the prejudices of race.   The aristocratic
principle has been known to found and preserve
powerful empires, to ensure their grandeur by fidelity
to noble traditions, by the enlightened protection of

popular interests. History has never shown a democracy and an aristocracy living side by side, uniting in the same enterprises, animated by the same ambitions, free from hatred and jealousy. And what is to be thought of a social order where in the midst of the most complete equality had sprung up a privilege founded neither on virtue, nor learning, nor services to the country, nor even upon wealth, but only on a particular kind of property—human property? This fatal antinomy of servitude and liberty is the key of all the political and social history of the United States. In allowing it to remain in the Constitution, the founders of the Union imperilled their whole work. The consequences of this culpable error were developed with frightful rapidity. The institutions were corrupted, and slavery never ceased to act as a dissolvent. When the source of an evil is very deep, it breaks out in numerous symptoms that often seem independent of each other, and of which the links can only be seized in going back to the first cause. The political history of the United States since the defeat of the Federalists, until the recent triumph of the republican party, was only the history of the alliance of Southern statesmen with the democrats of the North. And what was the object of Southern statesmen, for whom the Northern democrats were but too complaisant during fifty years? The maintenance and indefinite extension of slavery.

The Constitution invested the President with a very extensive and perfectly defined power. The democrats had succeeded in almost entirely annulling it; they had at least obtained from the first magistrates of the republic a sort of tacit renunciation of the exercise of their legitimate authority. The lustre that surrounded the presidential office had been dissipated by degrees. The first Presidents were named Washington, Jefferson, John Adams, Madison; those that preceded Lincoln, Polk, Taylor, Pierce, Buchanan. Who does not remember the deplorable weakness of Mr. Buchanan, treating with the audacious movement of the South, receiving its commissioners, entering into parley with them, authorising by his inaction the pillage of the arsenals and the seizing of the forts of the Confederation? Who does not remember that Mr. Lincoln, going to Washington to assume the Presidency, was obliged to go through Baltimore secretly in the night, and reached the White House like a fugitive? A year after, were there many sovereigns armed with as much power as he, who then, at the peril of his life, reclaimed a disputed authority?

The civil war has revealed and brought to life again the force of the executive power in the United States. 'The President,' wrote M. de Tocqueville, ' possesses almost royal prerogatives, which he never has an opportunity of using, and his rights, until now, are very circumscribed. The laws permit him to be strong; circumstances keep him weak.'

For a long while the President only reached the White House bound by a narrow programme and promises without number; his ministers were already named, and the offices had all been seized upon in the general scramble which follows the accession of the first magistrate of the republic. But before

circumstances unforeseen, new, and terrible there is
no imperative order: the farther Mr. Lincoln was swept
away from the programme of which at first he was
the still obscure and timid representative, the more
strength did he draw from his powerful prerogative.
'Honest old Abe' had only to stamp his foot on the
ground to cause an army of a million of men to
spring up. His mind, whose rustic simplicity was often
sharpened by a point of innocent irony, was confronted
with the most formidable problems and the most
solemn alternatives. In this part, which events that
no human foresight could have guessed called on him
to play, he was sustained only by his probity, and
by that Constitution which lent him its strength and
its majesty. The world was so unaccustomed to see
a President of the United States exercise his prerogative, that the peaceful solution of the 'Trent'
affair caused at least as much astonishment as satisfaction. Mr. Lincoln gave up to England the Southern
Commissioners seized by Captain Wilkes without asking
the advice of Congress, against the wishes of some
of his ministers, without even consulting the Senate—
the body politic, *par excellence*, which by its traditions, by its composition itself, eminently represents the
greatest and most durable interests of the republic. The
pacific lawyer of Illinois found himself the commander-
in-chief of an immense army and a powerful fleet. He
was able to remove M'Clellan the day after his victory
at Antietam. It was during the darkest and most
critical hours that he enforced his authority most
firmly. It was after the defeat of Fredericksburg, in

the midst of the threats and murmurs of the democrats, that he called the law of Conscription into activity. From the outset of the civil war he was authorised by Congress to suspend the habeas corpus.* The proclamation of martial law in the revolted territories, the creation of special provost marshals charged with the police of the army and the recruiting, and the Confiscation Bill, gave formidable weapons to the President, which he used but rarely, and with regret. At the opening of the struggle every one was surprised to see a government so weak and so helpless against revolt; later, its enemies willingly accused it of sacrificing liberty to the Union.

Public opinion and parties underwent profound transformations, together with the central power. Perhaps the programme of the party that brought in Mr. Lincoln in 1860 is still remembered. This platform contained no direct threat against slavery; the only ambition of the republicans was to circumscribe its domain and to revive the jurisdiction of Congress in the Territories. These latter had been divided by the Missouri compromise into two parts, one given up

---

* The Constitution declares that the habeas corpus can only be suspended 'in cases of rebellion and invasion, when the public safety requires it.' The article does not specify on whom shall devolve the right to pronounce the suspension of this Act. After animated discussions, it was admitted that this prerogative ought logically to belong to the executive, because the Constitution imposed on it the task of repelling invasions and suppressing insurrections. Mr. Binney, an eminent jurisconsult of Pennsylvania, has written a very remarkable paper on this question, which has not been without influence on the solution of this delicate constitutional question.

to free, the other to slave labour.   But the democratic party had procured the repeal of this compromise, and substituted the sovereignty of the first comer to that of Congress.   The republicans, on coming into power, proclaimed their respect for the constitutional rights of the South, and went so far as to promise the rigorous execution of the hated Fugitive Slave Law. Mr. Lincoln called round him not only statesmen of his own way of thinking, but he made a wide opening for those democrats who, alarmed by the excesses of their own party, and in view of civil war, felt the need of strengthening the Federal authority. Above all, he lent an attentive ear to the councils of the representatives of the border States, who, between the North and the South, seemed to be naturally called upon to reconcile hostile interests.   The Secretary of State, Mr. Seward, the most important statesman in the cabinet, gave his influence to this conciliatory policy.   Of a deep and far-seeing mind, hiding connected plans under an apparent mobility, too clever to deprive his political adversaries of all hope, he always caused the voice of prudence to be heard in the presidential councils, as well as that of a patriotism that had easily guessed that Europe would not remain an altogether disinterested spectator of the commotions of the New World.   Nevertheless the passions of the South were not to be reasoned with. The heat and difficulties of the struggle by degrees wore out the patience of the North.   The republicans were obliged to unite more and more closely with the abolitionists.   The connecting link that united

the two parties from the very beginning was Charles
Sumner, the celebrated Massachusetts senator, who
awhile before had very nearly paid with his life
for the courage he had shown in defending Kansas
against the rapacious ambition of the slave-owners, and
who, after Mr. Lincoln's election, had been appointed
President of the Committee of Foreign Affairs because
of the prestige of his name, and of his great knowledge of history and international law. For a long
time Mr. Sumner's position had been too important
to admit of his being the tool of any party. He had
never concealed his sympathy for the abolitionists, even
during the moment of their greatest unpopularity.
Without wholly sharing the views of Garrison, Wen-
dell Phillips, and their friends, he loved and respected
them, and recognised in them the intellectual guides
and, so to speak, the moral lights of the republic.
They had from the very first understood the issue
of the civil war. The sincerity of their belief, of which
they had furnished so many proofs; the energy of
their convictions; and that peculiar clear-sightedness
which is only bestowed by moral grandeur during
those epochs when human societies are overturned
by revolutions, soon assured them a new authority,
and their alliance became of inestimable value.
Nevertheless they were not brought together in a
day.

For a long time the republicans believed themselves strong enough to crush the rebellion without
recourse to the weapons that could be furnished by the
slavery question. In his message to Congress at the

beginning of 1862, the President spoke of emancipation for the first time; he warned the rebels that if the war continued ' all the incidents of war would take place, even at the risk of utter ruin '—a threat to be easily interpreted by the most short-sighted. A month later, Congress, at the proposition of the President, abolished slavery in the district of Columbia, of which Washington is the centre, allowing a large indemnity to the slave-owners. Reassuming the jurisdiction over the territories granted by the Constitution, Congress declared that slavery could no longer exist there, thus closing the virgin soil of the central continent to the Southern institution. When General Lee repulsed the army of M'Clellan on the banks of the James, and himself prepared to invade the Northern States, the Confiscation Bill was the answer of both houses to the insolent cries of victory of the Confederates. The President accorded a delay of sixty days to the secessionists to submit. After that time he had the right to declare their slaves free and to confiscate their property. The Bill freed all fugitive slaves, and forbid the military authorities to execute the Fugitive Slave Law; it also authorised the President to enlist coloured men, to hasten the suppression of the rebellion.

Shortly—overstepping the limits of the Confiscation Bill, which only assured liberty to fugitives within the Federal lines—the Chamber of Commerce of New York, which represents the largest interests of the first commercial city of the Union, requested the President to proclaim the immediate and unconditional emancipation of all the slaves in the rebel States. Mr. Lincoln, on September 22, 1862, decided to take this grave resolution; but, to give a fresh proof of his moderation, he announced that the proclamation would only go into effect on January 1, 1863. For a moment he seemed overwhelmed by the weight of the responsibility he had assumed as commander-in-chief of the Federal army, invested with full powers to suppress insurrection. The Constitution, in confiding to the presidential power the task of struggling against rebellion or invasion, could not leave it unarmed in presence of this danger, and long before, John Quincy Adams had declared in the Senate that, in facing such perils, the President could abolish slavery to save the nation. When several abolitionists went on September 24, 1863, to thank Mr. Lincoln, he refused to accept any praise, any ovation. ' What I did,' he said, ' I did after ripe deliberation, and under a solemn sense of my responsibility. From God alone can I draw the confidence that I have not committed a fault. I shall not attempt to defend my conduct by any commentary. My country and the world will judge me, and will act on this judgment, if necessary. I can say no more.' The emancipation proclamation was the object of violent criticisms in America as well as in Europe. Mr. Lincoln was reproached with only freeing the slaves of the rebels, and with leaving the slaves of the States still in the Union in chains. It was thought immoral that the maintenance of the rights of property of the masters should be held up as the price, so to speak, of fidelity or return to the Union. Is it necessary to say, in answer to this reproach, that Mr. Lincoln did not possess the right to abolish slavery in those States which had neither lost nor compromised any of their constitutional rights or privileges by revolt? His proclamation was a war measure, which could only be enforced against the enemy.

Events have replied to those who maintained that the great act of Mr. Lincoln would give the signal to a frightful servile war. It was not a simple proclamation that might arm the blacks against the whites; in emancipating the slaves, Mr. Lincoln knew he was not liberating them on the spot. He only meant to show the South that the North was determined to yield to her in nothing. He was punishing an arrogant oligarchy that had given the signal for a fratricidal war, he was destroying the reward of the victory that the slave-owners were promising themselves. It was thus the philosopher Emerson measured the bearing of this resolution, that sealed for ever the alliance of the republicans and the abolitionists : — ' It is not in the least necessary that this measure should be instantly followed by a marked and important result, that should affect the blacks or their rebel masters. The importance of this act consists in its causing our country to enter the paths of justice, in its obliging the numberless civil and military agents of the republic to be on the side of equity. Once taken by one administration, this measure cannot be revoked by another, for slavery can never overrule the disgust of the moral sentiment, but with the strength of immemorial usage. In our nineteenth century, it can never appear to us as a novelty or a progress. This act excuses the sacrifice of so many noble soldiers; it heals our wounds, it restores health to the nation. After such a victory as this, we can submit with impunity to many defeats. The proclamation does not promise us the immediate redemption of the black race, but it delivers it from our complicity and our opposition. The President has delivered on parole all the slaves in America, and they will never fight against us more. We have abandoned a false position to fix ourselves on the solid ground of natural rights; every ray of intelligence, every virtuous sentiment, every religious heart, every honourable man, every poet, every philosopher, the generosity of cities, the vigorous arm of workmen, the patience of our farmers, the passionate conscience of women, the sympathy of distant nations, these are henceforward our new allies.'

There was all the less reason for saying that the emancipation was an act inspired only by vengeance, ill-will, and hatred, that Mr. Lincoln at different times suggested to the loyal Slave States to efface from the State constitutions all traces of servile institutions, and pressed on Congress to put the financial resources of the whole Union at the service of those States that consented.

The government gave a manifest proof of its sympathies for the black race in recognising the black republic of Liberia, and entering into diplomatic relations with that of Haiti, which had never been done by any preceding administration. The presence of a black ambassador in the drawing-rooms of the White House would never have been tolerated by a Pierce or a

Buchanan. At last, the rights of citizenship of the coloured man were for the first time solemnly recognised. Doubtless they had been already acknowledged in several of the New England States, but until then the central government had never openly or explicitly given those rights to the coloured man. In opening to them the military ranks, the Executive was necessarily obliged to cover them with its protection. It was impossible to ask the blacks to shed their blood for the Union, without acknowledging them to be men and citizens. The Secretary of War exacted that the government at Richmond should treat prisoners of all colours alike, and threatened to reply to all acts not inspired by this sentiment of equity, by severe reprisals.

The civil war had not only brought the republicans and the abolitionists definitively together, it had also transformed the democratic party. A division had taken place between those who, though they criticised the cabinet on some points, considered the war an inexorable necessity, and, above all things, wished the reconstruction of the Union, and those who remained utterly devoted to the cause of slavery, and whose hostility did not draw back before treason. The first were familiarly known as *war democrats*; the others, or *peace democrats*, were a despised but active and unscrupulous minority. Among the democratic partisans of the Union many had taken sides warmly with the government, and had become its most solid supporters. Mr. Lincoln had skilfully left them an important part in his administration, as well as in the ranks of the army. Among these modified democrats, I will quote Mr. Stanton, the Secretary of War. His first entrance on the great theatre of public life was when Mr. Buchanan first refused to send reinforcements to Major Anderson, shut up in Fort Sumter, at the opening of the civil war. In consequence of this General Cass retired from the Secretaryship of State, and in the ministerial changes which followed Mr. Buchanan made Mr. Stanton Attorney-General. As soon as he was in the Cabinet, Mr. Stanton used all his influence against the Floyds, Thomsons, Cobbs, and all those who had been conspiring long before the signal for secession had been given. It was through the efforts of Mr. Stanton, Judge Holt (become Secretary of War), and General Dix that Washington was at that time kept in the Union. Mr. Holt of Kentucky also rallied to the Union, though he had all his life belonged to the democratic party. How many more could we not quote? General Halleck, called to command the army of the West after Fremont had retired, and for a long time commander-in-chief of the Federal armies; General Butler, not long before devoted to the interests of the democratic faction the most opposed to the abolitionists, now turned organiser of black regiments, and the most ardent advocate of emancipation.

Though many influential men had gone from the republican to the democratic camp, there were many left who sought to reestablish the party accustomed to exercise, and remain in, power. As it always happens during a war, the opposition was bolder and

E

stronger in proportion as the military reverses were more numerous and the operations slower.

In one of the darkest hours of the civil war, the extreme wing of the democratic party, which made no secret of its Southern sympathies, thought itself on the point of triumphing. After the bloody battle of Chancellorsville, Lee had crossed the Potomac; his army, emboldened by success, threatened Washington, Baltimore, and Philadelphia at the same time. This was the programme prepared by the secession leaders and their Northern accomplices :—Lee was to cross the Potomac, beat Hooker, demoralised by the checks he had received; an insurrection was to break out at Washington, Baltimore, and New York; Mr. Lincoln, Mr. Seward, and all the members of the cabinet were to be thrown into prison; the victorious insurrectionists were to call on Lee, who would enter the White House as master, and re-make the Union, for the good of the South and slavery. That was the programme sketched out after Fredericksburg and Chancellorsville. Even in case of fresh successes, Mr. Davis would probably have not attempted to carry it out to the end, and probably would not have cherished the senseless hope of reconstructing the Union for his benefit; but he allowed them to believe this to be his intention, in order to obtain the cooperation of his Northern allies, and to stir up dissension in the great towns, where the democratic party recruits its most numerous and active adherents. The nomination of General Meade to the command of the army of the Potomac, and the great victory of Gettysburg, baffled all these projects; but the powder was all prepared in New York, and exploded of itself. The largest commercial city in the Union was for several days the theatre of atrocious scenes. The movement of the Irish population, which has always been the obedient army of the democratic party, was nothing but the premature explosion of a long-standing conspiracy, whose ramifications extended as far as Washington and Richmond. The conscription was the skilfully chosen pretext of the leaders, but the infamous violence used towards the free blacks revealed the true nature of the insurrection. The saturnalia of a cause which retreated neither before murder, arson, nor pillage were not of long duration, and soon the echoes of great victories gained in the valley of the Mississippi stifled the last murmurs of treason.

If we attempt to sum up the political results of the war, what was the condition of the Northern United States towards the end of the first term of Mr. Lincoln's presidency? The most obvious effect of the civil war was the strengthening of the executive power. So terrible a crisis had restored to the presidential authority the strength that the Constitution had so wisely assigned to it, but which had been worn away during the long triumph of the democratic school. The necessary augmentation of the army and navy, the creation of numerous taxes destined to pay the interest of an overgrown public debt, contributed to extend the presidential patronage. The conservative interests, shaken by such violent commotions, rallied warmly round the central authority. A brisk reaction took place against the excesses of the democratic school; everything conspired to hasten it: the emission of gigantic loans, whose bonds circulated even in shanties and in all parts of the Union ; the forced adoption of paper money, all the holders of which were interested in the triumph of the government; the gradual substitution of the national banks, so called, to those already existing, whose credit was bound up intimately with that of the State; but, above all, the community of so many dangers faced together on the battle-field, so many emotions, and so many sorrows. Interests as well as passions brought the hearts of the people more and more to him who was the living expression of the national will.

With respect to parties, the influence of events had been none the less visible. During revolutionary epochs, parties are decomposed with great rapidity, and are obliged to look for new rallying points. While their framework is dissolved, their programmes are modified ; it becomes almost impossible to follow the currents of public opinion in all their windings, and we must be content with watching the main direction. Before the war the republican party had rejected the alliance of the abolitionists ; soon it sought them out, and banded with them against slavery Before the war the abolitionists were only a minority despised by statesmen. Soon their thought, their spirit, dictated the resolutions of Congress and of the Senate. Several years before, the abolitionists, hopeless of obtaining the abolition of slavery by constitutional means, openly preached disunion, and asked the North to break the tie that bound it to the South. For twenty years the war cry of Garrison had been, ' No union with slave-holders !' The abolitionists became the most ardent defenders of the Union, when the Union no longer meant slavery, but emancipation. As for the democrats, they still partly kept the prestige conferred by the long possession of power ; but the ground had, so to speak, given way under their feet. All the compromises, all the concessions that the party had obtained from the North in favour of the South, were claimed in the name of the Union ; and here was the South striking terrible blows at this same Union, and declaring itself its irreconcileable enemy. Then, as I said, the party divided itself into two factions. The first, the most numerous and influential, acknowledged the necessity of the war, and its opposition was confined within the limits of some questions raised by the civil war, such as the suppression of the habeas corpus and the conscription. The minority exhausted itself in useless efforts to establish a permanent agreement between the leaders of the South and the democrats of the North ; it was unable to shake either the patriotism of the nation or intimidate the government ; it did not even rise to the honours of persecution, and was able in a sort to conspire openly, even after the bloody troubles in New York, which it had brought about, and which had raised against it the indignation of the whole country.

CHAPTER IV.

THE PRESIDENTIAL ELECTION OF 1864.
THE CANDIDATES.

On the 7th September, 1864, the steamer 'Scotia,' on which I had embarked, came in sight of the low-lying coast of Long Island. In company with my fellow-passengers, I gazed on these shores, which were new to me. The blue hills of New Jersey soon came in sight, and we saw standing out against the dark and tremulous background of the sea the triangular sail of the pilot-boat. A small boat, manned by two oarsmen, came alongside of the gigantic steamer. In an instant the pilot sprang on deck ; he communicated the news to the captain, who ascended to the light bridge which connects the two paddle-wheels, ' Atlanta was taken,'— the democratic convention of Chicago had nominated General M'Clellan for the coming presidential election. The news of the great victory which had at last crowned Sherman's campaign in Georgia was received with triple salvos of hurrahs. The secessionists and blockade-runners made no attempt to protest against the general enthusiasm. The joy caused by the taking of Atlanta then became mixed with more complex sentiments, and we began to discuss M'Clellan's chances. The choice of the General was an astonishment to no one, but the news was not received with equal favour by all. During the passage I had heard few political discussions, but now party spirit awoke with a start, and before quitting the deck of the ' Scotia ' I began to feel myself in America.

The political spectacle which I was about to witness was something wholly new, and well worthy of attention. In England, and in other constitutional countries, we have seen ministers fall in the midst of war. The patriotism of a free people is not always so blind as to prevent a loyal opposition from demanding peace when it believes a war unjust and fatal to the country. Nevertheless, even in countries where the habits of free discussion are the most firmly established, it is difficult and often dangerous to struggle against that powerful and legitimate instinct which unites the honour of the citizen to the honour of the nation, against that natural love of glory which, fixing all its strength and will upon one symbol, makes of the flag the living emblem of the country. Thus almost always the executive power gathers new strength from war. Elsewhere, in constitutional monarchies, some things remain when a ministry is overturned : the sovereign, the army, public administrations. In the United States, the change of the Executive is a far deeper revolution. The President is followed in his retreat by all the officers whom he has named. A reflux takes place in all the currents of public life, like the irresistible ebb tide of the sea, which is felt in the least interstices of the rocks of the coast as well as on the widest shores.

The change of the whole executive power in the midst of war would seem of itself a perilous experiment;

but does not the experiment offer double dangers when the war is a civil war? Principles are then in opposition as well as armies. The spirit of discord enters into each province, each city, each hamlet, each fireside; passions are heightened, the noblest as well as the vilest instincts of humanity are roused during these times of trouble and decomposition : treachery crouches behind heroism, cowardice behind courage, and hate behind generosity.

At the opening of the war, when the cannon was fired against Sumter, party spirit seemed for a moment to abdicate before the spirit of patriotism ; a breath of enthusiasm had spread over the whole nation. It was confidently hoped that the rebellion would be crushed in a few months. The inevitable checks and slowness of the war permitted the old democratic party, over-thrown by the election of Mr. Lincoln, to reconstitute itself by degrees, to choose new leaders in place of those who spontaneously and loyally took their places beside the defenders and supporters of the government, to seek new rallying points, and to reform their ranks, which had been filled for so long by the majority of the nation. The war had seemed at first to have given a fatal blow to the democratic party of the North, which had shown itself during fifty years the faithful and compliant ally of the slaveholding oligarchy; but as time wore on, and the war still continued, the party took courage, and events seemed to serve its every wish—Mr. Lincoln's political moderation, who, coming to power in a most critical moment, called upon all and showed to the democrats, especially in the frontier States, an indulgence which often alarmed and irritated those who had nominated him to the Presidency; the attitude and political sentiments of M'Clellan attached, like most of the old graduates of West Point, to the traditions of the democratic party; the long-smothered and now open hostility between the young general and the Executive, his opposition to the emancipation policy and to the recruiting of black regiments, and the checks experienced in Virginia by the generals who succeeded him in the command of the army of the Potomac. Since the death of Douglas, familiarly called the 'little giant of the West,' the democrats had lost their leader. They found one in General M'Clellan: his campaign in the peninsula had been unsuccessful, but he had obtained a victory at Antietam which had given back to him some of his military prestige, and his name had thus regained a partial popularity among the masses. It was known that he was disposed to re-establish the Union by a political compromise, and his slightly enigmatic reserve suggested to many that he had received eventual promises from the leaders of the rebellion.

At times parties show a singular clairvoyance. Long before General M'Clellan had thrown himself into the Opposition, before he had written from Harrison's Landing, on the banks of the James River, while he was still commanding the army of the Potomac, a letter which was made public containing a censure on the emancipation policy and the principles which animated the Government in the conduct of the war, the leaders of the democratic party had cast their eyes on him as their candidate for the coming presidential election. Some even, those who were accustomed to consider Mr. Lincoln an intruder in the White House, went so far as to see in the commander of the army of the Potomac a republican Monk, whose mission was to re-establish what they called the old Union, and to proclaim peace on the continent. One might almost say that the democratic party had discovered a gene ral before it had found its soldiers. Nevertheless, its ranks were soon refilled, and the malcontents rallied again round their flag. The slowness of the war, the successive levies, the conscription, the disorder occasioned by the constant emission of paper money, necessarily sowed new seeds of opposition in the country. Notwithstanding, during the war, as well as before, the democrats and republicans separated principally upon the question of slavery. I know of no political phenomenon so strange as the blind attachment and devotion of a great party to an *institution* from which it derives no direct profit. The regret of the slaveholders for the old *régime* in States where slavery has been abolished, may be explained by the prejudice of their education, and the natural love of man for an authority without control : but it is difficult to comprehend by what secret power slavery had entered as a sort of religion into the hearts of so many Northern democrats who had never lived elsewhere than amongst free men. The hatred of the ignorant and semi-barbarous Irish population which the emigration has thrown upon the American continent may be attributed to a natural jealousy. An Irishman would see nothing below himself in the social scale if the law did not degrade the negro and take from him his citizen's rights. The democratic party — which finds in the great cities, and especially among the Irish, its noisiest and most faithful adherents — flatters the prejudices of the multitude, and uses them as a weapon against its adversaries.

There is, however, if I -mistake not, something besides ambition, something more than the love of power, in the sentiment which bound the leaders of this great party to the institution of slavery. There was mixed with it I know not what demagogic baseness, which confounded the ideas of independence and servitude, equality and oppression. The American democrat gave with the same hand to his adherents the joys of liberty and the pleasures of tyranny.

In proportion as the administration felt the force of liberal opinion and entered more and more decidedly into the path of the emancipation policy, the opposition of the democratic party became more impatient and more violent. With a little more foresight its leaders would have seen that they were mistaken, and were struggling against an irresistible current. The one advantage of war and force is to resolve with rapidity the questions that time and discussion can only decide slowly. In vain, in the beginning, the democrats, and even many republicans, repeated that there was no connection between the civil war and slavery, and that the sole object of the war was the re-establishment of the Union. The day when the men of the South took up arms against the Constitution of the States, they cut the

Gordian knot which was growing tighter every year. The good sense of the public was not led astray. It was not Mr. Lincoln who violently forced the nation into the path of political emancipation: the nation took this path herself with him. The emancipation proclamation of January 1, 1863, which gave liberty to all the slaves of the rebel States, was not dictated by the passing fancy of a solitary will; it was in harmony with the wishes of the nation, and with the greater part of the acts of the legislative power. We have not in Europe, perhaps, paid sufficient attention to the efforts of the Senate, the Congress, and the Legislatures to efface the last traces of slavery. Let me recall here all these measures: the abrogation of all laws relating to fugitive slaves,—the prohibition of the interior slave trade,—or from State to State,—the admission of coloured witnesses in the courts of justice of the United States,—free labour organised on a great number of plantations in South Carolina, Louisiana, Tennessee, and Western Virginia,—the enrolment of two hundred thousand negroes under the Union flag,—the warning given by Congress to the Federal Government not to employ any negroes who were still slaves,—the new treaty with England for the abolition of the slave trade,—the abolition of slavery in the district of Columbia,—the abolition of slavery in the State of Missouri,—the new Constitution voted by the State of Maryland, which emancipated all her slaves. Does not this nomenclature speak plainly enough, and does it allow us to believe that the emancipation policy was forced upon the President by a handful of fanatics?

The question of slavery, then, became again, as it was

before the war, the battle-field of all parties. The republican party, who met first in convention at Baltimore to nominate a candidate for the Presidency, announced openly in its programme that it would pursue the abolition of slavery as well as the re-establishment of the Union. The Baltimore convention, in supporting Mr. Lincoln's re-election, and in promising him the support of the republican party, declared itself for an amendment of the Constitution prohibiting slavery for ever, not only in all the territories, but in all the States of the republic. The language of the *platform* was simple and categoric: the war must be continued until the entire submission of the rebel States. Slavery must not survive the war. There was no hesitation in the choice of a candidate. Mr. Lincoln was nominated unanimously, and no other name was offered for discussion. It was not that all the leaders of the party professed a lively enthusiasm for Mr. Lincoln. Some were displeased with his slowness, his tergiversation; others found fault with his extreme indulgence of his favourite councillors, the incapacity he showed in forming a ministry whose members should be united by a common sympathy and common principles. Some made a crime of his ignorance of diplomatic affairs; and, to conclude, others again whispered that he was a politician of the lowest order, that he possessed none of the qualities and far-reaching views of a statesman—accustomed to place questions of persons above questions of principles, always endeavouring to conciliate the enemies of to-day at the risk of offending the friends of yesterday. At the

same time, all of these criticisms were made while the
party sat with closed doors, and were never given to
the public. The most railing republicans had always
felt the need of fortifying the moral authority of the
President, and their discontent had more than once
been smothered by their patriotism. Mr. Lincoln's
popularity had not been exposed to that work of
disparagement which in democracies wears out the
greatest reputations; his popularity was unchanged
in the feelings of the nation. The great trials of
the past four years had rendered him dearer to the
people; the instinct of the masses had, perhaps better
than the jealous sagacity of political men, penetrated
this strange character, where subtlety was mingled
with simplicity, goodness with irony, but where above
all there was so much honesty, patriotism, and disinterestedness. A small fraction, however, of the republican party had openly broken with Mr. Lincoln;
it had held its convention at Cleveland, and had
chosen for its candidate General Fremont. The
radical minority which met in the month of May
at Cleveland raised only vague reproaches against
Mr. Lincoln's administration; it reproached him with
having paralysed the enthusiasm excited in the country
by the taking of Fort Sumter, with having divided
the North, with having struck a blow at the liberties
of the country. It declared that, from an administrative, financial, and military point of view, the presidency of Mr. Lincoln had been only a series of
faults and errors. Meantime General Fremont did
not succeed in constituting a party. His staff was

composed of one or two ardent abolitionists and old democrats; behind this staff there was no army. Mr. Fremont had kept still a remnant of influence among the German populations of the West, but little by little his popularity declined, and he endeavoured in vain to recover it; it could not long be concentrated on this anxious and ever changing figure. When he found himself abandoned, Mr. Fremont retired from his candidature, and most of those who for a moment had gathered round him hastened to place themselves among the partisans of Mr. Lincoln. The democrats had not called their convention in the spring, at the same time as the republican party; they awaited events, and held themselves ready to profit by every fault and every defeat of Government. At last they thought the time had come, and they chose as it were the darkest hour of the year 1864, when General Grant, who had left the Potomac with a magnificent army, crossed the whole of Virginia, fighting a bloody battle almost every day, and at last, in spite of his indomitable energy, saw his efforts fail before the fortifications of Richmond. The hero of Vicksburg had found in Virginia a more disciplined and more redoubtable enemy than those whom he had combated in the West. He had hoped to overpower his adversaries by the number of his battalions, and to cut a bloody passage straight to the capital which so long had defied all the efforts of the United States; but these battles had but decimated his army, and he had been forced to fall back upon the banks of the James River, and to begin before Petersburg and Richmond the slow war of a siege.

The President had made a new call for 500,000 men, and the ranks were to be filled by conscription if it could not be done by voluntary enlistment. In Georgia the position of General Sherman occasioned the greatest anxiety. With no other communication than a single line of railway 200 miles long, Sherman had ventured as far as the centre of Georgia; he had begun a game where he could gain everything, but where he might also lose everything. The Southern journals exulted in seeing him approach Atlanta; they predicted that his whole army would be taken prisoners, and never be able to return to Chattanooga. Doubt, anxiety, and mistrust had cast their sinister shadows over the nation; lassitude had for a moment overcome the firmest courage.

During this time the democrats were at work, and circumstances conspired to facilitate more especially the efforts of those called the *peace democrats*, in opposition to the *war democrats*, who were ready to maintain the Union by force of arms, if the rebel States could not be brought back by a political compromise. The first were the least numerous, and public opinion had branded them with the name of *copperheads*, but they were skilful, active, and logical. They openly professed the doctrine of *state rights*, a doctrine which, if carried to its extreme limits, ends in the right of secession. Their sympathies were for Jefferson Davis and for slavery, and if they had not openly joined the rebels, it was because they still hoped to detach from the North the border States—those of the West, and even Pennsylvania and New York; they would thus have re-formed a new

Confederation, excluding only the abolitionist States of New England. It cannot be doubted that these projects were the favourite dream of some democrats. Mississippi had been given back to the Union by the taking of Vicksburg. The rebels could only hope thenceforward to form an independent government if they succeeded in obtaining the spontaneous and voluntary annexation to their confederation of the vast States of the West, and of the Mississippi Valley. And, if this new rupture took place in the North, might not they also detach the two great States of New York and Pennsylvania, where the democratic party had always been so powerful. The Copperheads had organised a strong opposition in all the frontier States where the influence of the slaveholders had so long been in the ascendant; they covered these States, together with those of the West, with secret societies recruited among the malcontents. General Price, the old Governor of Missouri, who had already invaded his native State in 1862, in the hopes of gaining it to secession, came back at the head of 20,000 men, and openly announced that he was about to make a last effort to wrest Missouri from the Federal army. In the State of New York, Governor Seymour was at the head of the most ardent and least scrupulous opposition. Tennessee and Louisiana were only maintained in obedience by the presence of the Federal armies, and the republicans watched in vain for the awakening of that Union element on which they had always counted to re-establish legal order in these States. All these circumstances had restored its old confidence to the democratic

F

party. Mr. Vallandigham, of Ohio—lately condemned for his complicity with the rebels to imprisonment for life, and who had been, by order of Mr. Lincoln, simply conducted across the Federal lines—had succeeded in getting to Canada. Returned to the United States, he gave free course to his bitter eloquence, and stirred up against him to whom he owed his liberty every dema-gogic passion. At New York, the two brothers Wood, who after the murderous outbreak which took place in that city after the battle of Gettysburg had retired for a moment into obscurity, reformed the ranks of their numerous democratic army always ready for disorder. Such were the allies who forced themselves upon those democrats who remained faithful to the Union and their country, and who were simply disposed to use their constitutional right to regain the power.

The convention of the democratic party took place at Chicago. The choice of this city was a flattery for the West, which was called to play a more and more preponderant part in the presidential elections, and in the general policy of the Union. Eighteen thousand or more persons met in this beautiful city, which, born but yesterday, has become the capital of the great lake region of America.

Governor Seymour was elected President of the con-vention, and Mr. Vallandigham was the principal author of the platform of the party. Divested of its phrase-ology, this document may be summed up in two pro-positions—an immediate armistice; then a convention of all the States, as well of the South as of the North, to settle the conditions of peace. In proposing an immediate armistice, the democratic party affirmed that the war waged during the three last years had been sterile and useless. This declaration, made in no measured terms, and which was a challenge, as it were, to the courage of the nation, roused a deep indignation in the North. No one can offend with impunity that delicate sentiment we call honour in individuals and patriotism in a nation. The Chicago platform was regarded as an insult to the country and the army; the injury was felt all the more keenly as the meeting of the democratic party was almost immediately followed by a succession of brilliant victories. Fortune again smiled on the Federal arms. One after the other came the news of the taking of Atlanta; of the glorious battles of Sheridan in the Shenandoah Valley; the capture of the forts which guarded the approach to Mobile, by the squadron of Farragut. General Grant had as yet obtained no decisive success, but his lines drew nearer together and extended all round Richmond and Petersburg, and new recruits came in every day to strengthen his army. All hearts were full of joy and hope; gold fell by rapid degrees. The discouragement of the long and oppressive summer months was succeeded by a return of confidence, enthusiasm, and manly and joyous resolution. Thus the months of autumn in the United States have a more brilliant splendour than those of midsummer: the horizons seem deeper; the light takes more varied reflections in the woods, which the approach of winter has covered with a magnificent livery unknown in our European clime. In spite of the smallness of their numbers, and their unpopularity,

the Copperheads, profiting by the general discouragement, had succeeded in dictating the Chicago platform;
they chose also from amongst their own ranks the candidate for Vice-President, Mr. Pendleton. For President,
the choice was made beforehand. The democratic party
had but one serious candidate to offer to the people
—General M'Clellan. A few days after the meeting at
Chicago, a committee went to New York, carrying the
resolutions of the democratic convention to the General. He was some time before giving a reply. He
was deeply irritated against the Government and some
of its members; he attributed the failure of his first
campaign in Virginia to the hostility of the Cabinet,
which had deprived him at a decisive moment of the
auxiliary troops on whom he had counted. The command of the army of the Potomac had been taken from
him almost the day after his victory of Antietam. After
the Chicago convention, one of the friends and councillors of the President, Mr. Blair—the father of Mr. Mont-
gomery Blair, who was Postmaster in Lincoln's Cabinet
—went himself, in spite of his great age, to General
M'Clellan, and endeavoured to determine him to repulse
the offers of the democratic party. He appealed to his
patriotism, showed him the dangers that the triumph of
that party, and the change in the Executive, might occasion. If the General had listened to the advice
of Mr. Blair, he would probably have soon received
another important military command, the clouds
which hung round his popularity would soon have
cleared away, and his political disinterestedness would
have been infallibly recognised by the American people.

But it was doubtless too late. The Chicago delegates awaited their reply; what had he to tell them? The press attacked the Chicago platform with lively indignation. Mr. Seward, in general so reserved, had for a moment descended into the political arena, and, in a speech at Auburn, denounced the framers of this programme as traitors in connivance with the South. From his camp at Petersburg, General Grant wrote a letter conceived in the same spirit, and made it his aim to show that there only remained one blow to strike to end the rebellion. To accept without comment the Chicago platform was to confess that the war had been an error; and so colossal an error, so fruitful in both public and private misfortune, was it not a crime? But was that the language befitting a captain who had often led to battle the soldiers of the Union, and sometimes to victory? Was it for him to lower his sword before the enemy? After some hesitation the General accepted the nomination; but he did it in terms which were an indirect disavowal of the platform of the party. He took the bride, but refused the dowry. ' I could not,' he says, ' face my brave comrades of the army and navy who have survived so many bloody battles, and tell them that their toil, and the sacrifice of our brothers has been in vain, that we have abandoned the Union, for which we have risked our lives so often.' Elsewhere he says again, 'The Union must be maintained at all hazards.' He separated himself thus from the *peace democrats*, and became the faithful organ of the sentiments of the *war democrats*; he knew that these last were the most numerous, although theirs had not

been the predominating influence at Chicago.   In their
eyes the war had no other object than the re-establishment of the Union.   As soon as the rebels should
show themselves ready to treat upon this basis, the
democrats would hasten to give them back full and
entire guarantees of all their constitutional rights, including the possession of their slaves. They considered
the emancipation proclamation and the arming of the
negro as dangerous measures, and as obstacles to the
re-establishment of peace. They said, with General
M'Clellan, 'The Union is the one condition of peace;
we ask no more.' Like him, they subordinated everything to the necessity of preserving the Union.

General M'Clellan's letter displeased the peace democrats, and some among them spoke for a moment of
calling together a new convention; but their ill-humour
was soon dissipated; they felt that the new President
could never cut entirely loose from those who had
brought him to power.

The Chicago platform remained the official expression, so to speak, of the opinions of the party : the
patriotism, the military honour of the old commander
of the Union armies had only added some stronger
accents to the language of the democratic convention.
But, as Mr. Charles Sumner well says, in a speech
which I heard him deliver in Boston, ' The rebellion
is but armed slavery, and if we yield to slavery, we
surrender to the rebels. The platform sacrifices the
Union; the letter professes a love of the Union, but
sacrifices emancipation, without which the Union is
henceforth impossible. The letter says, " The Union

is the one condition of peace; we ask no more." If the democratic candidate asks no more, others do. I ask more, for if we do not obtain more, the Union then becomes an empty name. I ask more in the name of justice and humanity, and that this frightful war may have its justification in history. The Baltimore convention asks more, Mr. Lincoln asks more, the American people ask more.' The result of the election justified Mr. Sumner's assertion; the American people chose between those who wished for slavery with Union, and those who wished Union without slavery.

CHAPTER V.

THE DUEL BETWEEN THE PARTIES.

WE have seen in the preceding chapter the conditions under which the electoral struggle took place. I shall now endeavour to retrace a few recollections of my voyage, and relate some of its episodes, that the reader may better understand the organisation of parties, and the working of democratic institutions, in the United States.

I arrived too late to attend any of the general conventions of the different parties; but I was soon enabled to witness a State convention held in Massachusetts. It is impossible to form an exact idea of the political institutions of the United States unless we study the organisation of the parties on the spot, and the system of conventions forms an essential element of this organisation. This system is applied to the interior government of the States, as well as to the government of the Confederation; to the administration of counties, districts, and towns, as well as to that of the State. The organism of American parties may be compared to that of vegetable growth: the meetings and committees of the townships represent the elementary cells; the State conventions, the fibres; the general conventions, the trunk. This comparison is all the more exact as the primary communal committees form the base of the whole politic organism, as that of the cell is the origin and substance of the whole vegetable edifice. The principle of self-government brought from England to the United States by the first colonists, has constantly enlarged the circle of its empire, but it has always remained fixed in its primitive centre, which is the township. Political life circulates incessantly from centre to circumference, and from circumference to centre, and keeps up without cessation the activity of those great bodies called parties. This powerful circulation is never interrupted, but it becomes naturally more rapid at the approach of any great political crisis. Before the presidential election, the members of each party meet together in all their townships, and choose delegates; these latter meet in their States, and designate their representatives for the general convention, which publishes its programme and chooses its candidates. Then an inverse movement takes place. New State conventions are called to ratify the acts of the general convention, and choose the names of the candidates for the functions of presidential electors; to these names the State convention adds those of the candidates for the vacant State functions. Each party thus forms its *ticket*; that is, a list which comprehends the presidential electors, the governor, the State officers, and the representatives whose seats are vacant in Congress. The day of the presidential election, each citizen chooses among the different lists, and modifies them at his will. The mandate of the presidential elector is in fact an imperative one, so that the name of the list which triumphs shows the name of the future Pre-

sident long before the electors have sent their sealed
vote to the Senate. These few explanations were necessary to make clear the character of the State convention
at which I was present in Massachusetts, when all the
parties had already chosen their candidates for the Presidency, in general convention. Special trains had been
provided to carry to Worcester, on the morning of the
14th September 1864, 1,625 republican delegates, sent
by the townships of Massachusetts. The manufacturing
town of Worcester, situated in the heart of the State,
owes to its central position the privilege of being always
chosen as the place of meeting of parties, rather than
Boston. The delegates, as I explained above, had been
elected by their political sympathisers in the primary
assemblies, and all brought credentials from the committees of their townships. Arrived at Worcester, they
went at once to a great building called *Mechanics' Hall*,
specially used for popular meetings. The principal hall
is of vast size, and can easily contain 3,000 persons. A
raised platform at one end served for the officers of the
meeting and the speakers. The hall was filled with
delegates. The auditors entered freely, and took their
places in a large gallery which occupied three sides of
the hall. A provisional board of officers was named, and
on the proposition of one of the delegates, the first committee was formed, composed of as many members as
there are electoral districts in the State, to organise defi-
nitely the board of officers of the convention. A second
committee was charged with the examination of the
credentials. These committees met round the desks of
the platform, and quickly made their report,   One of

the members of Congress was called to the chair, and
the meeting accepted a list of vice-presidents and secretaries. As soon as the permanent board was named,
the convention chose its candidates for the political ma-
gistratures of Massachusetts; that is, for the functions
of Governor, Lieutenant-Governor, Secretary of State,
State Treasurer, Auditor, and Attorney-General. Some
years ago, the Governor of Massachusetts, assisted by his
councillors, chose himself the magistrates who were to
second him. The democrats at last succeeded in taking
from him this prerogative, but that party at least never
succeeded in giving up the choice of the judges of the
law tribunals to popular suffrage, as in the States of
New York, Pennsylvania, and in the Western States.
The nominations to the State functions were made
without discussion, with the exception of the choice of
Attorney-General; this last was undecided for a long
time, and recourse was had to a regular ballot.

After the ministerial officers of State, the convention
named two presidential electors *at large.* These words
require explanation. The President of the United
States, as we know, is not elected by direct and
universal suffrage. The electors in the second degree,
chosen by the people in the State-elections, represent not only the mass of the citizens, they represent
also the federal principle. In consequence, the electoral
body is modelled exactly upon the Congress, where
each State invariably sends two senators, and more
or less representatives, according to the population.
The representatives correspond to electors named in
the same districts, and the senators to the electors *at*

large; that is, elected by the whole State. Besides the votes to which its population gives it a right, each State throws thus into the balance two supplementary votes, which represent in a certain manner the abstract principle of its individuality.

The convention of Worcester did not choose the district electors; these are named in the electoral districts. It only chose two senatorial electors. One of these, chosen in the midst of enthusiastic applause, was Edward Everett, who had been minister of the United States in England, and candidate for the vice-presidency in 1860. Attached during all his life to the conservative principles of the old whig party, Mr. Everett made a temporary alliance with that fraction of the democratic party which desired to see Mr. Bell President, in the hope of checking the triumph of that exalted and unscrupulous democracy who had chosen Breckenridge and Douglas as their candidates. The so-called Bell-Everett party did not survive the presidential campaign of 1860. The war broke out soon after the election of Mr. Lincoln, and Mr. Bell followed for a time the fortunes of the South. Mr. Everett, on the contrary, remained faithful to that Union whose glorious founders he had so often celebrated in such eloquent language. Then came a sort of second youth to this old man. The cunning and violence of parties had sometimes carried him away, and bent him at their will; but before this civil war he raised his head, and his noble patriotism found vent in accents which have been rarely surpassed in the annals of political eloquence.

A committee prepared and submitted a series of resolutions to the approbation of the assembly; the resolutions, developed at length, may be resumed in these terms—an energetic pursuance of the war, abolition of slavery, re-election of Mr. Lincoln, no armistice on any basis but that of unconditional submission to the arms of the United States. These resolutions were supported by several speeches. That of Mr. Bullock, of Worcester, captivated my attention. One other figure remains, together with that of Mr. Bullock, engraved on my memory—that of the minister who, according to the custom, opened the meeting with prayer. Still young, with long flowing hair and beard like the pictures of Christ, I see him still, motionless and with closed eyes; I hear his slow and deep accents echo through the immense hall in the midst of a profound silence. His eloquence was at the same time strong and tender; he called down the celestial mercy upon his people punished for having oppressed an unhappy race: but he offered to God, if it were necessary, fresh sacrifices with an ardour in which there was more of pride than resignation. With his unwrinkled, and at the same time careworn, brow, where strength had banished grace, this face appeared to me as a living image of the New England of olden times, pious, austere, and laborious, which in its rude wooden houses prepared itself for its lofty destinies. Had I not before me the direct descendants of those emigrants who brought first to the new continent faith and liberty? Not one of the 1,600 delegates sent from all parts of Massachusetts was personally known to me. By their simple dress, heavy shoes, and sunburnt hands, I recognised on all sides artisans, farmers, fishers of the coast. All seemed perfectly familiar with parliamentary usages ; they rose, spoke without embarrassment, without affectation. I have never seen more perfect order reign in so numerous an assembly. Each brought with him to this general convention habits long acquired in the meetings of their townships, cities, and electoral districts.

On their return to their towns, the delegates to the general convention convoke their partisans, and render them an account of their mission, in meetings which bear the singular name of *caucuses*. A short time after the republican convention, I attended the republican caucus of a small town of Massachusetts. The meeting took place in the evening, in the town-hall. I proceeded there by the light of an aurora borealis. The low arch from whence sprung the moving rays, which at times reached as high as the zenith, threw a strange, pale and troubled light upon the little hills covered with dwarf cedars, and upon the white houses and stone walls which form the boundaries of land in Massachusetts. The caucus was neither numerous nor animated. The first business was the preparation for a popular meeting where all the partisans of Mr. Lincoln were to meet; after that were named candidates for the office of *select man*. A candidate was named for each school district. The township had no less than eight schools for a population of 8,000 inhabitants, spread, it is true, over a great surface.

Schools in the United States are the elementary agglomeration which serves as a basis and support to the township. They are thus the cradles of the civil institutions, and primary education is the source of political education.

While the republicans were holding their caucus in one room of the townhall, the democrats met in committee in another. The entrance to the municipal edifice is never refused to a meeting of citizens for a political motive. All parties need liberty : in the hour of triumph they do not dream of depriving their adversaries of the rights themselves have invoked when out of power. Some days before the republican general convention in the Mechanics' Hall at Worcester the democrats of the State had also held their general convention there.

In Boston, long before the War of Independence, a Frenchman named Peter Faneuil left to the municipality of that city a considerable sum of money to build a public hall, with the condition that its use should never be refused to the request of a certain number of citizens. With this money was built *Faneuil Hall*, which is often called *the cradle of American liberty*. There were heard the first protesting voices against the tyrannical acts of the British Government. There the first abolitionists could speak to the American people, when elsewhere their voices were smothered. During the period of the presidential campaign, hardly an evening passed on which the doors of Faneuil Hall were not opened both to the democrats and the republicans. Thanks to the unlimited liberties which they enjoy, political parties in the United States can give themselves a very powerful organisation. The primary assemblies, district conventions, general conventions, form a sort of organism which is sustained and governed by party spirit, as the solar system is governed by gravitation. Party spirit, instead of showing itself destructive as in countries where it is not regulated, becomes here, on the contrary, a guarantee of preservation. It is easy to conceive, that these political organisms, which embrace the smallest towns as well as the *ensemble* of the confederation, cannot be changed or created in a single day; it is by no means easy to fill up so extended an outline. The democratic party which has been in office since Jefferson, up to the election of Mr. Lincoln, still keeps to-day a large part of the power which was acquired during that long period. The actual republican party was not born in 1860; it is but the last transformation of the old whig party, which through many vicissitudes has never entirely lost sight of two objects: the consolidation of the executive power, and the limitation of slavery. Political traditions could not be transmitted from generation to generation, in a democracy, without these great governments of opinion which reign in the peaceful dominion of ideas.

In countries where the electoral body is small, and where there exists a privileged class, a community of interests imposes consistency, as if it were of itself, to political action; but in the United States, where suffrage is universal, where the division of classes is scarcely marked, where reigns the most perfect equality, and at the same time the most entire liberty, the electoral body, were it not guided by party traditions, would become a sort of shadowy form, blown hither and thither by every idle wind. In such a society there is nothing but the moral action of parties, always vigilant and always active, which can serve as a defence against anarchy or despotism. It is strange also to observe how much party spirit loses its bitterness and intensity when every day it finds an occasion of manifesting itself, when it mingles in all the relations of public life, when it is not forced to wait for rare and solemn occasions to show its ardour. The presidential election, which is renewed every four years, agitates the country, it is true, to its deepest depths; but this emotion is not expressed differently from the ordinary and local emotions which have for their theatre only the State, the city, and the town. No one is alarmed by it, no one sees anything more than is natural in it, and the regulations of the great duel between the parties are all traced beforehand.

Although the organisation of parties in the United States must be considered as a political necessity, and as a guarantee of stability and order, we can nevertheless see some drawbacks. We can, for example, reproach it with warping the presidential elections, and giving up the choice of the chief magistrate of the republic, not as the Constitution directs, to an independent electoral body, but to a convention, which imposes its decisions on the presidential electors. We can also charge it with having enlarged beyond measure the importance of those men called politicians, and who are the active leaders of parties. The politician has nothing in common with the true statesman; he requires neither profound instruction nor a high character, nor even great eloquence: what he needs is, the art of understanding and directing men; a profound knowledge of the vices and qualities of the human heart, with a natural taste for action, intrigue, and patronage. The name of *politician*, in the mouth of many Americans, is almost equivalent to an insult. But we hardly see how parties could dispense with these daily instruments; there has never been an army without a staff. I could not help observing, at Worcester, that the work of the meeting was, in a certain manner, prepared beforehand; the lists of the committees, the resolutions, the names of the candidates —all that was not, and could not be, wholly improvised. In the meantime the leaders could do nothing without consulting and knowing the popular sentiment; they are political weathercocks, who mark without ceasing the direction of the great currents of opinion. The true statesman can always speak to the nation over the head of the politician, certain that, if he can be heard and followed by the people, he has nought to fear from parasites, who live by popularity alone. When the work of parties is terminated, when the electoral lists are completed, there remains still another task to accomplish. Then begins the struggle for popular favour, then it is that the most violent attempts are made to influence popular opinion by the thousand voices of the press, tribune, and even the pulpit. Popular orators, members of Congress, senators, and governors, begin the canvass—the electoral crusade. They go from city to

city, preaching to the people, comparing programmes,
discussing the claims of the rival candidates. Meetings
daily succeed each other. The most imposing one
which I witnessed was held at Faneuil Hall, in Boston,
on the 28th of September. The republicans, who had
met in the clubs of the different districts, crossed the
city with torchlights, banners, and transparencies, on
which were painted their favourite devices. When
I arrived at the great hall, three thousand persons
had already taken their places, and outside Faneuil
Hall there had been two temporary platforms erected,
occupied by orators addressing those who had been
unable to find places in the interior. From the platform where I was, among the officers of the meeting
and the orators of the evening, the hall appeared
to me like a sea of moving heads; all present were
standing closely packed shoulder to shoulder, and
from time to time irresistible currents swayed in divers
directions the animated mass, as the wind bends the
waving corn.

During four hours the orators held the attention of
the crowd. One of them, just come from Maryland,
carried the enthusiasm of the audience to its height
by evoking the remembrance of the soldiers of Massachusetts killed at the beginning of the war in the streets
of Baltimore, on their way to protect the city of Washington. 'I have come,' exclaimed he, 'to bring you
the price of that blood; it is the new constitution of
Maryland which abolishes slavery.' There was in the
eloquence of this young orator, who gesticulated with
violence, and who ran from one end to the other of the

platform, a southern grace which charmed and astonished the inhabitants of Boston, accustomed to less demonstrative speakers.   Mr. Charles Sumner pronounced the principal discourse of the evening ; his grave and sonorous voice was heard above all the noise of the immense crowd, while he developed, with an inflexible logic, the separate programmes of the democratic and the republican parties.   I observed attentively the coloured men mingled amongst the auditory.   Their sparkling eyes followed the least movement of him who so long ago had constituted himself their defender ; and on these humble faces I could read purer and truer sentiments than those in which vulgar popularities think to find their consecration.

Some time after, on my return from an excursion in the White Mountains, I stopped at the town of Springfield, situated in Massachusetts, on the borders of the Connecticut River.   During several days, geology and botany would have made me completely forget the presidential election if from time to time I had not seen an electoral flag floating over some half hidden village of New Hampshire and Vermont.   Scarcely was I arrived in Springfield when I heard from my room a great noise of music and drums ; and drawing near the window I saw, in the distance, a long cortége preceded by torches.   I inquired into the object of this manifestation, and learned that one of the democratic clubs of the city was about to hold a meeting upon the hill on which stand the buildings of the United States 'Arsenal. I followed the cortége, which defiled down the principal street.   Numerous spectators crowded the wide brick *sidewalks* (trottoirs), and I overheard, in passing by the different groups, some ironical remarks. ' Then there are some democrats left; I thought they were all dead; their procession looks like a funeral.' Nothing more—no cries, no insults, no blows. The procession soon turned, and ascended the hill by a wide avenue bordered with magnificent elms. On either side of the avenue I perceived pretty villas half hidden in the trees, and surrounded by gardens. Soon I walked beside the high massive iron fence which encloses the vast grounds, in the centre of which rise the noble arsenal buildings, surrounded by beautiful lawns; at night they might be taken for palaces, for there is nowhere to be seen the scattered materials and débris which in general are accumulated round a workshop. At last the crowd halted on the top of the hill, an improvised president rose from among the multitude, the meeting begins. And first they proceed to business, and name delegates for the meeting of the party; they choose a committee, to be charged with the preparations for a mass meeting of the democrats of Springfield. A little girl, scarce eight years old, is then raised up beside the president, and sings, in a sharp, piercing voice, a song in honour of General M'Clellan. I still recall the chorus :—

> ' We have another Washington,
> Let's vote for little Mac.'

At this point one of the orators sprang to his feet and made a long speech, the most striking point of which was a laborious comparison between the copper-head and another serpent called the black snake;

which naturally represented the black republicans and the abolitionists. Every allusion to the unfortunate blacks is seized upon with transport by the ignorant and brutal auditory, principally composed of Irish workmen. The orator never says negro, but *nigger*; and never pronounces that contemptuous name without a savage air of provocation. I could not avoid recalling the frightful scenes of which New York was but lately the theatre—of these poor blacks pursued through the streets, stabbed, and burned; of the asylum of coloured orphans fired and sacked. The moon was at the full, and shed a soft light on the crowd before me; on the fair faces of the women who mingled with the workmen; upon the elms, with their graceful, drooping branches. The crowd seemed, except at the moments when it uttered its rude hurrahs, so orderly, so quiet, that at times I could scarcely comprehend anything of what was passing under my eyes. What an abyss is the heart of man! Why such hatred under this clement sky, amidst all these gifts of nature, these triumphs of human intelligence? On one side I saw the walls of the arsenal, where an army of two hundred thousand men would find arms and equipments; and, on the other, a multitude whom the very name of the negro seemed to rouse to fury. The crowd helped me to understand the arsenal. Can a nation be at peace with itself when it is not at peace with humanity?

In great cities like New York, Philadelphia, and Boston, these processions through the streets serve not only to captivate the imagination of the masses; many hesitating electors compare the rival armies, and place themselves in the ranks of the strongest battalions; consequently, the acting committees do not hesitate to incur very heavy expenses to give the greatest possible éclat to these manifestations. I was in Philadelphia at the time of the great democratic procession; it took place a few days before the election, the evening of October 29th. The city of Philadelphia is divided into twenty-six wards; each ward was represented by a numerous troop of mounted horsemen, by standard bearers and transparencies and a car drawn by several horses, and lastly by a long procession of men walking in soldierly order. All wore round their hats wide bands of white paper, on which was inscribed the number of their ward. The most part carried torches, or long sticks with lamps suspended at their extremity. The horsemen were decked with scarves and garlands of coloured paper. The cars were ornamented with numerous flags, and one of these enormous carriages, drawn by six horses, was filled with young girls representing the different States of the Union. Among the white dresses and floating draperies, the rebel States were distinguishable by the long black veils and mourning garb.

On another car there was a small cannon, and from time to time the sound of a loud detonation mingled with the cries and hurrahs of the crowd. Small fire crackers went off on all sides, and long rockets ascended above the roofs of the houses. Occasionally Bengal lights, burning on one of the cars, illuminated the street with their soft splendour, and the long moving train of horsemen, cars, and banners was enveloped in a red or violet cloud.   All the windows were crowded with women waving their handkerchiefs, who answered with cheers the hurrahs of the cortége.   The transparencies especially fixed the attention of the spectators ; illuminated in the interior by a lamp, they showed on their four sides mottoes, caricatures, and portraits, and their bearers kept them constantly turning, to show them on every side.   Here we recognised among them the long thin *silhouette* of Mr. Lincoln, with a fat negress on each arm ; elsewhere the President was represented, carpet-bag in hand, hurrying down the steps of the White House.   I saw upon another these words ' Abolitionism the cancer of the nation,' and between these words was painted a gigantic cancer, with its red veins and knotted roots.   The most perfect order seemed to reign in the long procession, which was formed of not less than 5,000 men ; but I learned, the next morning, that the democrats had assumed a threatening attitude before the republican club-house, and had broken with brickbats the two large transparencies in the windows representing Mr. Lincoln and Mr. Johnson.   Many of the fine plate-glass fronts of the adjoining shops had been smashed, and a chance brickbat had killed a poor old Irishman who was probably of the same party as his involuntary murderer.

I witnessed still another democratic procession in Boston, on the very eve of the presidential election.   It rained in torrents, and the horsemen, banners, and transparencies were covered with a heavy fog ; the half smothered and smoky torches shed but a feeble light on the cortége. The democrats carried in a mock funeral procession the effigy of Mr. Lincoln; but this sinister pleasantry was turned against themselves by more than one witness. They celebrated in effect the funeral of their own party, and this sombre evening heard their last cry of hope and triumph. The next day, the 8th of November, Boston was so still and tranquil that one might have fancied it was Sunday. I took my way towards the buildings where the balloting had began. At the door I was offered on all sides the democratic ticket; the distributors gave me at the same time a thousand recommendations. 'Here is the only. true good ticket; beware of the red ticket, it's the bad one.' At the top of the stairs, a silent distributor put this red list in my hand, and I recognised the republican ticket. Each elector as he entered gave his name to the *tellers* (those who count the votes), who looked for his name on a list, and when it was found there his vote was accepted. I saw one of the most eminent lawyers of Boston arrive there, preceded and followed by ˋa negro. The coloured man enjoys in the State of Massachusetts all a citizen's rights, and, to be an elector, he has only to pay in common with every citizen his *poll tax*, which is only two dollars for a term of two years. During the days preceding the election there were many rumours of plots and conspiracies, and disorders which were to break out in New York and several of the great Western cities. Secessionists secretly come from Canada were to seize Camp Jackson, situated in the environs of Chicago, to deliver the 12,000 rebel prisoners who were kept there, to throw themselves with them upon the beautiful capital of the Western States, and to sack and destroy it. Detroit, situated just opposite Western Canada, was also to be surprised, sacked, and burned. Some of the conspirators were discovered and arrested. Chicago and the Canadian frontier were placed under a strict *surveillance.* In New York there was no less anxiety. The democrats, sure of the connivance of the municipality and of Governor Seymour, had openly declared that they would not allow free voting for Mr. Lincoln ; they had organised their forces, and held themselves ready for any violence. Some days before the election the Government sent General Butler to New York, and entrusted him with the command of the United States troops stationed in the environs. The mere name of Butler threw terror over the democratic ranks ; he announced in a manifesto that the election would take place as usual, and without the aid of mili tary authority, but that any attempt at disorder would be promptly repressed by the troops under his command. In the democratic meetings which preceded his arrival, the desperadoes had publicly declared that his life would be attacked, but he was soon seen slowly crossing New York on horseback in full uniform, followed by his staff. The day of the election passed without disorder, and the democrats had only the satisfaction of giving a majority of 37,000 votes to their candidate.

As early as the day after, and although the definitive figures were not ascertained, it was known throughout the Union that Mr. Lincoln was re-elected. From each

village, each city, the numbers were sent to the committees of either party ; the *employés* of the telegraph
and post offices and railways were occupied with little
else. The victory of the republicans was soon certain ;
it became a brilliant triumph when, to the votes of
New England and the West, were added the 26 votes
of Pennsylvania, and lastly the 33 votes of the State of
New York ; there remained to the democratic party only
the little State of New Jersey, and two slave States, Delaware and Kentucky. Mr. Lincoln received 213 votes to
General M'Clellan's 21. Not only had the republicans
given an enormous majority to their candidate, but they
had succeeded in sending to Congress a sufficient number
of deputies to obtain there the two-thirds majority
without which it was impossible that the Constitution should be amended. In the Senate, as well as in
the House of Representatives, the republicans were
certain beyond doubt of the majority of three-fourths of
the votes. The executive and legislative powers were
then in perfect harmony, and thus for the first time
since many years the legislative power found itself
armed with sufficient authority to undertake the revision
of the national Constitution, and to efface from it every
trace of that fatal institution which had brought upon
the country the scourge of civil war. An absolute
calm succeeded at once to the emotions, anxieties,
and agitations which preceded the 8th of November.
The triumph of the republicans had nothing noisy in it :
theirs was not the febrile joy which salutes the victories
obtained on the battle-field; it was mute, deep, and self-
contained. Even the minority bowed with respect

before the expression of the popular will, and was not insensible to the grandeur of the spectacle offered to the world by the American people, when in the midst of the convulsions of civil war, and among so many hostile interests of hate and passion, it accomplished, with the same tranquillity as in the days of peace and prosperity, the normal functions of its constitutional life.   Even the cannon before Richmond were silent, and the two armies during a tacit truce gave themselves up to the same pre-occupations.

CHAPTER VI.

FROM BOSTON TO NIAGARA.

BOSTON has been sometimes called 'the city of three hills.' A great part of New England is, like it, formed by gently-swelling hillocks. Before the country had a name, a great plane smoothed off all its roughnesses; an irresistible force passing over the hard syenites, granites, greenstones and conglomerates, has drawn a network of straight and striated furrows over them. Was it, as Agassiz thinks, an enormous glacier, covering the whole of North America, which left these traces, ground down the rocks, and modelled the country as it now is? Did a violent deluge roll, pell-mell, all the débris that throw their rough cloak over the silurian strata of New England? Or was it only icebergs, come from the pole, that dropped their cargoes of erratic boulders, as they still continue to do on the banks of Newfoundland? These are the questions I put to myself, towards the end of the month of September, in going through the cuttings of the railway that leads from Boston to Portland in Maine, and which beyond goes on to Canada, passing at the foot of the White Mountains, which I was on my way

to visit. Few of the people round me paid any attention
to the landscape; men and women read the morning
papers; soldiers, convalescent or on furlough, wrapped
in their blue coats, kept up the talk of the camp.   Only
a few Englishmen, *en route* for Canada, looked with an
air of wearied curiosity upon the rounded hills, crowned
with little cedars, the clumps of elms, maples, oaks, the
little neat white wooden houses surrounded with trees
and orchards, and the golden rods and the brown
clusters of the sumachs that grew all along the track.
Perhaps they were looking, though unable to find it,
for some cabin, some shanty, some trace of misery.
But if in America nature still retains here and there
some of the grace of the wilderness, if wild flowers
border cultivated fields, all the abodes of man, built
with care, have a certain air of decency and finish that
is a perpetual wonder to European travellers.

As far as Portland, the railway keeps near the sea,
which dances and sparkles beneath a radiant sun.   Its
fringe of foam beats capriciously against the savage
rocks of Nahant, kisses the sands of Marblehead, and
dies away at the foot of the beautiful pine forests of
Beverley.   The mouth of the Merrimac is crossed at
Newburyport, and, at Portsmouth, that of the Pisca-
taqua.   The rivers nearly all keep their fine Indian
names; the towns have mostly foreign names, and
those given by chance.   Marshy meadows extend
into the valleys, and are overflowed by the tide, which
leaves a salt deposit on the grass: the hay is kept in
ricks, perched on little piles to protect them from high
water.   From the sands and gravel that cover the coasts

of New Hampshire and Maine rise here and there, like walls, the worn and rounded hills. Pastures follow woods, and woods pastures ; the sharply-cut leaves of the maples stand out against the dark background of savins or the blueish green of the pines. You are never tired of admiring this rich vegetation, whose decay is more splendid than its maturity. At a distance the hill-sides look like a painter's palette. The oaks keep their natural colour till the end of September, but all the other deciduous trees are already touched by the hand of autumn.

Portland has a magnificent harbour ; the nearly ver-tical slates of the coast strike down below the water, and form an enclosure which the largest vessels in the world can easily enter ; the ' Great Eastern,' to whom so many ports are closed, can come in. There are twenty-five churches in Portland for a population of 25,000 inhabitants. The spirit of the Puritans has taken deep root among all these fishers and lumberers of Maine. A soldier returning to Bangor told me of the painful marches he had made in the last summer campaign in Virginia. ' Sir, we were forced to throw away everything ; knapsacks, blankets, and change of clothes. The day came when I had to throw away my pocket bible that had never quitted me for two years.' In the army he had been faithful to the Maine liquor law, and nothing but water had touched his lips. Per-haps the North had no better regiments than those from this State, made up of tall, robust, sober men, patient hunters, and bold woodsmen. The log-house of their forests, built of unsquared trunks, was the model of the shelters constructed by the Federals in their winter quarters. Since the opening of the war, Maine has given 61,000 men to the army and navy of the United States ; that is to say, a tenth of her whole population. In the one year of 1864 this State furnished 1,846 sailors and 17,148 soldiers, 3,525 of whom were veterans who re-enlisted.

The quays and all the railway depôts of Maine are piled up with pine trunks and boards. The chief centre of the lumber trade is, however, Bangor, on the Penobscot. The white pine (*pinus strobus*) 'is the most sought for, in the great forest that stretches uninterruptedly over the northern half of Maine, the largest part of New Brunswick, the north-east of the State of New York, and the adjacent parts of Canada. This tree, light in colour and with long needles, sometimes reaches sixty metres in height. It is used exclusively for masts, and the wood, cut into planks, laths, shingles, and pieces of all shapes and sizes, is sent all over the United States. The plateau between the Atlantic and the St. Lawrence is covered with resinous trees. The waters of Maine flow on the north into the St. John and the Chaudière rivers, on the south into the Penobscot and the Kennebec, which flow towards the fiords of the coast. An archipelago of lakes, if I may be allowed the expression, alone interrupts the monotony of the verdurous desert. The levels differ but little, and the boatmen pass from one to the other by short *portages* (an expression adopted long ago by the Canadians). According to an old Indian tradition, the Penobscot could flow either north or south as it pleased.

On leaving Portland, the railway that goes from Boston to Canada crosses a lonely and wooded region ; a mantle of sand and gravel covers with its undulations the rocky framework which crops out at intervals in higher and higher walls. Along the track there is often nothing left of the forest but trunks and blackened stumps : sometimes they are torn up, and the ragged roots make the first enclosures of the fields. The vocabulary of American geography is fertile in surprises : all of a sudden we are at Oxford, and a little further on at Paris. This unknown Paris consists of a few houses lost among the maples and oaks of the valley of the Little Androscoggin. The setting sun throws its rays on the gold and purple of the woods, and gilds the sleeping lakes where the river takes its rise. A little beyond we enter the valley of the Great Androscoggin, rushing with a joyful noise from the hills where the Connecticut also takes its source. We follow this valley as far as Gorham in New Hampshire, and on both sides the already solemn and grandiose lines of the chains which serve as ramparts to the group of the White Mountains are drawn out in the descending shadows. It is night when the train drops us at the door of the Alpine House. From the wooden portico I see the sparkling plume of the locomotive diminishing in the distance ; before me the crescent moon shines softly above the mountains that fill one whole half of the heavens.

I left early the next morning to ascend Mount Washington, the highest peak of the White Mountains : this mountain is 6,285 feet in height. A carriage-

H

road has been lately made to the very summit; it leads at first to the foot of the mountain, rounded like a shield. Ascending a wild valley, the road, intersected by torrents, goes through a forest where birches are more numerous than evergreens. Among these latter you very soon learn to distinguish the *pérusse* (*abies Canadensis*), whose light and delicate foliage makes a sort of lighter lacework against the blackish greens of the other pines. Emerging from this forest, you enter a vast amphitheatre shut in on all sides by mountains. A great wooden hotel, called the Glen House, has been built there. Opposite to the mountain and its enormous slopes, the immense hotel looks like a hut. A brown bear, fastened by a chain, walks sadly round the post that holds him prisoner. They have at least left him a free view of the woods where he was born.

The real ascent begins from the Glen House. Six strong horses slowly drag the heavy carriage up the ledges cut on the side of the mountain, through the rocks, the wild-flowers, the maples, the birches, and the pines. Here and there are the traces of a fire; the grey and naked rocks only support whitened trunks, that look like phantoms at a distance. The maples disappear first, then the birches; but this latter species has an extraordinary rusticity and power of resistance, for you find individuals of it at a very great height. The zone of pines has an indescribable look of sadness and desolation; everywhere we see dead trunks falling against live trees, torn branches, drooping mosses. Soon the pines, beaten by the winds, cling with more twisted roots to the rocks ; but the wind and the cold end by vanquishing that secret force that flows with the sap and carries it upwards. Vanquished, crushed, bent, the last firs are deformed dwarfs ; they crawl like monstrous mosses on the surface of the ground, and in the yawning interstices of the gneiss. Higher up, even in the region where the lichens cling like a tenacious mould to the peaks for ever beaten by the winds, Nature, as if to prove her fertility, sows here and there exquisitely beautiful flowers. This hanging garden sees the unfolding of the exotic plants of Labrador and Lapland ; but these delicate wonders are invisible to a superficial gaze ; and beyond the zone of the evergreens the mountain is nothing but a vast desert of stone. The gneiss which forms the summit, broken into gigantic rocks, shows its undulating and irregular veins of quartz, feldspar, and sparkling mica. From this great heap of rocks the eye follows with pleasure the sombre slopes, shaggy with pines, and the depths of the valleys where the rusty browns, the orange and the scarlet of the birches and maples light up the velvet background of the evergreens.

Going along, I enter into conversation with the driver, by praising his skill in driving six in hand. He becomes confidential, tells me he is born in the State of New York, that he is a democrat, and is going to vote for M'Clellan. He complains of the war, of the high price of everything, and above all of the draft. He went to Portland the day before, to buy a substitute from a friend of his, an old driver like himself, turned substitute broker. 'Do you think,' said he to me, 'that these dealers in men are any better than slave dealers?' Nevertheless, on questioning him, I find that his substitute will only cost him five hundred dollars, a sum which must be reduced nearly one-half if you wish to know its gold value, and which certainly does not seem very high after a four years' war.

A thin layer of clouds, which had obstinately stuck to Mount Washington ever since early morning, hindered me from the full enjoyment of the view from the top, the distinguishing characteristic of which is that nothing in it recalls man. You see only the unbounded forest; a few lakes scattered here and there like the fragments of a broken mirror on a carpet. Neither cultivated valleys, nor towns, nor villages; the undulations of the mountains hide the spot where man has made himself a little place. Is it wonderful that, in the immense loneliness of the woods, the Indians should have personified the mountains? The Anglo-Saxon race has not shown enough respect for the names they gave them. Mount Agiochook has become Mount Washington. Nevertheless, in the distance, Monadnoc and Kearsage* still keep their singular names, and from the interminable forest that stretches away to the north-east the masses of Ktaadn rise like a bluish cloud against the horizon. In this direction civilisation has as yet left but few traces. There is no need of going beyond the Mississippi to see Indians and virgin forests. You will come upon them only

---

* Nearly all the Monitors of the American Navy take their names from the mountains of New England.

a few miles from Gorham or Bangor. Under this sombre mantle of forests, which stretches in majestic folds on the damp and spongy soil, where countless vegetable generations have left their spoils, live, as they did so many centuries ago, the bears, wolves, lynxes, caribous, the awkward and gigantic moose, who, bending his branching horns backward, forces a path through the branches with his chest. With them also lives the primitive man known to the first emigrants.

Beyond the last villages you still find shelter and a rough bed among the lumberers in search of the tallest pines. Further on, you only venture with an Indian guide; there is no other bed than branches of arbor vitæ spread on the moss, and the only noises to be heard in the frightful solitude are the cries of unknown animals calling to each other, or the sudden shock caused by the fall of a secular tree—a solemn note which alone marks the flight of time. Such must have been the America seen by the first explorers. In these latitudes civilisation has occupied nothing but coasts and valleys. She has glided round immense mountainous provinces as water flows round rocks. The masts of American vessels that cross all seas, the boards of the houses of New England that shelter so many ambitions, calculations, and passions, come from regions where the Indian hunts in peace like his ancestors. The geography of one part of America is still nearly as uncertain as that of the Rocky Mountains. The geologists of New York State take Indian guides to explore the Adirondacs.

A one-story house has been built on the little rocky

plain that forms the summit of Mount Washington, called the Tip-top House; it is surrounded by blocks of gneiss, which protect it from the furious wind that blows almost incessantly at this height. The gusts are so violent on the top of the mountain that our driver thought it prudent to roll up the canvas that covered the open waggon, for carriages have been known to be caught up and thrown over the heaps of stone by the roadside. The ascent lasted five hours, the descent was hardly quicker; the carriage went down the steep slopes up which it had crawled in the morning with frightful jolts. From time to time heavy masses of mist were driven higher up, and permitted the gaze to plunge into the green and azure depths of the mountains. Then the wind would blow the mist down the valley, and the summit of Mount Jefferson, opposite Mount Washington, appeared above a thin cloud, like an island situated at an inaccessible height.

From Gorham you can cross the White Mountain to Littleton, in the valley of the Connecticut. It is a long and fatiguing journey, on account of the roads, which in many places are mended with half-rotten branches laid side by side. To make up for it, the landscape is admirable, for following the line of the White Mountains to the north, and of the lower range of the Franconia Mountains, which join the western flank of the chain, Mounts Madison, Adams, Jefferson, and Washington are seen in all their majesty, their peaks of nearly equal height supported by a common base. The mountain sides, steeper to the north, exhibit very distinctly the wide bands of the vegetable zones, one above the other. The thick dark line of pines runs above the variegated zone of the lower slopes, and the grey and purplish summits tower above all.

Emerging from a wood, a little village is reached, named Jefferson. On one side rear up the masses of the Presidential mountains, and on the other the mountains of Franconia, and those that shut in the valley of the Connecticut, stretch away in endless undulations. Mount Lafayette (3,200 feet high) and Mount Pemigewasset (4,100 feet high) raise their heads above a sea of mountains of all shades, colours, and shapes, that recede in a disorder full of grace. At Jefferson you can study what I should be willing to call the embryogeny of an American village. The farmer who settles in such a deserted region begins by burning the forest; the fire consumes the underbrush, and leaves nothing but the roots and the blackened trunks of the largest trees; these trunks cut, and laid end to end, make the first enclosures. They shut in a few oxen. You see the animals, with long red hair, straying about in this strange pasturage full of rocks; elsewhere, yoked together, they pull up the stumps, and break up and hollow out the ground, when the foundations are laid for the house, barns, stables and sheds, separated from one another because of the frequent occurrence of fires. The stumps dug out of the earth are spread along the enclosures, roots uppermost, and at a little distance they look like rows of deformed and monstrous cactuses. Stones piled one on top of the other serve to make walls. The farm-buildings are light constructions of wood ; the dwelling-house is usually built with care, clean, spacious, and at the well-closed windows smile round and rosy children's faces. Among the houses along the roadside, at some distance apart, I distinguish one in particular, where in a great room I see nothing but wooden benches ; it is the school-house, which is never forgotten.

On leaving Jefferson we return to the solitude of the woods till we reach Littleton. This township is situated on the Ammonoosuc, which falls into the Connecticut, whose waters, flowing through rocks, turn a large number of saw-mills. In this out-of-the-way corner of New Hampshire something still recalled the war and politics to me. At the door of the inn was a great placard, indicating the road to be taken by the collector of the new war taxes in the third electoral district of the State. The ratepayers were invited to come on specified days to the different towns where the collector was to stop, to pay the said taxes, if they were not able to do so at his office in Orford. In the rural districts, often of very large extent, the collectors, as one sees, are obliged to make their rounds from village to village to raise the taxes. The ratepayers receive by post, beforehand, letters stating the amount due from them. Those who delay over the date fixed are punished by a fine of ten per cent. on the sum total of the tax.

A small branch railway goes from Littleton to the great and beautiful valley of the Connecticut. The line follows all the sinuosities of the river, and crosses

it several times over tubular bridges roofed in. Now
the train goes through these galleries, now it rolls
over the top of them.   In the latter case the rails are
laid on the top of the flat roof, and you see on each
side the transparent water gliding over the rocks.
The valley goes through smiling mountains, among
which the river winds on a fertile plain formed by
alluvial deposits.   The ground is laid out in natural
terraces, which succeed each other like the steps of
a gigantic staircase.   The iron way follows these long
shelves, levelled beforehand ; fine fields, pastures,
flourishing towns and prosperous villages, succeed each
other on these broad terraces.   The river grows wider
and wider.   At Holyoke the waters are shut in by a
magnificent dam 330 metres long and 10 metres high.
This hydraulic force puts in motion several important
cotton factories, saw-mills, and divers other mills. Soon
after Holyoke the chimneys of Springfield come in
sight.   This town is one of the most flourishing in
Massachusetts.   The population, which in 1850 numbered 11,766 inhabitants, is now raised to 20,000.
The arsenal, one of the largest in the United States,
employs a great many workmen ; 200,000 rifles are
always kept there.   Certainly never was there an industrial town less black or less gloomy.   At a distance
the workshops look like palaces ; hydraulic force being
almost the only one employed, the sky is never darkened
by coal smoke.   Pretty villas are, as it were, buried
in the foliage of elms and maples ; nothing tarnishes
the green blinds, the white pillars of the verandahs,

the wood painted in all colours, the mouldings and cornices of freestone.   Industry does not yet drag in her train rags, misery, social degradation, brutality and ignorance, in New England.   Man is looked upon as a product fully as important as exportable goods; the workman is ranked above the work.

Springfield is not very far from Albany, the political capital of the State of New York.   The western part of Massachusetts is first crossed, which is the most mountainous and picturesque part of the State.   For some time the route follows one of the tributaries of the Connecticut; it then enters the great basin of the Hudson. Near Albany you come upon the Catskill Mountains, whose crests assume those quadrangular shapes, simulating battlemented towers, ruins, and gigantic stairs, which almost always characterise sandstone mountains. The valley of the Hudson rolls far away out of sight, with its woods, its fields, and its many villages.   The transition from Massachusetts to New York is clearly defined. In this latter State the fields and enclosures are larger, the farm-buildings more spacious; per contra, the dwelling-houses are smaller, and not so clean.   At Albany travellers leave the cars, and go aboard a steamboat that plies constantly from one side to the other of the Hudson.   These steam ferries, without either prow or poop, are really moving streets; in the middle of the deck is the place for the carriages, omnibuses, horses, drays; on each side long waiting-rooms for foot passengers.   When the boat reaches the landing, the end of the wide deck is adjusted to the level of a moveable platform; carriages and foot-passengers, without a moment's loss of time, pour out in all directions, and the boat, without turning, goes back to the other side.

The Hudson River is one of the principal arteries of the commerce of the United States. It was on its waters that, in 1808, Robert Fulton made the first trial of steam navigation. Great would be his surprise if he could see, to-day, the gigantic steamers, with piled up stories, that go incessantly between New York and Albany, carrying hundreds of passengers! Those last built are undoubtedly the finest specimens of river boats in the world. Besides these great floating houses, the river carries all the time thousands of sailing vessels. Large ships ascend as far as Hudson, and schooners go to Albany and Troy (a distance of 166 miles from the mouth), where the tide is still perceptible. Besides its river and its railways, Albany possesses canals which connect Lakes Erie, Ontario, and Champlain. This town is one of the greatest lumber markets of the whole world. It receives the white pines of Michigan and Canada, the oaks, wild cherries, and poplars of Ohio, the common pines of Pennsylvania and New York. There passes through it, besides, an immense quantity of cereals, wool, and tobacco. The little establishment founded by the Dutch in 1614 has become a considerable city, which has forty churches, eleven public schools, ten banks, a capitol, a city-hall, an observatory, a university, a medical school, a normal school for the school-masters and mistresses of the State, and numerous charitable establishments. At Albany you enter the great current of emigration that flows to the North-western States. The German families going to settle in Michigan, Illinois, and Wisconsin, take tickets in New York, that enable them to go through without stopping at Detroit and Chicago. The train on the line of the New York Central was so full of women and children that I had some trouble in finding a seat. In passing through the suburbs of Albany I saw many German signs and names. Here *lager beer* is sold, there Rhine wine ! Though New York has a larger German population than any other city in the world except Vienna and Berlin, it may be affirmed that the true German does not stop willingly on the Atlantic coast. He loves solitude and independence too much. He is still to-day what he was when Tacitus so faithfully depicted his manners. In the colonisation of the West he plays the part of pioneer ; he loves isolation, he clears up the forest, and brings the first harvests out of the earth. His robust mate readily follows him to the fields, and does not shut herself up in the house like the American. Their yellow-haired children grow up in the desert, in the woods and furrows, and begin to work early. When the task of the labourer is ended, that of the Yankee begins ; the producer is followed by the speculator. The American brings among these isolated, suspicious, sober, economical, still half-savage families, tied to the soil, the spirit of enterprise, commercial and civil institutions, the solidarity of public life, education, temptations, tastes, and the habits of an advanced civilisation. With the peaceful, slow, and laborious German all is muscle ; with the thin Yankee, whose eyes sparkle with a sombre fire, with anxious forehead, and long and mobile neck, all is nerve. The mind of the one and the body of the other know neither stop nor rest: one creates wealth, and the other puts it in circulation; one works, the other is always busy inventing more perfect tools. They are not very fond of each other, but they are necessary to each other. The Yankee, with an adventurous and supple intelligence, always ready to seize an opportunity, as generous as he is grasping, a lover of general ideas, a political and religious rhetorician, social and ambitious, has too much contempt for the slow patience and the taciturnity of the German. He does not understand this dreamer who prefers above everything the great horizons of the solitary plains, this soul which lives an interior life, and for whom independence is the best reward of labour; but these two great races naturally complete each other: one finishes what the other begins, and from their marriage will one day spring, at least in the West, a new race in whom the fine mental and physical qualities will find a better equilibrium.

On quitting Albany the road climbs by a rapid ascent the slope of the valley of the Hudson. Farms and woods follow each other on the rich table-land that overlooks it; the yellow corn-stalks are tied up in sheaves in the fields, that extend far out of sight; red cows stray about the pastures. Here and there the loam of the plateau grows poorer, and becoming sandy, bears only little white pines. From time to time you see the boats going up the Erie Canal, which runs parallel to the railway for some time.

Schenectady, situated on this canal, is one of the oldest of the Dutch settlements. In 1690 this town contained only one church and sixty houses, and was burned by a party of French and Indians. It continued to be the principal commercial link between the Hudson Valley and the West, until 1825. The Mohawk, a tributary of the Hudson, has rapids below this point, and all merchandise used to be carried to Albany over the high road; to-day the canal, which connects the Mohawk with Lake Erie, and the railways, have reduced the cost of transport by nine-tenths. Locomotives cross above the canal and the river, on a bridge 330 mètres long. After Schenectady you ascend the valley of the Mohawk. At Little Fall, the waters are precipitated between rocks that assume the boldest shapes and look like dismantled fortresses. The canal runs along by the railway at the bottom of a narrow valley, and you see it engulphed in a fissure of the mountain. From time to time the current is dammed in, and supplies the hydraulic force of several industrial establishments. Further on the valley opens out and is covered with rich pasturage and roaming herds. At Frankfort (another reminiscence of Germany) an immense chimney, surrounded with brick factories, is a sort of centre to an agglomeration of pretty little white wooden houses, in which the workmen live. Out of breath, the locomotive stops at length at Utica. This town, settled by some obscure Cato towards 1793, contains to-day six great hotels, twenty churches, publishes several daily papers and five weekly ones; it has five banks, is lighted by gas, has several cotton and

wool factories, foundries, tanneries, and railway workshops. In 1830 it was still a village; its municipal
charter dates from that time. The most interesting
establishment is the insane asylum, belonging to New
York State. Dr. Brigham, who was at one time its
head, founded a paper in 1844, called 'The American
Journal of Insanity,' and intended to spread more
humane ideas concerning the treatment of the insane.
Dr. John Gray, the present head of the asylum and
editor of the journal, faithful to the same ideas, forces
the insane to cure themselves, and leaves them almost
entirely at liberty. His system consists in making an
appeal to whatever reason is left them, to watch over
and conquer their disease. Madness, according to him,
is never hopeless at the outset; it takes possession, at
first, of only a corner of the mind. He explains to the
sufferer his ailment, frightens him with a picture of
incurable madness, and teaches him to use his will
against the phantom that haunts him. I am told that
in most cases this method produces wonderful results;
but its success undoubtedly greatly depends on the
tact, firmness, and moral qualities of those who apply it.

Trenton Falls are at some distance from Utica.
They are reached by a branch railway, which goes
through a wild and pastoral country, and crosses
Canada Creek, a small branch of the Mohawk. On
nearing Trenton the locomotive, dragging after it a few
old and worn-out cars, timidly crosses a light wooden
bridge thrown at a great height over a torrent. Cart-
loads of gravel are being thrown down to build up
an embankment; but the crossing still seems dangerous,

and the traveller is not quite at ease until the locomotive has ceased to roll over the slight wood-work.   I
went early to the falls, after a night passed in a wretched
inn ; I crossed a little wood, and going down a rustic
flight of steps found myself at the bottom of a gorge,
in front of the lower cascade.   It would be difficult
to imagine a more unexpected landscape : nothing
announces it.   The Canada Creek flows at the bottom
of a narrow valley, which is a sort of cutting in the
plain ; the bed of the river is hollowed in the calcareous strata, laid one above the other like the leaves
of a book ; thin, and of an even thickness, they trace
a series of parallel and horizontal lines over the
walls of the valley.   On both sides, just above the
level of the water, these beds form little sidewalks,
sometimes wide, sometimes narrow.   We walk slowly
on over these natural pavements, treading under foot
innumerable fossils of the silurian period.   The waters
fall dark and foaming over the steps of this natural
staircase.   Holding on to the iron chains fastened into
the stone, we walk along the narrowest places between the rock and the torrent.   When we come to a
cascade the sidewalk turns into steps ; we go quickly
up the slippery steps in the midst of a liquid and
transparent dust on which the sun paints beautiful
circular rainbows.   Reaching the level of the fall, we
can look at our ease at the waters gliding over the
edge of the rock, which take a fine yellow tone, due to
the chemical composition of the blackish calcareous
strata they have washed ; they almost seem to be
mixed with pitch or bitumen, or, you would have said,

flowing masses of melted glass, such as ordinary bottles are made of. This hue disappears in the foaming flakes that constantly rise and fall at the foot of the cascade, and whose whiteness wearies the eye. The second fall is the highest and the most picturesque. The glittering sheet that bounds and drips over the black rocks is framed in by the wooded sides of the valley; the pendant and melancholy branches of the arbor vitæ droop over the boiling waters; the silver-trunked birches and the maples cling in disorder to the walls of rock and crown the summits, mingling their richly-coloured autumn foliage with the sombre pine tops. Here and there a red creeper looks like a streak of blood. Among all my recollections, nothing surpasses Trenton Falls for harmony, beauty of hue, or richness and contrast of colour. It is a landscape of limited dimensions, but perfect finish. Nothing in it recalls man. Not a house, not a road, not even a visible path, not a rustic hut, or wooden bench; the utter solitude, the sadness of this forgotten valley, the low and monotonous murmur of the water, everything conduces to repose and reverie.

After returning to Utica, I crossed the rich and monotonous plains of the State of New York, to Niagara. During all this route the face of the country never changes: wide natural meadows surrounded by light wooden fences; here and there a village, made up of houses bordering long wide avenues of trees, and in the midst of gardens and orchards, groves and woods, where white pines mingle with maples, birches, oaks, and elms, whose branches bend in regular curves

I

like an aigrette of feathers. I was never weary of admiring the brilliant hues of the foliage; every species has its autumn livery: the maple, with its scarlet, red, crimson, or ruby, is recognised at a great distance: the elms make a yellow mass, green still struggles against the red and yellow in the sugar maples. The setting sun gilds the wide plain, and glistens through the tufts of trees; no description gives any idea of the splendour of the sight. Light clouds, like unshaken fringes hung on the edges of the horizon, seem to float in purple, fire, or blood; the furrows, the rough fields, and the newly cleared up plain are transformed, and seem like a pink or violet lake. The distant elms shine like slender branches of amethysts or garnets: but these fairy twilights do not last long enough: the sun hardly rests on the horizon, and the irisations fade away by degrees to a light amber that grows more and more opaque.

Between Utica and Niagara there are two important towns, Syracuse and Rochester. In 1820, Syracuse was a village of 300 inhabitants; to-day it has a population of over 30,000 souls, twenty-five churches (four of which are Catholic), and eight public schools. Its prosperity is owing to its salt mines, the largest in the United States. At a depth of 100 mètres a water is raised which contains ten times more salt than sea water. The wells are dug and the water pumped at the expense of the State of New York, the proprietor of the mines. The water is given out to workers, who concentrate it for the fabrication of salt, and who pay a slight tax on every cubic foot. At Syracuse there are, besides, many manufactories and workshops for agricultural implements, steam-engines, iron-stoves, paper-mills, tanneries, and mills. The Erie Canal crosses the town from east to west; it meets at right angles the Oswego Canal, which runs towards the north in the direction of Lake Ontario. The town is laid out in wide quadrangular streets; the railway runs through one of them in the most populous quarter. While the trains go at a slackened pace before the great hotels, shops, and the high stone and brick houses, children, at the risk of being crushed, amuse themselves by jumping on the little platforms that are placed at each end of all American cars.

Rochester only began to be a city in 1834. In 1855 it had a population of 44,000 inhabitants. The Genesee River supplies it with an almost unlimited hydraulic force; perhaps, indeed, its mills are the most active of any in the United States. On a length of 4 kilomètres, the river falls 75 mètres. Three successive dams are 37, 17, and 25 métres high. 600,000 barrels of flour are annually ground in Rochester. The Erie Canal goes through the heart of the city, and crosses the river on a fine aqueduct in stone, 280 mètres in length. A second canal goes up the valley of the Genesee and runs into the valley of the Alleghany, which, at Pittsburg in Pennsylvania, changes into the Hudson, after joining the Monongahela.

I reached the village of Niagara in the night, and went to one of those immense hotels built for the thousands of tourists who every year visit the cataract.

I could distinguish at some distance two deep tones—one that came from the rapids, the other from the falls; the first higher, the second more grave and solemn. In the morning I hurried to Niagara. The waters of the great lakes of North America here reach Lake Ontario, the last and lowest of the inland seas, through a deep cut made in the narrow strip of silurian rocks that unites Canada West to the State of New York. This natural passage is like a gigantic lock placed by nature between Lakes Erie and Ontario, the level of the first of which is 100 metres above that of the second. The waters flow from south to north. Before reaching Niagara, they descend a long gently inclined plane, whose uneven and rocky bed forms the rapids. At the end of this plane they separate into two branches, pass to the right and left of an island called Goat Island, and, at the other extremity, reach the precipice where they are engulphed. Between the little island, which seems to hang over the abyss, and the American side, is the smallest cataract, the edge of which is as straight as that of an immense factory dam. The waters run from east to west perpendicularly to the general direction of the valley. On the Canadian side the crest of the great cataract has the shape of a horseshoe. The waters roll over this half-circle in such thick masses that the clouds of spray that rise from the foot of the fall ascend more than 300 mètres. A little stone tower has been built on the extreme point of Goat Island. The observer standing on the top sees the waters coming in the distance, and foaming among the rapids; every step of rock is marked by a white moving fringe; here and there a rock torn from its bed, or a pine trunk, is surrounded by a higher and more furious crest of water. The liquid mass, hurried along by its own irresistible weight, falls at last into the circle of the horseshoe. The circular sheet, green at the top, is chequered below with silver streaks, that shiver and undulate like plumes beaten about by the wind. The beautiful cerulean line of the summit alone keeps its repose, and the moving waters pass for ever beneath its motionless level. The quietness is such that their bold parabola is still perceptibly distant from the vertical at the moment they break at the foot of the cataract, at a distance of 50 mètres. I went down into a slight wooden tower that covers in a cork-screw staircase, to the bottom of the valley on the Canadian side, and followed a little path that winds over the black and fetid calcareous schists that build up the lower part of the wall over which the river falls. At the top of this wall a thick bed of hard, compact limestone overhangs the thin schists, which crumble away, and which the water wears unceasingly. From time to time rocks are de-tached from this limestone table and fall at the foot of the cataract. The rounded sheet of water makes a sort of vault, under which, well covered with water-proof clothing, we can proceed some distance. I noticed two women, who had come down in monstrous accoutrement, and who had not the courage to pene-trate into the rain and thunder of the cascade. A boy of fifteen, who was with them, went alone with a guide, a stout black man, who dragged rather than guided him, as far as they could go. I see them yet, the black supporting the boy with one hand against the wall of rock, and pointing with many gestures with the other to the wall of water.   These two confused figures, one timid, the other energetic and almost threatening, have remained engraved on my mind, I hardly know why.   On the American side, you can also go down to the foot of the cataract through a wooden turret, and be wet through in a moment in a hollow called the ' Cave of the Winds.'   To go from one bank to the other, you cross the river in a little steamer at a very short distance from the cataract, the waters having a very weak current after their fall.   A little farther on, you come to the magnificent suspension bridge, thrown across the valley at a height of 83 mètres, which joins the New York Central Railway to the Great Western of Canada.   The locomotives roll over the top of the trellis of beams, which is 266 mètres long, and carriages and foot-passengers pass below. The general view of the falls is much the best from the Canadian side.   The dark mass of Goat Island is suspended between the two dazzling sheets ; the cloud that rises boiling up from the horseshoe seems to issue from an underground cauldron.   Above the greenish threshold of the long water-course, the foaming fringes of the rapids draw parallel lines as far as the sombre wall of pines that encloses the sad horizon.

I have never seen a good picture of Niagara. There is but one painter who would have been capable of rendering the terrible majesty of such a spectacle— Ruysdäel. He would doubtless have chosen a day when the waters are the darkest, when great sweeping clouds throw heavy and threatening shadows, when the pines bend under a cold and furious wind. The Canadian fall brought the great Flemish landscape painter to my mind at once. On that side nothing interferes with the severity of the picture. The rapids on the American side are spoiled by houses and factories. You wish to make a solitude round this place; there should be nothing but waters, woods, and rocks. You long to tear down those hotels that look like barracks, those shops where imitations of the industries of the primitive Indians, such as bows and arrows, mocassins, screens of brilliantly coloured feathers, birch-bark boxes embroidered with coloured moose-hair, glass beads, and snow shoes, are sold to the too confiding traveller. A small Indian tribe still lingers in the neighbourhood of Niagara village; but this is not the place to look for the red man, with his diadem of eagle's feathers, his necklaces, his many-coloured belts, and his fringed leggings. I saw only two squaws sitting on the trunk of a tree, wrapped in dark hoods. In the vestibule of the Cataract hotel I also met a man with a copper-coloured complexion, dressed with flashy finery; his shining black hair was carefully curled; and a great pin of imitation diamonds shone on his shirt, of a dubious whiteness. His obsequious smile showed white and regular teeth. I turned with pity from this degenerate representative of a noble race that civilisation degrades before annihilating.

CHAPTER VII.

DETROIT AND CHICAGO.

CANADA WEST, crossed in going from Niagara to Detroit in Michigan, offers but little interest to any but the agriculturist.   The forest still covers wide surfaces; wherever it has been cleared up, broad fields spread out where the golden balls of the pumpkins shine through the corn stalks.   Around the houses, apple-trees bend under the weight of their own fruit.   What can be said of St. Catherine's, of Hamilton, of London? All these towns look alike, and the train only stops in them for an instant.   Geography is hardly acquainted with these places, half towns, half villages, where dwells an obscure population, without a distinct nationality, without either past or future—the uncared-for servant of a far off, and more and more indifferent metropolis.   Hamilton, a large and prosperous town built in stone, overlooks Lake Ontario, which shines in the sun like a steel buckler.   At first the road follows the lake, then rises by wooded slopes to the plateau of the Canadian peninsula.   The western extremity of this peninsula is bounded on one side by Lake St. Clair, and on the other by Lake Erie.   At ten o'clock at night I reached Windsor, situated on the straits that connect

the two lakes. On the opposite bank, Detroit, lighted
by the full moon, seemed to rise from the waters. The
lights of the port shone in the distance, and the coloured
signals of the steam-boats glided in every direction. A
ferry-boat quickly crossed the canal, and its red fires
were reflected on the rippling surface of the water.
The strange scream of the whistle of the boilers alone
broke the silence of the night. The Great Bear, dimmed
by the light of the moon, seemed to set on the sleeping
town.   There was something fairy-like in this picture,
and, in spite of the sharp cold of the night, I remained
on the deck of the steam-ferry that was carrying me to
Detroit, while the many emigrants with whom I had
travelled all day threw themselves on the supper prepared for them in the saloon.   While I admired this
immense canal, which is nearly two miles wide, I remembered with a pride mingled with regret that the
French were the first to bring civilisation to this place,
where the name is the only French thing left.   When
a thoughtless government gave Canada to England,
was it not here that a hero, Pontiac, alone renewed
the struggle, and fought heroically for France, and at
the same time for the independence of his race ?   Alas !
France no longer knows this noble martyr, and his
name is now only to be found in an unknown county
of Illinois.*

The next morning the charm was broken. Detroit,
which the night before I had seen as it were transfigured
by the luminous vapour of the moon, now showed

* See *History of the Conspiracy of Pontiac.* By F. Parkman.
Boston, 1857.

itself as it really is, a half-built town, where wooden sheds are near neighbours to gigantic stone and brick stores, where immense avenues, marked out for a capital, are bordered everywhere by waste and unoccupied lands.   It is indeed a Western city, where extremes meet; here they are building, there they are pulling down in order to build up again.   All styles are mixed together—sheds, wooden houses, villas with white wooden verandahs; great blocks of brick and stone, where stores fill every storey, and signs shine all over the front; Greek temples with wooden columns and naked facades; Gothic churches, whose angles have not yet been rounded by time, and to which the ivy planted yesterday vainly tries to give an air of age.   After stone sidewalks as wide as streets come plank walks or ruts. German country carts made of two long boards supported against four posts, and dragged by rustic horses, go along side by side with fine drays painted red, and horse cars. There are, of course, a few monuments, a town-house, a court-house, a custom-house, a bank built in the Greek style, a theatre, a museum ; but in the West the hotel is always the real monument. In the great marble-paved halls, there is an incessant crowd of travellers, idlers, and speculators, busy reading the papers, the monstrous handbills, the telegrams, the price of gold, or the book of the hotel, where the names of the new comers are inscribed.   Black servants run in all directions ; a smell of brandy and tobacco-smoke comes from the bar, full of noisy groups.   The ladies receive their visits in the drawing-rooms, covered with rich and glaring carpets ; now and then a young girl tries the last waltz from Paris on a piano whose worn-out notes only give out a dead false sound. In the enormous dining-room stretch out the tables where you can sit at any hour, and where under different names you eat the same meal three or four times a day. Beside a woman elegantly dressed, whose white hands covered with rings handle her fork with dainty slowness, sits down a stout farmer, who has devoured in an instant all that is set before him. A child drinks a glass of iced milk, while an officer on furlough drinks a bottle of Catawba. Active and smiling negroes stand behind the taciturn eaters, attentive to their slightest wish, and always ready to satisfy it. In the West, the hotel and the political meeting are organs and instruments of social intercourse ; life is too busy for those social re-lations which require leisure, the disinterested love of intellectual things, the half serious, half frivolous pur-suit of a conventional ideal. Democratic roughness ignores or despises shades, degrees, and classifications : among so many equals a man really feels alone. Every-body has his own house, where he shuts himself up with his wife and children. But at the hotel the American sees new faces, he hears people talking about something besides his own business, he learns to love order, neatness, luxury, and large and high rooms ; his manners are formed on those of the strangers with whom he mingles. He watches the motions, listens to the smallest words of the celebrated people—generals, states-men, orators, or writers—whom chance has brought be-fore him for a day. Among these continuous streams of new comers, among so many different faces, he learns

the grandeur of his country better than on a map.   If
he is unable to go to all the States, all the States come
to him.   His horizon is enlarged, and from the centre
of his great continent he can look to the Atlantic
coast, the Gulf of Mexico, and as far as the valleys of
California.   The hotel is a sort of abridgment of the
Confederation.

From Detroit to Chicago the agricultural State of
Michigan is crossed in a straight line.   Nothing catches
the eye on this fertile plain.   You do not travel in the
West ; you are carried from one place to another.
Among the woods and fields, you pass at one bound all
the phases of civilisation ; here fire slowly burns the
last trunks of a part of the forest about to be put under
cultivation ; cows still stray about the pastures, full of
china-asters and golden-rods, and among the blackened
stumps and scattered rocks.   In the first enclosures the
plough turns slowly round the last stump ; on the cleared
up fields the share easily draws even furrows.   The
first shelters are shanties put up hastily ; later, the
emigrant, grown richer, builds a larger house, the wood-
work is painted yellow or white, and green blinds are
at every window.   In the most important centres, rise
brick and stone buildings.   The stations only differ in
name.   Who imagined giving to one of them the name
of the Hellenic hero Ipsilanti ?   Chelsea and Albion
come next ; you stop a moment at a place called Paw-
Paw on the most recent maps, but which has already
taken an insignificant English name.   The railway follows for a long time the sleeping waters of the harmo-
nious Kalamazoo, which creeps along between woods of

yellow maples. At nightfall the bare prairie assumes
the aspect of a black and motionless lake, without
reflections. The plain is unbroken by any undulation
on the southern shores of Lake Michigan; its smooth
surface exactly reproduces the ideal form of the earth
imagined by astronomy: the circumference of the
horizon is as unbroken as that of which the sailor
in his vessel is the moving centre. This rapid flight
across a dreary, silent, unlimited desert seems like a
dream. A few lights shine out at last on the dark
background of the horizon, like stars when they first
rise. Chicago is reached.

Chicago is the queen of the West; it is the capital of
the great corn-growing States. Thirty-three years ago
Indians roved freely along the banks of Lake Michigan,
where now stand churches, hotels, monuments, and
houses for 180,000 inhabitants. The immense chequer-
board, cut up by wide streets, stretches out of sight,
north, south, and west. To the east is the port, where
a multitude of vessels crowd together. They come into
the little river that gives its name to the town, and which
in the middle divides into two branches; it is crossed
by twelve turning bridges, which connect the different
quarters of the town. Little steam-tugs, that look like
great floating insects in the water, are incessantly
dragging boats loaded with corn. Chicago is a colossal depôt; it receives on one side the cereals of the
West, on the other all the manufactured products that
the Eastern States send in exchange; consequently some
of the streets are as animated as the City in London.
There is building everywhere; old wooden houses are

torn down to make room for large high houses : they already build for the future. The fine marbles of Athens (the Athens of Illinois) are cut, wood is carved, the fine bricks of a light golden colour are mixed with stone. There is no town in the Union with a street that can compare with Michigan Avenue, with its long row of beautiful houses facing on the lake. They are not mere repetitions of each other, like the houses in the fashionable quarters in New York. Many among them have Mansard roofs, and it seemed to me that there was in general a tendency to the imitation of French forms, which is also visible in the furniture ; our habits and fashions are more prized on the banks of Lake Michigan than on those of the Thames. On the other hand, the churches, almost all in the Gothic style, are in the most detestable taste. There is a street, whose name I forget, where there are almost as many churches as there are houses. All sects are crowded together, and the congregations, not being very numerous, do not build monuments vast enough to make an imposing architectural effect. The Gothic churches in particular, which look like reductions, have a poor, mean, and often grotesque appearance. Religious architecture, however, all over the United States, is placed under particularly unfavourable circumstances. I made the calculation that on an average there is throughout the country a church to every thousand in-habitants. There is no need of vast naves, spacious transepts, inaccessible vaults, in the temples where these little congregations meet together, and which they are obliged to raise at their own expense. In Protestant communities the church loses all that is gained in religious feeling.

If Chicago is, so to speak, the representative town of the West, its *rôle* can be represented by two kinds of establishments—*elevators*, and slaughtering-houses, called *packing-houses.* These are the two fountains of the West from which bread and meat flow unceasingly. I went first to see an elevator. Imagine an immense building without windows, very high, and divided on the inside into several storeys; the ground floor is cut in two by a long gallery, where two trains and their engines can come in. The cars come from the surrounding depôts, where the company owning the elevator stores the grain brought in by the different railway lines. The Chicago River flows on one side of the elevator, a canal on the other connected with the river, so that boats can lie alongside the building as easily as trains can go inside. When a car loaded with grain has gone in, a door on the side is opened, and the corn pours out into a deep trench that runs the whole length of the track. Let us follow its progress. An iron axle turns at the top of the enormous building, put in motion by a 130 horse-power steam-engine. This shaft supports a drum at intervals, on which runs a belt to which buckets are fastened. These come down, and are filled with corn in the lower trench I have already mentioned, and raise it to the upper storey: a few turns of the wheel bring the corn to the roof, and there it is emptied into a square wooden box of great size. Once stored in this box, it is weighed, like carriages going on to scales, then it is passed on to

definitive reservoirs, where cereals of all sorts and kinds
are already classified. For this purpose a wooden spout
is fixed on the lower orifice of the reservoir where the
weighing takes place. This moveable spout can be
directed at will into any one of the twenty canals that
disgorge themselves into great towers that fill up almost
the whole body of the edifice. When the corn is to
be sent away from the elevator, it has only to be left
to its own weight; it pours down intosacks on the
lower storey, or into boats by quadrangular wooden
canals, such as every one has seen in mills. The
river of nourishment flows, flows incessantly, and
spreads in all directions in the Eastern States, and
towards the Atlantic ports.

The elevator that I examined in detail can hold
three hundred thousand bushels of grain. It might be
feared that the reservoir thus filled would burst, but
the wooden towers are very solidly built, and the
whole edifice is surrounded with thick brick walls.
Thirteen elevating wheels raise each one 4,000
bushels an hour, so that 52,000 bushels can be stored
in that space of time. The whole building can be
filled in half a day. The use of these gigantic reservoirs is easily understood. The producer can bring at
his own convenience a given quantity of cereals; it is
weighed and numbered, and he receives a certificate of
storage negotiable on the Chicago market. The company takes a commission of two cents (a cent is the
hundredth part of a dollar) on the bushel stored, and
agrees to take care of the corn for a space of time not
to exceed twenty days; after this time depositors must

pay half a cent a day per bushel. The expenses of the company amount to 175 dollars a day. This figure allows us to easily compute the profits realised.

Elevators, we see, are nothing but docks for corn; they are to be found in all places where there is an extensive trade in cereals, at Chicago, Milwaukee, Buffalo. Chicago possesses eighteen, that can contain in all 10,000,000 bushels. The largest hold about 1,250,000 bushels. In 1845 the quantity of cereals shipped on the lake at Chicago was only 1,000,000 bushels; in 1854 this figure had risen to 12,000,000; from the 1st of April 1863, to the 1st of April 1864, to 54,741,839 bushels (comprising 18,298,532 of wheat, 24,906,934 of Indian corn, 9,909,175 of oats, 683,946 of rye, 943,252 of barley). The total tonnage of the ships that during the year 1861 entered the port of Chicago—steamers, tugs, brigs, and schooners—amounts to 232,970 tons.*

* I borrow the following figures from the documents of the Board of Trade of Chicago :—

Years	Wheat	Indian Corn	Oats	Rye	Barley	Total Bshls
1859	10,759,359	4,217,654	1,174,177	478,162	131,449	16,753,795
1860	15,892,857	13,700,113	1,091,698	156,642	267,449	31,108,759
1861	23,855,143	24,372,725	1,633,237	393,813	226,534	50,401,862
1862	22,508,143	29,452,610	3,112,366	871,796	539,195	56,484,110
1863-64	18,278,532	24,706,934	9,909,175	683,946	943,252	54,741,839

Part of the wheat is sent out as flour: there are nine great mills at Chicago. In 1863–64, 1,507,816 barrels of flour were exported from this town. The war lent a great activity to the raising of oats, as can be verified in our Table. The railways radiating towards the South were continually encumbered with trains carrying oats to the different armies.

K

These figures prove that the war did not interrupt the development of agriculture in the West. Financially, the whole weight of the gigantic struggle in which the Union was involved bore upon the Atlantic States. So far from being impoverished, the West is enriched. Before the civil war, mortgages had taken alarming proportions. The year 1848 had been marked by an extraordinary prosperity, and at that time the farmers, flushed with success, had all made heavy loans to buy lands and undertake ameliorations of all kinds. Unfortunately for them, from 1850 to 1857, corn brought less and less remunerative prices During the crisis of 1857, it fell to twenty, fifteen, and even ten cents a bushel. The West thought herself ruined, and almost lost the hope of paying her debt. Before the war, Indian corn was worth thirty cents, wheat about seventy-five cents. Since the introduction of paper money, prices have naturally risen. In October 1864, Indian corn was quoted at one dollar, and wheat one dollar thirty cents. The farmer was thus enabled to pay back in paper what he had received in specie. The increase of prices not only allowed him to free himself very rapidly; he has also been able to lay up and invest money, in land, or in the Federal loans. The war has swept out of the Western States that multitude of bank bills that used to inundate them; they have been sent East, and *greenbacks* alone pass current. It is but true to say that salaries have notably augmented: day labourers, who used to receive from twelve to fifteen dollars a month, now demand twenty-five; but the use of various agricultural machines has much lessened manual labour, and many agriculturists on small farms are not obliged to have recourse to extraneous help. In proportion as recruiting thinned the population of the West, emigration came to fill it up, for it always flows towards the States the farthest from the Atlantic. By the help of all these circumstances, the West has been able to grow rich by the war, and the prosperity it enjoys has singularly heightened the sentiment of fidelity to the Union. Those who dream of detaching the North-Western States from the central and Atlantic States know very little of the feeling of the population which fills the immense provinces which have become the granary of the Union. The doctrine of secession has not yet made a single convert there, and those who delight to trace out in imagination the limits of an occidental confederation must be sought elsewhere than in the West.

After bread comes meat. After my visit to the elevator, I went to one of the slaughtering-houses of Chicago. The *packing-houses* are situated away from the centre of the town, on the prairie, which surrounds it on all sides. At some distance from the populous quarters you come to suburbs where wooden sheds are scattered here and there, apparently by chance. Streets nevertheless are already marked out, and wide avenues stretch out of sight. The road is not paved : carriages sink into sand, or jolt over a road made of planks laid side by side. Before the houses wooden sidewalks are supported on posts. Let us follow one of those great herds across the plain, that guides on horseback drive slowly to the pens near the packing-house. For a few days the oxen are kept fenced in, and browse on the thin dry grass of the prairie. When the time comes they are driven to the slaughter-house. Bundles of hay toll them along to the door, where they are waited for. The moment an ox crosses the threshold, he is seized by the horns, and dragged by a cord wound round a windlass. A blow of a club finishes the poor beast in an instant. Iron hooks are passed through its hind legs; it is strung up, its skin taken off, cleaned out, and cut in two. The two dressed halves are carried to a great wooden anvil; all around stout butchers make their hatchets fall incessantly. Once cut off, the pieces are seized by hooks, salted, and packed into barrels. On such a scale, butchery becomes almost grandiose. You see the great bleeding carcasses swung along the beams on which they are hung; the hooks by which they are suspended run on little iron rails. One after another the immense quarters come upon the anvil, where the sharp chopping knives ring unceasingly. In the busiest days of October and November, 340 oxen are sometimes killed in a day at the packing-house I visited. There is room for 700 oxen cut in two in this great beef factory. Only imagine 1,400 halves hung on long parallel beams! 350 workmen are constantly employed. Besides 340 oxen, they kill and prepare 1,800 hogs every day. A long quadrangular boiler full of hot water is ready for the carcasses. They fall one by one, after receiving the death-blow, into the last compartment, where the water is nearly boiling: they float in it a few minutes, then the butchers seize them, clean them, and scrape them with little iron

candlesticks. These are the quickest and most convenient tools that have yet been found for taking off the
hard bristles. The butcher, holding the candlestick by the
socket, scrapes backwards and forwards with the sharp
edge of the saucer, and removes the bristles in locks.
All this time the carcasses float on the water, which is
kept at boiling pitch by a jet of steam passing constantly through it. The hog, thus scalded, very soon is
caught in a sort of iron cradle, which turns it over and
throws it on a table. There it is cleaned again; it
takes the tender and delicate rose colour of a sucking-
pig: then iron hooks are passed through its hind legs,
the animal is hoisted up, and suspended by the feet.
With a single stroke of the knife, the belly is ripped
up; hands are plunged into the puffed-up intestines, the
greenish bile, the fat, and serrated ribbons of tripe.
The blood flows off in gutters; nothing is lost; everything is gathered up and set aside. The hog, dressed
and split, is hung up in a storeroom, where it dries
before it is cut up. There is something Homeric in this
perpetual massacre, and you end by finding a savage
poetry in these bloody scenes. You forget the revolting
side of it, to think of nothing but the order, the
activity, and the grandeur of the results obtained. Is
the miserable workman who buys cheap meat in the
suburbs of London or Liverpool aware that he owes
it to these rough butchers of Chicago, whose arms are
dipped in blood all day? The slaughter-houses are
great laboratories where the necessary materials of
human life are amassed : the wild flower of the prairies,
the azure gentian, the grasses that wave in the wind

blowing from the Rocky Mountains, have passed into those muscles which are to-day the sport of the hatchet and the knife, and which soon are to become the blood of a people.

The meat trade has been developed at Chicago as rapidly as the corn trade. A few years ago Cincinnati was the principal pork market, which procured for it the name of Porcopolis; but to-day Chicago has gone ahead. By the lakes, canals, and railways that radiate from it in every direction, this town can distribute meat more rapidly and economically than any other. In 1863–64, 904,659 hogs were put in barrels in the fifty-eight packing-houses of Chicago; during the year 1862-63, the figure rose to nearly a million; in 1857–58, it was only 99,262: it has therefore increased ten-fold in six years. During the year ending March 31, 1864, 300,622 head of cattle had been brought to Chicago, instead of the 209,655 of the preceding year. Large quantities of oxen are daily driven through the town, and are sent by the lake to the Western States. For example, the city of New York, that in 1863 consumed 264,091 head of cattle, received 118,692 from Illinois. Is there a curiosity to know what this town of millers, butchers, and merchants does for primary education? It has founded 17 district schools and a high school. During the year 1863, these schools were daily frequented by 10,000 scholars on an average. The school funds, which consist of lands granted by the municipality, are estimated at 900,000 dollars; the income derived from these is added to the school-tax voted and raised every year. During the year 1863, the budget of the primary schools was 146,655 dollars, which allows us to calculate the average expense per scholar to be 12 dollars 67 cents.

The great public works undertaken at Chicago can compare with those of the largest capitals. A network of magnificent sewers extends under the whole city. The houses have water on every storey; this water is brought from the borders of the lake, and raised by powerful steam-engines into a large reservoir. But the many packing-houses, tanneries, and the divers establishments along the river send a great deal of impure matter into the lake; and to obtain a more healthy water, Mr. Chesbrough, the city engineer, conceived the bold project of getting the waters of the lake a mile from the edge, by means of a tunnel dug beneath its bed, and connected with a hollow tower, perforated by openings from interval to interval. These doors can be opened at will, so during the summer, for example, only the water from the bottom of the lake, unheated by the sun, would be allowed to come into the tunnel. This fine work is being executed, and the wooden tower that was to serve as an inlet for the waters was already finished when I left Chicago.

After my visit to the packing-houses of Chicago, I was taken to Camp Douglas (this name is to be found everywhere in Illinois), where above 10,000 Confederate prisoners were detained. Twelve long parallel rows of wooden houses had been erected for the Confederates; the vast camp was surrounded by a palisade, round the top of which ran a wooden balcony, where Federal sentinels walked backwards and forwards. I was not admitted to the interior of the great enclosure. I only saw a few prisoners, returning from work, crossing the great squares with their guards. All round these courts were stretched out low barracks built in haste, and with only one storey. Most of the prisoners still wore their grey uniform, and those soft felt hats that seemed to be the favourite head-gear of both armies. The Southern prisoners have always been treated with the greatest humanity in the North; their food was the same as that of their guards, and their fate was not in reality more unhappy. In the South, on the contrary, it is stated that the Northern prisoners have often been subjected to most barbarous treatment; the tale of their sufferings is the most lamentable page of the war, and shows to what degree the institution of slavery can harden the heart. The keeper of the Ander-sonville prison in Georgia boasted publicly that he had killed more Federals than Lee on the battle-field. I saw Camp Douglas on the 17th of October. A short time afterwards, on the eve of the presidential election, the police of Chicago arrested malefactors, from Canada and the Southern States, who had planned to fire the town in several places, and, under cover of the fire, deliver the 10,000 prisoners guarded in the camp. Doubtless this conspiracy was already suspected at the time I was there, as for many days no one had been admitted within the palisaded enclosure.

CHAPTER VIII.

THE POPULATIONS OF THE WEST.

No matter how quick and well-directed may be the impulse given throughout the West to works of art, industry, commerce, and public education, the most interesting thing to be found there, after all, is the people. We get tired of seeing schools, churches, monuments, factories, banks: we are never tired of studying men. In our old Europe history, political institutions and traditions have created a sort of social hierarchy that enslaves the individual as much as it protects him: what is a support is at the same time a barrier. All the tasks are allotted, all the places taken; individual force multiplies its action, in being concentrated on unchanged and definite objects. The artist, the scientific man, the musician, the manufacturer, should aim at perfection. High cultivation envelopes the select intelligences as with a subtle web, spun of doubts, reserves, and contempts, through which joy and enthusiasm can scarcely penetrate: the temptation is greater to be a spectator than an actor. In several towns even of the Atlantic States, whose history is comparatively old, the family spirit, the spirit of coteries, and the spirit of provincialism are already as intolerant as in Europe; and if the chain of traditions is not as long, it is fully as

tenacious. A people without traditions lives in the West
—a new, simple, creative people—childish still, though
civilisation has put all the weapons of maturity into its
hands.   Everything seems easy to it, everything beautiful.   It is joyous, impatient, and intoxicated with
a chronic enthusiasm.   Indeed, its language is stamped
with a perpetual exaggeration. What name did Illinois
give its favourite statesman, Douglas ? The Little Giant.
I could hardly help smiling when I heard, every
other minute, an ordinary man, unknown out of his
town or country, spoken of as ' a splendid man.'   That
is the formula of the West ; talent quickly assumes
the proportions of genius, mediocrity those of talent.
Political eloquence too often disdains the artifices, the
cold irony, the severe deductions of logic ; is too often
contented with invective, noisy declamation, and coarse
jokes.   Newspapers have the violent tone of pamphlets.
The only religious doctrines that succeed in profoundly
stirring the popular conscience are the Calvinistic. They
shake souls that would be insensible to philosophical
teaching or mysticism, by their terrible logic and
brutal simplicity : they need the full view of a hell:
the belief in predestination puts them at their ease:
they can only rest in a sort of fanatic tranquillity that
ignores all finesse and all criticism.   The spirit of
analysis has as yet touched nothing : rule and measure
are unknown. Not only does the Western man admire
everything, but he wants you to admire with him.   He
goes into ecstasies before a church, a picture, or a monument, never suspecting that they may appear monstrous
to you, and naively enjoys the pleasure you do not

experience. Open and generous, he shows and gives all he has; and his hospitality has really something royal about it, for everything he touches is transformed, seen through his imagination. At Chicago, I was shown a room where dusty bundles of maps, papers, and modern books were kept : that was the library of the ' Historical Society of Chicago,' and I was informed that the Prince of Wales had been shown solemnly over it during his visit to the town. Everywhere, where I went over libraries, it was thought necessary to tell me, ' This is not the Astor Library (the largest in New York and the United States) yet, or the British Museum, but we are only beginning.' Generosity, like enthusiasm, knows no limits. A young man, who made a large fortune in a few years distilling brandy, has just given a million of dollars to the city of Chicago, to build a new opera-house. For several years the Observatory of Harvard College has possessed a magnificent telescope, that in the hands of Messrs. Bond has rendered great services to astronomical science. Chicago wished to outdo Boston, and has just made the acquisition of an objective a third larger than that of the University of Massachusetts. One rich merchant has been found to buy it, another to pay for mounting it, a third to give the other instruments; so that now the Observatory of Chicago is furnished with everything but an astronomer.

After enthusiasm, confidence is the most characteristic trait of the populations of the West. They seem to know neither those anxieties or timidities that debilitate men elsewhere. In countries where every-

thing is still to be created, there is so much to do that
every man is welcome. He feels that he is needed;
he can discuss his services and make his terms. It
seems as if every citizen, as soon as he was up, read
over the official statistics published every year by the
Government. He recites them all the time: 'Our
resources, our exportations, our territories, our corn,
our mines.' These words are repeated over and over
again in conversation. All this seems to belong to
each individual: indeed, everybody is ready to be
merchant, farmer, miner, one after the other; everyone
is on the look-out for fortune, and follows it, no matter
where it leads him. Now-a-days, everybody knows
the story of Mr. Lincoln—a true representative of
the West: first boatman, then woodsman, farmer,
lawyer, representative, and President of the Republic.
Grant and Sherman, the best Union generals, are
Western men.

Politically, the Western States are more deeply imbued than any other part of the Union with democratic
principles. Popular sovereignty has become a dogma
and a religion there; it knows no rules, and it casts off
all restraints. Political mandates are more imperative,
and of shorter duration than elsewhere. Universal
suffrage chooses the representatives of the judiciary
power, as well as those of the executive. Society is too
mobile and fluid to voluntarily imprison itself in forms.
The laws are being constantly modified, and the States
amend their constitutions as soon as they feel the
slightest inconvenience or defect. Popular sovereignty
does not readily bend before the engagements entered

into by past generations. The Western citizen says, rather, with Lowell's Pioneer : 'The serf of his own past is not a man.' Is it the tyranny of public opinion that makes individuals more versatile, or the versatility of individuals that makes public opinion more tyrannical? In a laborious, hurried, ardent society, that never looks back to the past, and for whom the future never seems to come quickly enough, every one wishes to feel himself drawn along by the most rapid current ; there are no asylums, or cloisters, or strongholds, or peaceful retreats for the discontented. Elsewhere, the worship of a sect, the caresses of the patrician classes, the solitary pleasures of study, the enjoyment of the arts, may soften the regrets and strengthen the fidelity of those who are vanquished ; but a man would need a heart of steel to resist the current of opinion where there is no other recognised authority, where it enslaves civil, and even interprets the divine, law. When the sea retreats from a part of its bed that it has covered with sand, you can observe strata that with time harden into sandstone of some solidity : thus, in the oldest States of the Union, democracy is no longer a fluid and constantly shifting sand. Already, secular interests, rooted traditions, long antagonisms, local institutions, introduce conservative forces into the State. The individual can deal much more easily with these divergent and often contrary forces than he can escape that unique sovereign and overwhelming force that draws all along with it in a young democracy. It is in the old States alone that new ideas spring up, and that superannuated ideas live on. Massachusetts alone was able to be a fortress to the abolitionists for many years. There, too, the doctrines of the old Federalist party resisted the longest and the most strongly the triumphant democratic school. This State will long remain the guide and, so to speak, the intellectual protector of the country; for it is there that the rights of the individual intellect are the most loudly proclaimed and the best maintained.

As long as the moral influence of the Atlantic States lasts over the Western ones, there is no reason to be too afraid of what you might call the democratic intoxication of these latter. It must also be borne in mind that the spirit of anarchy cannot make great progress in a community bound to the soil and principally devoted to agriculture. In every fresh furrow drawn by the plough, the conservative instinct and love of country spring up with the young corn. His foot planted on the centre of the continent, the robust farmer of the West feels himself its king and master. The true America, in his eyes, only begins on the Western slopes of the Alleghany chain: the national pride that burns in his heart is not fed by democratic passion alone; it is also inspired by the sight of those boundless plains, open to his ambition, by those giant rivers, some running to the polar regions, others to the tropic seas. The old States have remained in many respects dependent on Europe. They borrow from it not only goods and machines, but ideas. The West entirely escapes this European influence. By I cannot tell what inexplicable charm, what powerful fascination, those who go towards the Rocky Mountains never look back to the Atlantic.   The emigrant from New England never regrets on the prairies the hills where he was born; the Irishman never dreams of going back to his damp island; the German himself, faithful still to his native language, becomes unfaithful to his country. From these varied races springs a new race, strong as the generous soil that rears it, proud and independent. The love of liberty and the feeling of equality become like congenital passions for it; its political convictions are not, as with the European, arms against a tyranny; it is not obliged to wrap them in formulas; its faith is a living faith. It is of the American of the West, above all, that it can be said that he not only believes himself to be, but that he is, the equal of all around him.   A little alkali removes a spot of acid on silk, but every woman knows that the acid always leaves a slight mark. The democratic spirit of the West is the virgin material that nothing has yet tarnished.

One of the most important causes of the prosperity of the West would remain unknown if its territorial laws were not studied.   Elsewhere surveys follow centuries of possession; here the survey precedes colonisation.   The farmer is not the only pioneer of the wilderness ; he is accompanied, and often preceded, by the geometrician.   Who has not been struck, looking at the map of the United States, by seeing so many rectangular lines, simply drawn by the degrees of latitude and longitude ?   Elsewhere, rivers, mountains, and the geological construction separate provinces ; on the territory of the American Union, geodesy has traced ideal frontiers.   It ·has fixed, with that rigour

which characterises all scientific operations, the limits
not only of the States, but those of the municipal
boundaries, and, within these, the limits of individual
property. The maps of Illinois, Wisconsin, and Minnesota look like great chequer-boards; the lands are
divided into squares that are six miles long and six
miles wide. These groups of townships lie on the
meridian, and the series they make from north to south
is called the range. Every township is subdivided into
thirty-six sections, that contain one square mile, or 640
acres. The section is cut into quarter sections of 160
acres, that can be once more divided by four: the
square of forty acres is the smallest territorial fraction.
As the degrees of longitude come nearer and nearer together as they approach the pole, the townships could
not be all of the same size, if the ranges were not interrupted from time to time. From interval to interval,
a new terrestrial parallel is taken as a basis. The
angles of each township are marked by fixed limits, and
the traces of all the geodesic determinations are preserved on the maps of the territorial agency.

These great surveying operations began in times
past on the Ohio River. The vast network of lines
that form the unchangeable frontiers of the territorial subdivisions has since spread in every direction
as far as the Mississippi, and beyond this river to
the sources of the Missouri. Like works have been
undertaken in California and Oregon, in Washington
territory, and some day the two nets will join at the
Rocky Mountains. The traveller who comes from the
Atlantic States to the great plains of the West cannot

fail to be struck with the contrast between the irregular lines of property in the old States and the rectangular figures of lands in the new States. Thanks to the system of numeration that has been adopted for the townships and the sections, a lot on the prairie can be looked up as easily as a house in the streets of a great city. It was not enough to protect property from all usurpation in a country without police, open to all adventurers, where nature herself had traced hardly any limits, and offered no protection; it was necessary to make the acquisition of land as easy as the titles were secure. The State has never made concessions of lands, but it sells them on the most liberal terms. Any one may buy a lot of 40, 80, 160, 320, or 640 acres, or a cluster of like lots, for $1,25 an acre. The law exacts immediate payment; but in 1841 a preemption law made an exception in favour of pioneers already settled on unsold lands. On condition that they do not buy less than 160 acres, a delay of twelve months is granted, and in some cases a still longer delay for the payment to the Treasury. An adventurous emigrant, who wishes to profit by the advantages held out by the Preemption Act, chooses a lot, settles on it with his family, builds a house, clears up and sows the land. He sends a written declaration to the territorial officers of the district, in which he states that he is an American citizen, or, if a foreigner, that he intends becoming a naturalised citizen. If the lot he occupies has already been offered for sale, but without finding a buyer, he is obliged to discharge his debt to the Treasury after twelve months' possession,

L

and receives with his receipt a definitive title to the property. If the land is comprised in the geodesic network already marked out, without having yet been put up to sale, he is only bound to pay the sum of $1,25 per acre, on the day the lot is offered at public sale by the territorial agents, which can only happen after several years' possession.

During my stay at Chicago, I went to the office of the Illinois Central Land Company. The company which built the lines from Chicago to Dubuque and Cairo is at the same time a land company, for it had at the beginning a grant of a wide strip of land each side the line. A farmer in search of a lot finds at the company's office not only detailed maps of the unoccupied sections, but he can examine there samples of arable lands taken from all the territorial subdivisions, and a collection of all the agricultural products raised on the parts already under cultivation, every species of grain, stalks of Indian corn as tall as young bamboos, gigantic ears of sorghum, leaves of tobacco, and cotton pods. An intelligent agriculturist can see at a glance the resources of the State, and the quality of its lands.

The company builds churches and school-houses beforehand in the townships to which it wishes to direct emigration. It makes the following terms to the farmers : it cedes them 80 acres at $10 an acre, if the payment is immediate, or they have the choice of freeing themselves by paying $48 down, and giving the same sum at the end of the first, second, and third years of possession. At the end of the fourth

year the annuity amounts to $236. At the end of
the fifth and sixth years to $224. The seventh and
eighth, which are the last, are $212 and $200. Since
the war the farmers have realised profits that have
enabled them to discharge their debt to the company.
There are few States that can dispute with Illinois for
the fertility of its black soil; the fat loam that covers
this region, as large as England, raised, in 1861, 35
millions of bushels of wheat, and 140 millions of bushels
of Indian corn, to say nothing of oats, rye, barley,
potatoes, sweet potatoes, hemp, flax, beets, tobacco, and
sorghum. During the year 1863, Illinois exported four
millions of tons of cereals. These immense plains, that
have as yet but a population of 1,700,000 souls, will
one day maintain without difficulty from fifteen to
twenty millions of inhabitants.

Figures of statistics are too cold and too empty to
make a durable impression on the mind; it is difficult
to understand the grandeur of the West, and to predict
its future, without crossing its endless plains. How
many times, standing on the platform of the last car,
have I not looked at the vanishing ribbon of the track
that runs in a straight line to the horizon. Beyond
the cultivated fields that here and there lined the road,
the solitary prairie stretched into the distance, sometimes even as a lake, now gently undulating. Now and
then a cloud-shadow swept over the tall grass, that
alternately in light and shadow seemed to move like
the waves of the sea. For how long a time have these
great gardens of the desert been useless to man? The
Indian has left no more trace than the buffalo, the elk,

the beaver, or the wolf, that still howls by night on the prairie. The fires of savage tribes have not destroyed the flowers of the wilderness. How often has the plain adorned itself with their rich harvest, and how often has the summer withered them! But civilisation is able to tear its idle ornaments from the desert. She never gives up what she has once seized, and a few years suffice her to lay the foundations of an empire.

These thoughts kept coming to my mind during my journey from Chicago to the Upper Mississippi. Among the iron roads that radiate from Lake Michigan to the great river, I chose the most northern, that goes through the upper part of Illinois and the whole State of Wisconsin. In this latter State you are in almost complete solitude; houses are still very rare, a great many fields are not yet fenced in, and the yellow stalks of Indian corn mix on the edges with the golden rods, or the coarse herbage of the swamps. In the midst of the wilderness, the belfry and the roofs of a rising village appear at long intervals surrounded by orchards. At Portage City we enter a very wooded country, and the soil becomes sandy; in the valleys, the sandstones make walls that look like ruined towers and fortresses. This barren region is covered with woods of oak and maple, with every now and then a few pines. The train stops for an instant at a place called Kilbourne City: I look on every side to see the city, but see nothing but a wooden shed, in front of which strays a solitary pig. At Sparta, a boy on horseback comes to get the bundle of newspapers that the conductor of the train throws to him, and then starts off at

full gallop towards the little village which, in the midst
of these wild woods, bears the name of the proud city
of Peloponnesus. A few blueish outlines presently
indicate the bluffs that border the Mississippi; the
railway leaves the wooded plains of Wisconsin, and
goes down gradually through the yellow cuttings of
sand, edged by thick brushwood, straggling creepers,
and wild-flowers, to the wide alluvial plain, where the
river meanders lazily along. Willows and alders mark
the courses of little canals that run in all directions.
Herds of oxen stand motionless, and, so to speak, buried
in the midst of high grass. Fields of wild-flowers sway
to and fro in the light wind. Here at last is the river
with its sandbanks, its innumerable islands with their
crumbling shores, covered with elms and maples. You
see high bluffs each side of the valley, whose promon-
tories retreat one behind the other, and are at length
lost in the mists of the horizon.

La Crosse is the name of the station where the train
stops. All along the Upper Mississippi you could almost
believe yourself in a French province, if you looked at
nothing but the names. Below La Crosse on the Mississippi, Prairie du Chien—pronounced Prairie du Chene
by Americans—and Dubuque; to the north, in fertile
Minnesota, you come to St. Paul's, the capital of the
State, and to the falls of St. Anthony, that were named
in the year 1680, by Father Hennepin. The end of Lake
Superior, that lies near the sources of the Mississippi,
is still called Fond-du-Lac; but this name is on the
point of degenerating into Fondulac. Though La Crosse
has been marked on the maps this long while as a

town, it is only ten years old, and nevertheless numbers 10,000 inhabitants. The tide of emigration for the last few years, has spread with great rapidity over the fertile lands of the Upper Mississippi. St. Paul's has already 9,000 inhabitants, eight churches, several hotels, three printing-presses, schools, and a capitol. La Crosse, in spite of its shops fronting on the river, its stores, and its elevator, whose bulk overtops the railway station, still wears a look of poverty and neglect. Cows wander at will over the sands, where quad-rangular streets are already marked out. Civilisation seems a long way off. In the bar-room of the hotel, round the reddened iron stove, sit silent and almost ferocious-looking groups. We can look at these faces of adventurers, so common all through the valley of the Mississippi; the beards are rough and uncared for, the clothing coarse, the felt hats pulled down over gloomy eyes that seem to follow some sinister shape in the empty space. At La Crosse I saw real Indians for the first time. Four men, wrapped in long red blankets, a woman enveloped in a grey cloak, and a half-naked child, were gathered round a great wood fire on the river's edge. The men were bareheaded; their thick black hair, that looked like a bunch of tangled horse-hair, floated in the wind, and almost covered their gloomy faces. Near them, rudders and oars were strewed on the ground; from time to time they threw sticks of wood on the fire, and the chilly group was in a blacker cloud of smoke. At some little distance the steam-boats showed their white upper storeys above the level of the river. I had before me at the same time the old masters of the Mississippi and its present possessors. The smoke of the fire lit by the Indians rose side by side into the sky with that puffed out by those powerful engines that to-day transport the traveller from the mouth of the Mississippi to the borders of Lake Superior. Was not the whole history of America in this picture?

CHAPTER IX.

A BORDER STATE—THE INVASION OF MISSOURI— SAINT LOUIS.

AFTER crossing the Northern States, and those of the West and Atlantic, I turned my steps towards one of those frontier States where civil discords have left their deepest traces. The time will come when this denomination of Border-State, still frequently employed in America, will cease to have any signification. Slavery alone had traced, in the very heart of the vast territory of the Union, an imaginary border line; the war has already half effaced it, and the reconstruction of the re-entering States will finally cause it to disappear entirely. The boundaries of the American republic will soon only be Canada in the North and Mexico in the South. But at the time I visited the United States the word Border-State had kept all its old signification, and civil war made it all the more apparent and sinister.

The Border-State which I proposed visiting was Missouri. I returned from La Crosse to Chicago by Milwaukee, a beautiful city, whose prosperity is fully equal to that of Chicago. I crossed over all the fertile plains of Illinois, and stopped at Quincy on the Mississippi. My intentions were to embark there, and to proceed to St. Louis by the river. I arrived at Quincy in the night, and repaired at once to the only hotel of the town. All through the day, in the train, I had heard people round me constantly speaking of the invasion of Missouri, where the rebels were committing great excesses. As is always the case on such occasions, a thousand rumours were rife, and the alarm had spread even as far as Quincy. On reaching the hotel I learned that during the evening the gas, both in the town and at the railway station, had been suddenly extinguished by an unknown hand. The porter of the hotel had been patrolling the streets in common with the other inhabitants, but, judging from his pallid looks, it did not seem to me, in case the rebels should cross the river and attack the town, that much confidence could be placed in this defender. The public room, in the midst of which stood a red-hot stove, was filled with groups of rough-bearded, long-haired men. Almost all were reading newspapers. Certain faces among them had an almost savage expression. I still see enter a poor lame soldier leaning on his cane, and attenuated by fever. An officer, with his large beaver hat, with its band and gold tassel, on his head, sits down at the nearest table and examines with much solemnity the letters which the train has just brought him. The landlord comes to tell me that I cannot have any supper, because it is after eleven o'clock ; he seems astonished that I insist, being very hungry, on having at least a piece of bread. American travellers, in such cases, have a sort of resignation and passive indifference which always astonishes me in a people so headstrong, and so opposed to all trammels. Both men and women accept without a word the small miseries of travelling with a fatalism mingled with contempt. Railroad companies have singularly tried this patience. I have scarcely ever been in a train which arrived at its destination at the hour indicated; but there never appear in the newspapers in the United States those complaints that the English are constantly addressing to their papers. An annoyance once over, the American hastens to forget it. Owing to her position upon the limits of the free and slave States, and to the junction of the two great rivers of the American continent, Missouri became necessarily one of the battle-fields of the war—far from the centre, and from those provinces where the greatest efforts of the combatants were expended, but also for that very reason condemned to be the theatre of most frightful scenes, where the most savage and violent passions, unchecked by honour and military discipline, had free course. At the time of the first difficulties, the largest part of the Missourians were at no pains to conceal their sympathies for the rebels. The partisans of the Union scarcely numbered one-third in a State which was bound by all the ties of political traditions, and above all, by the institution of slavery, to the new confederation. After the first election of Mr. Lincoln, it was an even chance whether St. Louis, and with this city the whole State of Missouri, were not lost to the cause of the North. Already the partisans had armed themselves, formed a camp at the gates of St. Louis, and were preparing to suddenly promulgate their 'ordinance of secession.' A few courageous and devoted Unionists silently organised the forces of the republican party, and recruited new allies, especially among the German population. On the 10th of May, a little before the term fixed for the ordinance of secession, Captain Lyon, at the head of a handful of volunteers, repaired to Camp Jackson, entered it without striking a blow, and dispersed those who were assembled there. One hour of daring prevented a vast province from uniting its fate to that of the rebels, and perhaps spared to the North years of efforts and sacrifice. At repeated intervals the rebels endeavoured, nevertheless, to wrest the State of Missouri from the Union; blood flowed in the streets of St. Louis, which became the seat of a military department. More than 40,000 Missourians entered the Southern armies. One of the late Governors of the State, Sterling Price, who still enjoyed a great popularity, especially among the rural populations, was named General, by Jefferson Davis, and invaded Missouri for the first time, at the moment when General Fremont held the command at St. Louis. The invasion was repulsed; the Unionists who had fled before Price's regiments were able to return to their firesides. But security was never entirely established. Armed bands long traversed the country in all directions. The fidelity even of those who had served the Union cause was severely tried when they could no longer doubt that slavery would never outlive the civil war. The Union sentiment had never been unmixed in Missouri. With many of its inhabitants it was wholly subordinate in their attachment to the servile institution. The nearer this fatal institution seemed to its ruin, the more obstinate became their efforts to save it. Some time before the presidential election of 1864, and while the partisans and the enemies of slavery were occupied on all sides, General Price announced that he was about to invade Missouri; he quietly finished his preparations, made his enrolments in the southern counties of the State, and his troops soon attained the number of 20,000 men. The draft, the enrolment of the blacks in the armies of the republic, the emancipation policy, the long inter-ruption of the commerce of the Mississippi, had con-tributed to augment the number of malcontents, who only waited for a leader to declare themselves in favour of secession.

General Rosencranz commanded at St. Louis, but for a long time he showed no disposition to check the movements of Price. His inaction allowed the rebel cavalry to show itself at Hermann, a very short dis-tance from St. Louis, on the Pacific railroad; and at Pilot Knob, which is also very near the city. The government had sent Rosencranz to St. Louis, in spite of some military faults in Tennessee; he had been es-pecially chosen, as a Catholic, to give a sort of pledge to the Catholic Germans of St. Louis. During the first campaigns of the war, he had acquired a great repu-tation; the newspaper correspondents delighted to represent him as a Christian hero passing from prayer to battle and from battle to prayer. But at St. Louis, as in Tennessee, Rosencranz showed himself inferior to his task; he allowed Price to cross at his ease the whole of Missouri. At the time I was at Quincy the rebel general had cut all the bridges of the Pacific railroad, and dispersed the workmen occupied on the works of this line, which is destined to so great a future, and which is already finished as far as Warrensburg. His marauders frequently appeared on the Hannibal and St. Joseph's railroad, which connects the Missouri and Mississippi valleys. While Price turned in the direction of Kansas, to strike a decisive blow among the population of this young State, wholly devoted to the Union, the partisan leaders roved around him, especially two ruffians named Bill Anderson and Quantrell; this last already famous from having the year before surprised the city of Lawrence, in Kansas, and for having massacred there two hundred unarmed persons.

Anderson and Quantrell had regular commissions from their government, but they acted the part of highwaymen; they demanded a ransom alike from their friends and foes, and their names spread terror along the right bank of the Mississippi. At Quincy, the river is already very wide. The town is of very recent construction, but it will necessarily grow with great rapidity, for it is situated on one of the railroad lines which connect the two banks of the Mississippi. The great square, planted with elms, is surrounded by warehouses, where all the farmers of the neighbouring counties come to make their purchases. The port is encumbered with sacks, barrels, boxes; from all sides great herds of cattle are brought to be shipped on the river steamers. These steamers in nowise resemble those which we see on the lakes and rivers of Europe. The Americans have not preserved in the river boats the form of sea-going ships. At the time of low water the Mississippi becomes extremely shallow, and its bed is composed everywhere of sand-banks which are constantly moving; so that the only boat which is suitable at all times to navigate this great river is a *flat boat*, which draws but very little water, and carries its freight on a vast surface. The Mississippi steamer is, properly speaking, only a steam flat boat, surmounted by a house. Upon the lower floor, but little above the surface of the water, the boilers are placed, almost in the bows of the boat; these are not, as is the case with our boats, buried in the hold, and at night the open doors into which the fuel is thrown shine at a distance on the river like two great red eyes. Behind the steam-generators is the engine. The cylinders are almost always horizontal, and im-mense horizontal cranks put the wheels in motion; these wheels are very narrow, and placed far aft. Between the engine and the extremity of the flat boat there remains a vast space, in which the freight is accumulated. Upon the boat on which I had em-barked there were crowded oxen, horses, and mules destined for the army of the Mississippi. Although this boat, the 'Sucker State,' drew only three feet of water, the long droughts had reduced the volume of the river so much that nearly all the freight was laden upon two ordinary lighter flat boats fastened on either side. A staircase led from what might be called the ground floor to the first storey, which is one long nar-row saloon, on either side of which open the numbered doors of the cabins; these have a second exterior door, opening upon a balcony, which runs the whole length of the boat. At the hours of meals the interior saloon is converted into a dining-room ; at one end is the bar, where all day long liquors of all sorts are prepared, the principal element of which is generally whisky. The saloon and cabins have a flat roof, covered with bitumen, and above that is a second storey much smaller, where are lodged the agents and officers of the steamer. This storey again is surmounted by the pilot-house, a sort of little square observatory, which commands the whole ship, and where the pilot steers the rudder-wheel.

The river was so low that it was found necessary to stop the first night a little above Hannibal, on the Missourian bank. We took on board, by the light of torches of pitch-pine knots, a great drove of half-wild oxen. They were only to be induced to step upon the plank leading to the deck by screams and blows. The black sailors and the herdsmen, armed with long poles, rushed about in all directions : the frightened oxen gave vent to long bellowings ; some, mad with terror, leaped into the river. We could see faint lights flitting through the woods. This frightful scene lasted more than two hours, after which everything became quiet. In this latitude the nights are of an admirable splendour : Orion shone with marvellous brilliancy, and the Great Bear, bending on the horizon and reflected in the river, appeared almost as bright. At the forward end of the saloon, the men stand smoking round the iron stove, which is replenished with coal from time to time by a negro. Some few savage-looking *river rowdies* are playing cards, some read the last Quincy and St. Louis papers, while others converse in low tones, and from time to time I hear the names of Price, Lincoln, and M'Clellan. There are some faces which would not discredit the Missouri hordes : the long rough hair and hands, the skulking looks, and the wide felt hats slouched down over the eyes, recall involuntarily the ruffians who follow Bill Anderson and Quantrell. At the other extremity of the saloon are the women and children, and the men who accompany them, or who are admitted to the honour of conversing with them. The Missouri refugees on the boat relate the atrocities committed by the guerillas. I will repeat only one of these tales, because I happened to verify its exactitude at St. Louis. After General Price had left the little town of Glasgow, Quantrell and Anderson entered it. Anderson, accompanied by a captain, went to the house of an old Unionist, very rich and much respected, Mr. Benjamin Lewis : he asked to see Mr. Lewis; he was told that he was not at home, upon which he threatened to fire the house. Mrs. Lewis sent for her husband. At this time Mrs. Clark, mother of the Confederate General Clark, was visiting her, and also Mr. Yorth, brother-in-law of General Price; but Anderson would not listen to their entreaties, and when Mr. Lewis appeared, he said to him; "I have heard of you, you have done more harm to our cause than any other man in this State." He then demanded all the money he had. Mr. Lewis brought him nearly 1,000 dollars, saying it was all he had left. But Anderson was not satisfied with this, and Mrs. Lewis then went out with Mrs. Clark and Mr. Forth to try to obtain more money among their friends and neighbours, leaving her husband alone with Anderson, who began striking the old man on the head with the butt end of his pistol, knocked him down, and with his companions continued to beat him while on the ground. One after the other placed the barrels of their revolvers in his mouth, and threatened to fire. At last Anderson ordered him to rise, still threatening him with his pistol. Four hours passed, during which the unfortunate old man was exposed to their fury. At two o'clock, a lady, cousin of Mr. Lewis, arrived, and asked the captain who accompanied Anderson how much they required for his deliverance. Anderson exacted 6,000 dollars. This sum was given up to him, 5,000 in paper and 1,000 in gold, and then only the ruffian consented to retire. Some days after, Mr. Lewis came to St. Louis, in a most deplorable state, covered with contusions, and the agitation he had gone through during the four hours his life was threatened had greatly injured and shaken his health.

My cabin companion was a young farmer of Kansas, who was taking his nephew, a boy of ten, to St. Louis. He was deeply engaged in reading the English translation of De Tocqueville's 'Démocratie en Amérique.' The book bore the mark of 'Leavenworth Public Library.' His conversation interested me deeply. Ten years since he settled in Kansas, and he had seen Leavenworth founded and attain its present population of 20,000 inhabitants ; also Lawrence and Atchison, which

M

have but 3,000. These three cities are the most important in Kansas, where the population is much scattered in farms and small towns. There is not a province in the Union where the love of the Union is more strong and passionate. Civil war visited Kansas long before it broke out in the rest of the country. There, too, was kindled the first spark which ignited the whole blaze. The remembrance of John Brown is still living there, and the heroic figure of the rude old farmer who led his sons to war like the Maccabees already belongs to legendary song. ' His soul is marching on,' says the refrain of the grandest of the songs inspired by the war : wherever I met a group of Union soldiers, I heard it ; 'His soul is marching on,' but it was in the solitudes of Kansas that it first saw liberty struggling against tyranny, and prepared for the final combat. Since the beginning of the war, 30,000 volunteers have been enrolled from the State of Kansas : 10,000 farmers, organised as militia and accustomed to carry arms, awaited Price's army, determined to defend their hearths and altars. At the time I descended the Mississippi the only defenders of Kansas were 1,000 Federal soldiers, commanded by Curtis, and garrisoned at Fort Leavenworth.

The ardent and exalted fidelity of this State to the Union is not inspired by vulgar motives, for there is but little pecuniary interest to bind them to the provinces of the Atlantic, or even to those of the West. Situated on the right bank of the Mississippi, Kansas is, as it were, on the Pacific slope, notwithstanding the Rocky Mountains, which rise like a wall between its ter-

ritory and the Californian provinces. Its principal
communications are opened with the regions crossed by
the great chain of the interior. Why should Kansas
send grain to Illinois, which is overflowing with it?
Placed on the confines of cultivated countries, she
sends her cereals to the district of Colorado, to Santa
Fé, to the silver mines of Virginia City, to Nevada, to the
gold mines of Idaho. Her commerce is a commerce
of caravans: cattle, flour, washing apparatus for the
auriferous sands, everything destined for those metal-
lurgic oases so long unknown, and where the gold fever
now draws a numerous population, comes either from
Kansas or from the Mormon country. The second
day the boat was again moored at night on the Missourian bank, at a short distance from the mouth of the
Illinois river. The morning after, we arrived in sight
of Alton. Above the rocky promontory on which the
town is built stands the immense penitentiary which was
used as the prison for the rebel soldiers. The bayonets
of the sentinels flashed brightly in the rays of the
morning sun, and idle soldiers lounged upon the quay.
A few moments before our arrival at Alton, a young man
who had seen me drawing on deck came to me, and
timidly begged me to make for him a sketch of the
prison at Alton. In spite of his rough uncombed hair
and beard, and sparkling eyes, the expression of his face
was so candid and simple that I acceded to his wish. I
could not refrain, however, from enquiring why he
preferred that point to any other: he blushed, and
told me that many of his friends and townsmen knew
the place well, and would be glad to have a sketch of

it.   A few days after, I learned at St. Louis that there
had been, on the part of the guerilla bands, a plan to
surprise Alton, and deliver the prisoners; it was not
carried out, however; so my sketch was useless, even if
it left the hands of my young unknown, whom I have
since suspected of having served in the armies of the
rebellion.

A little below Alton, the Missouri and Mississippi
mingle their waters : those of the Missouri are muddy
and full of clay, and have a much greater volume; so that
the Mississippi, hitherto clear and limpid, becomes
grey and troubled, and remains so nearly all the rest
of its course.   At last we come in sight of St. Louis;
vast workshops, magazines, and receiving houses stretch
along the quay, where, crowded together, we find a
veritable fleet of white steamers.

There was but little animation in the port: nearly
all the steam-boat fires were extinguished, and on the
banks of the quay there were few bales or hogsheads.
At first sight, the city seemed to me both dismal and
dirty.   The brick houses which are near the river are
nearly all in a state of dilapidation.   St. Louis, although
entirely modern, has already in many parts the air of
an old city.   The little post founded by Laclède and
Chouteau has been for twenty years the commercial metropolis of the centre of the continent.   St. Louis aspires
to-day to extend her influence to the Californian coast ;
her Pacific railroad is already finished as far as Dresden,
beyond Jefferson City, the political capital of Missouri.
With the natural advantages which she possesses, mistress of the largest river of North America, St. Louis

would have increased with far greater rapidity had she not been exposed to the enervating influence of slavery. The 'Missouri compromise' delivered over to this fatal institution a country whose latitude should have preserved it, and which offered to free labour vast fields of admirable fertility. This was the first triumph of an encroaching and unscrupulous policy. The South promised then never to claim for her '*peculiar institution*' any territory situated beyond the 36th degree of latitude. How this promise was kept, and how a series of humiliations for the North and triumphs for the South plunged them both into a civil war, every one knows. For Missouri herself, slavery has ever been a scourge; it has taken from her all spirit of enterprise, emigration, and industrial effort. The iron forges and workshops of Missouri cannot be for a moment compared with those of Pennsylvania, and meantime Missouri contains mountains of iron-ore in the Ozark hills. The metallic masses of Iron Mountain and Pilot Knob rival in quality the celebrated ore of the Isle of Elba, of Sweden and Norway.

The French population of St. Louis has from the beginning been attached to the institution of slavery, and still remains so; there is, mingled with its fidelity to the old colonial traditions, a sort of instinctive distrust and contempt for all that most interests the invading races by which it is surrounded. It is a melancholy spectacle for a Frenchman to see this population, rich, amiable, and estimable, but by its own fault absolutely deprived of influence: whilst all around it goes on and progresses, it alone remains stationary, and by its own wish. It never descends to the political arena, and has not yet given a single statesman to the republic. The Catholic clergy, although very rich, and by its virtues worthy of all respect, shows no other pre-occupation than that of preventing the Catholic children from attending the public schools, which are free, and where education is wholly laic. St. Louis calls involuntarily to mind this or that small French town, at once timid and fault-finding, idle and indifferent; governed by men whom she scarcely knows, or even whom she does not know at all; careless or ignorant of her municipal and political rights; contented with herself, without at the same time expecting anything from herself. Then take from her all national pride, the distant echo of the voices of the capital, and that deep and hidden sentiment of solidarity which cements as it were all minds, and, to sum all in one word, the assurance of a great destiny for the nation, and we have a perfect picture of the St. Louis of the French.

On the other hand, we find the St. Louis of the Americans and Germans. There is not one single French newspaper in this great city, while, on the contrary, there are a vast number of American and German papers published daily. It is perhaps amongst the German population of St. Louis that we must look for the most ardent defenders of the Union, and the most resolute enemies of slavery. But, less familiar with the habits of public life than the emigrants of the Anglo-Saxon race, the Germans as yet show in the political struggles a too unreflecting enthusiasm, a certain simplicity which is too easily satisfied with sounding phrases, and an obstinacy

which wears itself out in miserable personalities. By
flattering their demagogic vanity, the enemies of
Mr. Lincoln had succeeded in making them adopt
the candidature of General Fremont, at the beginning
of the presidential campaign of 1864; and when the
General retired from the lists, the radical Missourians
gave but a lukewarm support to the republican candidate. But although the extreme radicalism of the
German population may have been some embarrassment to the government, it is but just to admit that
the Germans have shown a strong attachment and
devotion to their new country. Understanding, from
the beginning, the aim and end of the civil war, they
embraced the cause of the Union and emancipation
with an ardour and passion the rebound of which
has even been felt by the populations beyond the
Rhine. The part they took in the war, the courage they
showed on the battle-field, their constant hostility to
slavery and the democratic party, henceforth assure to
them an important place in the politics of the United
States. The encroaching, jealous, and exclusive Anglo-
Saxon spirit—accustomed to absorb and conquer
everywhere—will be forced to consider this new
strength which grew up in the hour of difficulty
and danger. In California, as well as in Missouri, the
Germans have been found as American as the Yankees;
civil war has signed their naturalisation papers. The
true friends of the United States can only find in this a
cause for congratulation. There are in the Germanic
race qualities and elements which are destined to re-
juvenate the Anglo-Saxon race. The high culture of

Germany has but few representatives on the other side of the Atlantic, and as yet Germany sends to America scarcely any others than the poorest and most ignorant of her children; but they carry with them the mysterious germs which, in the old country, have borne such marvellous fruit. In the land of their adoption these germs will not always lie dormant; to the boldness and tenacity of the Anglo-Saxon race they will add something new, something more simple and poetic. In a purely physical point of view, much may be gained by the mixture of the two races: one is too nervous and irritable, the other too heavy and rustic ; but their intellectual union will doubtless bear even more precious fruits.

The situation of Missouri was, at the time of my visit there, far from satisfactory. Since the taking of Vicksburg the Federal gunboats circulated freely upon the Mississippi, but commercial intercourse between St. Louis and New Orleans was entirely interrupted. The army transports alone gave a little animation to the river. Guerillas still often fired on the steamboats, and destroyed all security for travellers. The violence of parties was extreme ; the democrats complained of Mr. Lincoln's emancipation policy, and their own candidate for the functions of Governor of the State was no other than the cousin of Sterling Price, who had twice invaded Missouri. This cousin, also of the name of Price, had, in 1860, remained faithful to the Union, and Mr. Lincoln, wishing at the same time to reward his fidelity and to give a proof of his conciliatory disposition, made him Brigadier-General in the army of volunteers.

This did not prevent General Price, in the month of October 1864, from supporting the candidature of M'Clellan ; and in a popular assembly he boldly declared that, if Mr. Lincoln were re-elected, Missouri would be forced to consider whether it would not be for her interest to join her fate to that of the States of the new confederacy. On the other hand, the republicans thought themselves abandoned and almost betrayed by the government ; they found fault with Mr. Lincoln for the smallest concession to the democrats ; they had obtained in a convention the gradual abolition of slavery, but they feared that the emancipation measure would remain a dead letter if their enemies succeeded in regaining their power. On all sides the Unionists were exposed to the greatest dangers ; the inertia of the military commander of the province had again delivered up the State to bands of robbers and assassins. Both parties complained of the draft. Missouri had already given thirty thousand men to the Northern armies, nearly forty-five thousand had followed the Southern flag, and now a new contingent, based upon the census of the population of 1860, was again required from the State.

The most interesting visit I made in St. Louis was to Camp Jefferson, situated a few miles beyond the city. I went there by the horse railroad, and saw on the way one of the eleven forts, now entirely abandoned, that were erected by order of General Fremont, when he commanded at St. Louis; more to hold the city in awe than for its protection. The wooden houses of the camp surround the great parades, beside a park which was once used for agricultural exhibitions. In the midst of beautiful black oaks, with their straight trunks and angular branches, rise rows of slightly-built houses, which have all been converted into hospitals: besides these, quantities of small wooden houses have been erected to lodge the sick soldiers, the negro families, and the Southern refugees. The hospital of these last, which I visited the first, presented a lamentable spectacle: on all sides were women and children, worn and emaciated by hunger, the fatigue of their long marches, and illness. They pointed out to me a poor old woman who had come alone from Texas to St. Louis on a little worn-out horse. While I made my melancholy way between the rows of beds, I saw an old man in the last agonies of death, uneasily moving his emaciated arms, which had already the appearance of dried bones. A fetid odour of drugs and cooking made the air, heated by iron stoves, still heavier. On the outside of each bed we saw still spread on the grey woollen blanket the scanty rags of clothing that the fugitives had brought with them. A few bold-eyed women were talking and laughing among themselves, and their gaiety near these deathbeds seemed cynical and lugubrious. Have those who kindled the fire of civil war ever contemplated these pictures? If they have seen them, can they avoid feeling the pangs of remorse?

The military hospital had quite another aspect. The clean white beds were almost all empty; garlands of coloured paper trained in festoons between the wood columns and along the ceiling; above the doors and the iron bedsteads were hung great cards on which were printed, in large letters, verses from the bible, mottoes, and patriotic sentences. Most of the patients were coloured men : one among them had had his feet and hands frozen during the operations of the siege of Vicksburg. The convalescents were sitting in little groups; some wore their hair braided in little tails, which stood up straight all over their heads; their clean blue uniforms were brushed till they shone again. After the hospital, I went through the cabins which had · been hastily built to accommodate the refugees, both blacks and poor whites. In the quarters of the former, the little coloured children seemed to leap out from every corner: the women were cooking. An old woman, with a bright gay face, passed us carrying a bushel of yams. ' Why do you not buy potatoes?' said my guide to her; ' they are not half so dear.' She replied—with a shake of the head, and an ·indescribable grimace— ' Cos I can't bear 'em.' An old man with beard and hair perfectly white sat on a stool near by, warming himself in the sun ; he must have been at least eighty years old. ' Why,' I asked him, ' did you leave your home in the South?' ' To do same as you, sah ; rest when I'm tired : Uncle Sam won't make *me* work no more.' The houses apportioned to the white refugees were filled almost exclusively with women and children ; I saw but few men, all either too old or too weak to work. The members of the same families remained together. The unfortunate creatures looked at us with a strange curiosity; the women, especially, willingly entered into conversation. They seemed to be entirely strangers to either shyness or embarrassment; some of them, engaged in combing their hair, crowded round us without taking the trouble to interrupt their occupation. Our guide, who had recently established in the camp a school for the children of the refugees, asked a young girl, whose delicate and still childish face indicated her age as certainly not over sixteen, 'Do you go to our school?' 'School,' replied she, tossing back her long fair hair with a look of surprise and disdain; 'I'm a married lady, sir.' All the Southern (white) women are ladies, but this fact does not prevent them from coolly smoking short clay pipes, like soldiers and sailors.*

The young *lady* who was so much shocked at the idea of going to school was forced to confess that she could not read; she did not appear in the least ashamed. The poor whites, who in the South form the intermediate class between the great proprietors and the blacks, live in a state of the profoundest ignorance. It was from this rude, uncultivated, and semi-savage class, accustomed to a complete dependence, that the South recruited her armies : she had managed to inspire them with horror for all that might regenerate them. These soldiers, whose blood had been poured out on so

---

* This abuse of the word 'lady' is very common in the North as well as the South. There is a current story of a clergyman saying in a sermon : 'Who were last at the cross? Ladies! Who were earliest at the grave? Ladies!'

many battle-fields, believed that they were fighting for independence, while in reality they were fighting to have masters. The soldiers of slavery were themselves the slaves.

After leaving the camp we saw a company of Missourian cavalry just returned from an expedition to Pilot Knob. The squadron halted before the gates of the camp, and was waiting till its quarters were assigned to it. Both horses and men seemed equally tired, having had no rest for several days ; the blue jackets trimmed with yellow, the long cloaks, the black beaver hats, were white with dust ; the long boots, and Mexican stirrups of leather, were covered with thick layers of hard dried mud. Each man had a musket at his saddle-bow, and a revolver in his belt. They had been beating the country in search of guerillas, and had themselves more the appearance of partisans than of regular soldiers. Most of them were so worn out that they dozed sitting on their horses ; some for greater repose sitting sideways, others with their legs crossed upon the pommel of the saddle. There were among them some splendid military figures. I remember particularly a young captain who had got down from his horse, and who stood leaning against the saddle, his long sabre touching the ground ; with his smiling and martial face, his brilliant teeth beneath a long blond moustache, he looked as gay and as fresh as if he were just returning from parade. From the bold visages of these Missourians it was easy to guess that they would fight like demons, but preferred these adventurous expeditions to the life of a camp, and to the long operations of regular war.

The hospitals of St. Louis were constantly visited by the members of the *Western Sanitary Commission.* The sanitary commissions were wholly independent of the State, and had their offices in every great city in the Union. They in noways interfered with the action of the medical corps, nor with the officers of the army; they endeavoured solely to render their task more easy. The generosity of the American people furnished them with resources which permitted to add everywhere the superfluous to the necessary— fruits and antiscorbutics to the usual rations of camp and hospital, some warmer articles of clothing to the army uniform. These same resources served to found schools for the freedmen, and to diminish the sufferings of so many unfortunate victims of the war, either black or white. Few of the Sanitary Commissions have had a more difficult task than that of the West. The subscriptions and patriotic gifts found their way more easily to the great Commission at Washington, and to its branches in Boston, Philadelphia, and New York. The Commission of St. Louis and the Mississippi Valley grew from the smallest beginnings. After the first battles in Missouri during the summer of 1861, nothing was ready for the wounded; there were neither beds, nor fires, mattresses, blankets, nurses or medicines. At the time I was at St. Louis, the commission had already received 275,000 dollars, in money, and contributions of various articles to the amount of $1,250,000. The President of the Commission, Mr. Yeatman, was spending $2,000 per day; on all sides vast hospitals had been erected; the Com-

mission had founded in several cities *soldiers' homes,*—
establishments where soldiers on their way to the
army or to their homes were lodged and fed gra-
tuitously ; the Commission distributed, through the
medium of the surgeons of the army, in the camps and
hospitals, blankets, stockings, flannels, preserved vege-
tables, wine, fruit, books, and in short everything that
could add to the comfort of the soldier. Boxes arrived
daily from all parts of the Union, containing the most
varied objects : from Maine to Minnesota, from Boston
to St. Louis, there is not a village that has not sent its
offering; but it is from Massachusetts that the most precious and abundant aid had come. Not only has this little
State given largely both in money and in garments, &c.;
she has sent surgeons, nurses, and schoolmistresses.
The Rev. Thomas Starr King, the Unitarian clergyman
of San Francisco, whose patriotic eloquence was so
influential in California, and who obtained from this
State the sum of \$300,000 for the Sanitary Commis-
sions of Washington and St. Louis, was from Boston.
Dr. Elliot, the Unitarian clergyman of St. Louis, who
with Mr. Yeatman of Tennessee, an ex-slaveholder, was
the soul of the Commission at St. Louis, was also from
New England. I saw one of his nieces, who had just
arrived in St. Louis to take charge of a school of
coloured children, passing, at the age of twenty, all
day long among the benches of a schoolroom. A democrat angrily exclaimed before me one day, 'This
war is the conquest of America by Massachusetts.' He
was right, but it was not a conquest by the sword.

When I left Missouri, all was still confused and

uncertain; a short time after my departure, Price was beaten by the rude troops of Kansas, reinforced by a few Federal troops and by Stoneman's cavalry. At the first repulse the army of invasion, demoralised by its own excesses, melted away; and General Price carried with him but a few scattered remnants to the solitude of the interior of the continent. His second call upon the inhabitants of Missouri had been as vain as the first. He had come, he said, in his proclamations, to deliver them from the tyranny of Mr. Lincoln, and to give them a last chance to rise up against the government of Washington; but his only recruits were robbers and ruffians. General Rosencranz, in spite of the weakness he had shown, still kept his command till the presidential election of the 4th of November, after which it was taken from him. Missouri gave her vote for Mr. Lincoln; and at the same time her electors chose their governor, the members of a new legislature, and those of a convention charged with remodelling the State Constitution from the ranks of the most radical fraction of the republican party. The terrible lessons of civil war had not been lost on the inhabitants of this unfortunate province, ravaged in every direction by civil war, and twice condemned to all the horrors of invasion. The new Convention bravely began its work. It would not allow a single day of existence to the fatal institution justly considered as the cause of the war, and it effaced from the Constitution every word which could recall it.

CHAPTER X.

THE MIDDLE STATES—CINCINNATI—PHILADELPHIA.

IN Missouri I had witnessed in all their bitterness
the political passions which had compromised the cause
of the Union.   In the Middle States, which I visited
next, I observed American society under its calmer
aspects.   It was towards Cincinnati that I turned my
steps after leaving St. Louis.   I crossed the river early
in the morning, in the ferry-boat, to take the railroad
upon the left bank.   The city was enveloped in a
light mist which slept upon the river.   Seen through
this veil the white steamers resembled vast piles of
cotton.   From St. Louis to Vincennes we crossed the
Southern part of the State of Illinois: this region,
entirely peopled by Southern emigrants, Missourians
or Kentuckians, is familiarly called Egypt; it is the
black spot of Illinois, the land of ignorance, barbarism,
and poverty.   We crossed beautiful forests, where the
trees of the South already mingle with those of the
North.   I never before saw anywhere so many different species confounded in such picturesque disorder.
From time to time we caught a glimpse through the
thick trees of a woodcutter's cottage, or a poor farm-
house surrounded by rich fields.   At every station
stood idle groups waiting for the newspapers.   Stop-

N

ping at one of them, I left the train for a moment, and heard a violent discussion between a Union man and some democrats, who addressed him in threatening tones; judging from the ferocious looks of the inter-locutors, one would guess that it was not far, in this country, from words to actions. 'If Lincoln is named,' cried one of them with frightful oaths, 'we shall see a change here.' The train went on again in the midst of a long cloud of sparks, and followed its course straight through a forest of black oaks, elms, maples, acacias, cherry-trees, walnuts, and birches ; the dead trunks were covered with vines already turned a deep red and yellow. Vincennes, on the Wabash, one of the nu-merous branches of the Ohio river, is one of the old establishments of the French Canadians, and is now the seat of a Catholic bishopric. In any other coun-try the Wabash would be considered a great river ; in America it is not even mentioned. After Vincennes we are in Indiana. The country still retains the same characteristics. We see only log-houses in the forest clearings: a few trunks of trees, the interstices between them being filled up with mud and clay, a rude chimney built of rough ill-joined stones or of wood plastered with mud, one window and one low door, compose the log-house. Upon the mound formed by the accumulated mass of refuse, wood, stalks, and dead leaves, the pigs wander at liberty ; sometimes a half-naked child with long fair hair comes to the door and watches the train of cars. Heavy German waggons circulate through the muddy streets of the villages. At almost every station I see the blue cloaks of the Federal soldiers, who have fastened their horses to the wooden fences.   After a whole day passed in the splendid forests of Indiana, we reach the Ohio, or the *Belle Rivière*, and the railroad follows its winding banks from Aurora to Cincinnati.

Cincinnati is the most populous and the most important city of the beautiful valley of the Ohio.   It has been a flourishing city for many years, but the war has given a new impulsion to its principal commerce, which is the sale and salting of pork.   Chicago is already beginning, as I have before said, to dispute with Cincinnati the name of *Porkopolis*, under which it has long been familiarly designated.   There is an immense activity in the street and on the quay ; the two gigantic piles of a suspension bridge are already rising on either side of the river, and soon the railway trains will pass above the vessels and steamboats.   On all sides rise immense constructions where the most various materials are employed : the silurian limestones which glitter in the sun, the greenish sands of the carboniferous soil which present the delicate shade of the ' Swiss molasse.'   The architects have given free course to their fancy, and the style of the houses cannot be accused of monotony, though we may not always admire the design and proportions.   All styles are mingled, or rather, in the midst of these Moorish, Gothic, Italian, and French forms, all style is lost. The environs are charming.   By the steep and narrow streets of the suburbs I reached the summit of Mount Auburn, a hill which commands the city on the north.   The slopes on the Cincinnati side are parched and sterile, and a few dilapidated houses hang on the outcropping schists. In these strata the geologist finds a rich harvest of silurian shells of the utmost delicacy. The top of the hill commands the whole valley, and the city lies around it like an immense crescent. The confused mass of roofs, steeples, smoke-stacks, and workshops is shut in by the hills, dotted here and there by white houses at all heights. The sparkling ribbon of the river traces its majestic curves in the centre of the vast picture. On leaving the heights of Mount Auburn we enter at once into a pastoral country full of soft undulations, and whose magnificent trees scattered here and there in the midst of the fields form as it were a boundless park. The sugar maples mingle with four different species of oaks, walnuts, ashes, and the pale birch tree. The beautiful velvet lawns, and the graceful distribution of the trees of the country-houses which I saw on a splendid avenue called Clifton Avenue, reminded me of some of the most beautiful residences in England; but where could one find in England a sky of such admirable transparence, and that clear and brilliant light which gives to every object such powerful relief, such rich and crystalline tints.

On returning towards the valley I admired the position of Cincinnati, spread out in a vast cup of verdure. In 1812 all was silent and deserted in this place, which now echoes to the voice of a human multitude. I heard in the distance the cries of mounted soldiers who were conducting a great herd of mules to a little stream which empties itself into the bend of the Ohio. The smoke of the boats marked with a long black line the curve of the great river. Beyond, among the sombre pine trees, a few white spots indicated the place of a cemetery—a city of the dead already nearly as populous as that of the living. The evening mists were already creeping along the Ohio, and, slowly mounting, softened the red roofs of the houses. I left the heights with regret, and only reached the city as the night closed in.

The railroad which took me from Cincinnati to Pittsburg crosses the whole State of Ohio. In the environs of the city we passed before the long rows of wooden houses of Camp Dennison, the parade-grounds, and villas converted into hospitals, scattered among the fields and the groves of trees. The railroad winds for a long time through the smiling valley of the Little Miami, past great farms, immense corn-fields, meadows where grand old trees are left standing, and lovely woods gilded by the autumn. It crosses the river Scioto at Columbus, a fine and visibly flourishing city, full of wide streets, in nearly all of which run the American horse-cars : the new and well-built houses have nearly all the high roofs, à la Mansard. Beyond Hanover we enter the fertile valley of the Miskatung river ; immense fields of maize extend between the hills covered with purple woods ; the railway runs parallel for a long time with a canal which goes from the Ohio river as far as Cleveland, on Lake Erie. As we approach the Alleghanies, the landscape assumes a more sylvan aspect ; pines begin to mingle themselves with the green trees, and noisy streams rush down the wild valleys.

At some distance from Steubenville we came upon a train of merchandise which was off the track, and were kept waiting nearly an hour; and in order to make up for lost time, and arrive at Steubenville to meet the train coming from Cleveland, to which our own was to be attached, the locomotive rushed down with frightful rapidity along the bending curves of a little valley, through which a foaming torrent bounds along among a forest of pines. We regained the time we had lost at the risk of being thrown, by the centrifugal force, off the track, which follows the capricious meanderings of the water-course. The train, going at full speed, had the greatest difficulty in stopping in the station at Steubenville, and wrung from the breaks the most frightful and dismal sounds. Without stopping a moment at Steubenville, the train starts at once for Pittsburg. At the end of some time we stop again in the open country; everybody leaves the train to seek information, and we learn that, in a cutting at a short distance, a baggage-train had run over a cow and gone off the track. All the American locomotives are provided with a *cow-catcher*, a sort of double ploughshare, which can throw to the right or left any of the cows that often wander upon the track; but in a narrow cutting, with only one track, the cow-catcher can only throw the unfortunate animal from one side to the other, and the train is thus easily thrown off. We waited a long time till the obstacles should be removed. I left the cars, and saw the dark lines of the first chains of the Alleghanies, like long horizontal walls. It was soon plain that the track could not be easily cleared, and we were forced to adopt heroic measures. On the other side of the broken-down train was another, which, like our own, had been stopped. The destination of the two respective trains was changed; the travellers coming down the line came and took our places, and we went, in our turn, and occupied the cars they had just left. The operation was none of the easiest. When the change of both travellers and luggage was fairly completed, it was very late, and we only arrived at Pittsburg towards one in the morning.

The city of Pittsburg is built on the cape at the junction of the Monongahela and Alleghany rivers, which, in mingling, form the Hudson. The French, as early as 1754, had built a fort there, which received the name of Duquesne. Before the War of Independence, Washington, then a young officer of militia, declared that Fort Duquesne was the key of all the Western domains. On the 25th November, 1758, the English general, Forbes, took the fort, to which his troops, by acclamation, gave the name of Pitt. In 1845 Pittsburg was almost entirely burnt, but was soon rebuilt; and the black coal-smoke now falls upon a *Court House*, built in the Doric style, which cost a million, and upon hundreds of churches. On the left bank of the Alleghany is Alleghany City, connected with Pittsburg by several bridges : a magnificent penitentiary has been erected there at a vast expense. At Lawrenceville, one of the suburbs of Pittsburg, the United States have an arsenal. At a glance you recognise a great centre of industry. A heavy smoke hangs constantly over the innumerable workshops of Pittsburg and its environs. Hills rise on all hands, on whose sides crop out the black layers of coal: the railroad cuttings lay them quite bare. The miner is not obliged to descend in a well, sunk at vast expense, to seek the combustible; he has only to cut galleries and enter the mountain. On the sides of all the valleys the openings may be seen from which waggons emerge, and, coming down light inclined planks, carry the coal to the level of the railroads or water-courses. The soil contains too many riches in its depths for any one to take the trouble to cultivate it, and its wild and savage aspect shows only too plainly this indifference of its inhabitants: the woods are cut down without mercy, to construct the scaffoldings for the galleries of the mines. Here and there a few groups remain which have been spared by the axe, and whose beauty makes one regret that man should have been forced to ravage the surface to extract from this privileged land the treasures it conceals. All through the Alleghanian chain, iron ore is found intermixed in the beds of coal. In 1864 the divers coal districts of this State furnished twelve million tons of mineral coal.* The average price of coal during the same year was $6 50c. per ton.

* Pennsylvania, Ohio, and Western Virginia have principally supplied the East with coal; in 1860 Pennsylvania furnished

The value of the coal production may be estimated at seventy-eight million dollars, which in gold, at the rate of 200 (and all through that year, 1864, gold was rather above than below this rate), represents thirty-nine millions of dollars. The coal extracted in 1860 was only valued at fifteen millions. We may judge by these figures what a tremendous impulsion the war, and the new tariffs of 1860, have given to Pennsylvanian industry.

The quantity of cast-iron produced in 1864, in Pennsylvania, is estimated at about 700,000 tons. The price of cast-iron was subject to singular fluctuations; it rose from $30 the ton to $70, and then fell to $60. The average price during the year 1864 was $53, which gives for the general production $37,100,000 in currency, or about $18,500,000 in gold; but this cast-iron is transmuted into iron rails, cannon, machines, and agricultural implements. When it has gone through all these transformations, it represents at least a capital of eighty million dollars in gold.*

Conemaugh is a centre of industry in the very

9,397,332 tons of anthracite, valued at $11,869,574, and 66,994,295 bushels of bituminous coal, valued at $2,833,859. Total value, $14,703,433. In 1850 the value of the total production was $7,529,683. In 1860 Ohio gave 28,339,900 bushels of bituminous coal, valued at $1,539,713, and Virginia 222,780 bushels, valued at $222,780.

* The quantities of iron manufactured in Pennsylvania during five years w

1859	.	.	286,332 tons.
1860	.	-	313,000 „
1861	.	.	310,000 „
1862	.	.	381,000 „
1863	.	.	430,000 „

heart of the Alleghanies. Immense iron-works are built up against the high banks of rubbish taken from the galleries of the mines; long thick clouds of smoke from the chimneys overhang the whole city. The dwellings of the workmen, all built on the same plan, somewhat resemble those small rows of houses we see in the outskirts of London; with the exception that here they are isolated, while in London they are built in long monotonous brick blocks, each house touching the other. We are glad to leave Conemaugh, and to return to the solitude of the woods. Dark fir-trees and blue pines grow on the banks of the torrents, and the rocks are everywhere shrouded in a mantle of shining rhododendrons. The shapes of the Alleghanies are extremely striking. At times I could almost fancy myself in the mountains of the Jura, so much do the two chains resemble each other; only in America it is not the jurassic, but the carboniferous strata, that we find rolling in heavy undulations. As in our own Jura, these majestic folds form long, straight, parallel chains, which are separated by longitudinal valleys, at times of a great height. The dark forest walls are interrupted by transversal valleys, like the *combes* of the Jura, or the *cluses* of Switzerland, so that each chain, with either end terminating in a combe, has the shape of a caterpillar; and the aggregate of chains, running from Pennsylvania to Tennessee, may be properly compared to a legion of caterpillars placed one after the other in several parallel curves. The great streams do not follow the longitudinal

valleys; they wind from one combe to another, and
add thus to the savage grandeur of these gigantic
cuttings. Wherever we follow their course, we find
the terrestrial strata folded in immense arches and
symmetrical curves; the joints trace majestic lines
which show how formidable was the crush which
accompanied the upheaval of the Alleghany. The
combes are narrow defiles, but the longitudinal valleys are generally broad, and widen sometimes into
little plains, where the water-courses have but a slight
inclination.

The topography of the Alleghanian chain gains peculiar interest from the fact that the mountainous region
played a very important part during the war. The
Upper Potomac follows the deep indentations of Western Virginia; at Harper's Ferry it mingles with the
waters of the Shenandoah, which descends a beautiful
longitudinal valley, wide and fertile. This interesting
region is as it were shut in between two long parallel
walls; to the west rise high chains, where no railroad
can enter or any large army engage itself; the east is
bounded by the low chain of the Blue Mountains, the last
buttress of the Alleghanies. Beyond extend the great
wooded plains of Western Virginia, which during four
years have been the battle-field of the principal armies
of the North and South. At several points, the wall
which separates these plains of the Shenandoah valley is
interrupted. Several combes, or, to use their American
name, gaps, are like so many natural gates by which
troops can be thrown into the great valley. Masked
by the curtain of the Blue Mountains, an army could

move rapidly upon the Potomac, and harass at will the rear of the corps placed between the river and Richmond, or, crossing the fords of the Upper Potomac, throw itself upon Maryland and Pennsylvania. The *Great Valley* (so the valley of the Shenandoah is commonly designated) was the favourite route of General Jackson, who played so important a part during the first campaigns of Virginia. In the spring of 1862, when M'Clellan threatened Richmond, Jackson, profiting by the fact that Banks, who remained in the valley with a few thousand men, was amusing himself with fortifying Strasburg, boldly threw himself into Fort Royal gap. Banks, in danger of being cut off, was forced to fall hastily back on Winchester, where Jackson arrived at the same time and dislodged him. This movement spread alarm at Washington : all the available troops were despatched to confront Jackson, who successively defeated them. General M'Clellan, not receiving the reinforcements on which he had counted to free himself from a situation already difficult, gave orders for a retreat, and thus the fruits of more than a year's labour were lost. Twice the Southern army, coming down the great valley, was able to threaten the capital of the Union at the very moment when Richmond seemed in the most danger, and these aggressive movements were only stopped —the first time at Antietam, and the second at Gettysburg. Placed at the confluence of the Shenandoah and the Potomac, the town of Harper's Ferry was never able to stop the current of invasion; for this place, protected on the side next the valley by a line of heights which bear the name of Bolivar, is commanded by the hills, which upon the opposite bank of the Potomac attain over 500 yards in height. The only means, therefore, of shutting from the Southern armies the way which has so often allowed them to frustrate all the combinations of the Federals, was to burn the barns, the mills, and to destroy everything which could serve for supplies and provisions. Sheridan made the great valley pay dearly for the privileges conferred upon it by nature, and the fame of those names which will remain indissolubly connected with the history of the civil war.

From Pittsburg to Philadelphia the road crosses diagonally the whole Alleghany range. The first important chain is Chestnut Ridge, which is crossed at Blairsville. The Conemaugh river rushes from the mountains through a narrow combe, and by being dammed from time to time furnishes a water-power to the manufactories. For the most part of its length it has been possible to canalise the river: along the rapids, a regular canal follows its course at a short distance. The gorge is so narrow that in some places there is barely room for the canal, the river, the tow-path, and the railroad. The front axletrees of the railway carriages and locomotives in America are moveable, so that the train can follow the boldest curves; the traveller gains by this, for he does not plunge into the darkness of tunnels so often as in Europe. After the Chestnut Ridge we come to the highest chain of the Alleghany proper. At the western foot lies Cresson, a most charming spot, and summer watering-place. As yet there is only an immense wooden hotel, over which waves the starry flag, a few pretty Swiss cottages, and a park newly planted. Shortly after we penetrate into a transversal valley ; the train mounts by degrees, describing zigzags upon a very strongly-inclined plane. One shudders at the idea of the train running off the track when one glances down from the top of the gigantic mountain slope to the bottom of the valley, where the torrent seems only like a silver thread seen here and there through the arrowy pines. As the road rises, the landscape seems to grow ; and in each opening of the valleys rise the green and blue plans of the, more distant chains, whose horizontal lines fade one behind the other. At the foot of the chain we reach Altoona, lost in a solitary longitudinal valley. Soon after we enter the rich valley of the Juniata. · The Juniata is a magnificent river, which after long windings empties itself into the Susquehanna at Cove: the road follows the right bank of this river as far as Harrisburg.

Harrisburg is the political capital of the State of Pennsylvania. A splendid tubular bridge, supported on eighteen grand piles, crosses the river there. This admirable work was in great danger of destruction at the time of the second invasion of Maryland and Pennsylvania, by the rebel army, in 1863. The vanguard of Lee was at Kingstown, only thirteen miles from Harrisburg, the 27th of June 1863. Two days later, General Lee moved his head-quarters to Carlisle ; the alarm spread throughout Pennsylvania, and already the work of defence round Pittsburg had

begun : the victory at Gettysburg obtained by General
Meade obliged the rebels to evacuate Pennsylvania,
and threw them on the other side of the Potomac.
During this short invasion, the German populations
were submitted to numerous requisitions. The Dutchmen, the name always given to the Germans everywhere in the United States, did not even dream of resisting the invaders; in the great drama in which they
found themselves involved by chance, they seem to
have wished to preserve the simple rôle of lookers-on.
Certain regiments raised in Pennsylvania, especially at
the beginning of the war, showed themselves inferior
to all the others in courage, in solidity, and in military
intelligence. Of all the States in the Union, Pennsylvania, although one of the oldest, is perhaps the State
where the population is still the least homogeneous. We
can easily trace its ethnographical map. The northern
plains are occupied by people of the Anglo-Saxon
race ; the banks of the Juniata are peopled by Scotch,
Irish Protestants, and *Yankees*, who mix only in the
southern part of the valley with the *Dutchmen*. The
Germans are masters of all the fertile land which separates Harrisburg from Philadelphia. Careful and thrifty
even to the verge of avarice, they leave to the English
race the cares and emotions of politics ; their only
thought is to extend their rich domain, and year by year
to drive the Americans proper from the lands which
still remain to them. The tremendous barrier of the
Alleghanies has kept them aloof from the great current
which carries both men and ideas from New England to the remotest region of the boundless West.

The German of Pennsylvania dwells isolated in a sort of intellectual oasis; he has only been gained over by contagion to the doctrines which reigned sovereign so long in Philadelphia, the 'city of Brotherly Love'; and he has only chosen and adopted those which suited best his egotism, his love of quiet, and his simplicity, leaving aside everything noble and elevated, everything which required a sacrifice, or imposed a struggle of conscience. In Philadelphia itself the Quaker influence is scarcely visible. This large and beautiful city, at the same time commercial and industrial, differs but little from the other Northern cities of the United States. The streets, which cross each other at right angles, may perhaps be a little more monotonous and more regular; there is perhaps more affectation of cleanliness in the houses, with their steps of white marble which are daily washed; the coping of the doors and windows is also in white marble; and wooden shutters painted white replace the green blinds one sees elsewhere. In the houses whose inmates are in mourning, the shutters are closed, and tied with long black crape bands. Although the whole aspect of the city is indescribably grave, composed, and decent, I nevertheless did not see a single man wearing the severe and traditional costume of Penn, nor a woman whose head was covered with the high snowy cap of the Quakeress. Beside the twelve Friends' meeting-houses (the word meeting-house takes the place of church with the Friends as well as among the New England puritans), built with the utmost simplicity, the Episcopalians have erected thirty-one churches, some of which have an almost monumental appearance ; the Presbyterians have as many as fifty-one, the Catholics fourteen, without counting a vast cathedral which has just been finished ; the Baptists are very numerous and have thirty-one churches, the Lutherans eight, not to mention several other sects of less importance. This enumeration shows at least that Philadelphia has not lost her religious character ; she remains equally faithful to her philanthropic traditions : her hospitals, her medical schools, are worthy of their old reputation. She has asylums for the deaf and dumb and for the blind, dispensaries for the poor, establishments of all sorts for orphans, for indigent women, societies without end for the education of prisoners, coloured children, &c. Her penitentiary system has been copied by many countries. The vast cellular prison, which has the shape of an immense wheel, seems to have served for the model of our prison of Mazas ; the buildings assigned to the prisoners form the spokes of the wheel, which converge to a common centre and are separated by angular courts. The isolation of the prisoner is no longer as complete as at first; they see human faces more frequently, and exchange a few words with their guardians as well as with the persons authorised to visit them. It was from the roof of the Girard College that I saw the whole of this vast edifice. This college is a Greek temple, which is wholly built of marble, even the roof. Girard was a Frenchman who emigrated young to Philadelphia, and who, having amassed a large fortune in the Quaker city, left to it his whole property to found an orphan school. He

o

specified in his will that no priest whatever should be allowed on any pretext to enter its walls, that the ground should be surrounded by a wall ten feet high, and that the building should have a marble roof : to support the weight of such a roof they found nothing better than a gigantic temple.   Imagine the Madeleine filled in the interior with schoolrooms and dormitories for four hundred boys.   The wall, ten feet high, prevents the monument from being seen.   The exclusion of clergymen has become a dead letter, as no one enquires the profession of the visitors ; and in fact I was assured that the administration of the college has fallen entirely into the hands of the Episcopalians.

Perhaps the most interesting study to the philanthropist and the economist which the city of Philadelphia affords is the dwelling-houses of the working class. Since a long time the problems which are but beginning to occupy our attention in Europe have been resolved there. Almost all the streets, where the working classes and even the small proprietors live, have been built by associations.   Nothing could be simpler than the plan which they have adopted.   Several house builders form themselves into a temporary association ; they buy their ground, and pay for it in part by means of a mortgage loan.   Each one furnishes to the association his special work, masonry, carpentry, wood-work, glass, &c.   As soon as the houses are built they are sold, and the profits divided in proportion to the work of each man. Half Philadelphia has been built in this way, and the workmen construct for themselves also houses which make an extremely good appearance ; they are healthy, airy, and provided with everything conducive to comfort and salubrity. The peculiar feature of the Philadelphia workmen's association is that they are temporary ; the agreements vary with circumstances, prices, and the number of the associates. It is not a conclave of economists or administrators who preside over all, imposing programmes, drawings, and an elaborate method of book-keeping. In the United States there is a horror of all trammels, systems, and uniformity. There is certainly not a city in the world where the working population lives with the comfort they enjoy in Philadelphia, and we must add that they owe this superiority solely to themselves and their intelligent activity. The education of the people commences in the public schools ; 56,000 children receive instruction in fifty-five schools, called grammar schools ; numerous libraries are accessible to all. The press of Philadelphia gives to the population eight morning and four evening newspapers, and twenty-nine weekly papers, to say nothing of religious and literary periodicals without end. The city of Penn has not forgotten the words of its founder : 'It is in vain that the Government is good ; if the men are bad they will spoil the Government. What preserves a Government is the wisdom and virtue of men; these not being hereditary, must be propagated by the education of youth.' Shall I venture to say, nevertheless, until the last few years, the wisdom and virtue of Philadelphia have been too often comparable to that of the Pharisees. Under the cloak of religion and philanthropy, bigotry, selfishness, lust for gain, and hardness of heart were frequently hidden. The Quaker city was one of the last refuges of the infamous traffic of the slave trade ; the courageous efforts of the abolitionists of New England found there but little encouragement or support. The democratic party has long reigned despotic in a city where the tide of emigration constantly brought in new recruits ; but since the breaking out of the civil war Philadelphia has emerged from her long moral apathy ; the Federal cause has stirred the slumbering fires, and found there numerous enthusiastic and resolute defenders. In this respect Philadelphia does not differ from the largest part of the Union ; in nearly all the provinces the public conscience was hardened by prosperity. Accomplice of slavery, the North had at last confounded the ideas of servitude and liberty ; the long practice of sophisms, compromises, and political lies had by degrees nearly extinguished that virtue without which Montesquieu says no democracy can live. It often happens that a sudden misfortune breaking in upon the joy of careless and frivolous youth better prepares it for wisdom and the severe responsibility of a riper age, than all the moralist's lessons. It is allowable to say that the civil war has not been without benefit to the American republic, for it has restored her in a manner to herself and to her noble traditions.

In crossing the United States twice, in different directions, I found everywhere the expression of these sentiments ; the language was the same in all latitudes ; those political differences which it was once so easy to observe between the New England States, the Border States, and the Middle States, have gradually faded away. Those passions and doctrines which have only their centre in the New England States have spread like an inundation over the whole surface of the country; the shock occasioned by the war was communicated even to the lost and forgotten populations of the high valleys of Pennsylvania; on the endless plains of the Central and Western States, nothing could avert its course. The waves roll more slowly across the Atlantic. Everywhere the provincial spirit abdicated before the national spirit. We can, nevertheless, even now trace out in the grand Confederation certain natural groups, founded at the same time upon history and geography. The New England States lying closely round Massachusetts will long continue to give the keynote to the nation's politics, religion, and literature. The region which from Maine to Washington is open to the Atlantic, will always remain accessible to European ideas; the great commercial centres of Boston, New York, and Philadelphia will be the bond between the old and new world. Beyond the chain of the Alleghanies extend vast provinces where the American genius, isolated from the rest of the world, shows itself already more original and independent. I have shown in the Western States a population imbued with democratic passions, confident in its destinies, with no other curb than labour and national pride. The Central States fill the vast zone which, extending between the great lakes of the northern continent and Ohio, separates the Atlantic States from the Far West. The business of these great Middle States, Indiana, Ohio, and Pennsylvania, is to serve as it were as mediums between all parts of the republic. Their mass is too compact ever to be divided; what could, for example, bind it to any Confederation whatever, when by the State of Pennsylvania it extends to the Atlantic ? Even at the moment when fortune seemed to smile upon the arms of the rebellion, could any man have the wild pretension of annexing to a black empire provinces which had never known slavery, and whose population was becoming daily more and more imbued with all the ideas, all the sentiments, and all the passions of the Northern States?

The manifest and inevitable solidarity of the Middle States with those of the East on one side, and on the other with those of the North-West, authorises us to regard as improbable a rupture between the Atlantic and the Mississippi ; and so long as the vast resources of a zone so rich, so thickly settled, and so extensive remain in the same hands, so long we have a right to consider as chimerical any attempt of the Southern States to escape from the Union which commands and envelopes them on all sides.

The Middle States form, as I have endeavoured to show, in a political point of view a great conservative mass which separates the two extreme wings of New England and the Western States, where the ebullition of new doctrines is always the most tumultuous. Political life is always, if I may so express it, more intense at the extremities than in the centre ; the absolute independence of the pioneer, the pride of the Yankee, founded on high intellectual culture, on the long practice of free institutions, exercises at either end of the territory the same influence. Between the oldest and the newest States dwells a calmer people more opposed to novelties, less easy to move, and less excitable, except when the question touches the very existence of the nation. The frontier States were long neutral ground, where the incompatible ideas of North and South managed to live side by side. On the breaking out of the war these provinces became the battle-field of the two rival armies. They learned, at the price of terrible sacrifice, that they could not separate their cause from that of the North. Wiser with experience, they will soon be the most ardent champions, as they are already the most active centres, of the emancipation propagand. It is there perhaps that we must seek for the most resolute and the boldest statesmen, those who are most deeply preoccupied with preventing the return of civil war, and with disarming the partisans of slavery. May the day soon come when the word border States shall cease to have a meaning; and when, under common institutions, the Union shall reign in all hearts from Maine to the Rio Grande, as she now does by force of arms. If these recollections have shown what marvellous energy American society has put forth, after four years of civil war, my end is attained. When the still bleeding wounds are healed, it will be seen that the war has fortified far more than it has weakened the Union. It has revealed to the American people the extent and depth of the feelings that attach them to it. In exacting the most terrible sacrifices from them, and in condemning them to bitter grief, it has carried them at one bound from youth to maturity. It has restored to the Federal constitution its primitive character, and given back to the executive power the strength which

the democratic school had gradually wrested from it.
It has put an end to the fatal contradiction between
servitude and liberty; it has given the nation a greater
confidence in herself and in the grandeur of her destinies, in the nobility of her own ideas, purified and henceforth without alloy.   It has been shown that liberty is
strong enough not only to arouse men against tyranny
for a single day, but to found institutions, a nation, and a
country. After so many sacrifices made by the American people for the Union, the loss of so much blood and
treasure, can we doubt that this people will hesitate at
the sacrifices, henceforward far lighter and far easier,
which will be necessary to consolidate its work ? Can we
believe that it will too easily listen to the instigations of
rancour and anger, that it will rashly rush into the com-
plications of a foreign war ?   It has reconquered all its
territory, but it has not the least desire to extend it.   It
knows better than any one how much the difficulties it
had to contend with were increased by the very immensity of this territory. Its ambition does not dream of annexing new provinces.   It is of far greater importance
to the American people to obliterate in the old ones all
traces of the war.   Neither is it to be dreaded that in
the flush of triumph it will show itself without pity for
the vanquished; all will be forgiven to those who cease
to be the enemies of the Union. The North will itself
draw the South from the abyss of ruin and misery into
which it voluntarily plunged : it offers her its capital,
its labour, its machines, its schools, its municipal institutions, the aid of its intelligence and activity, and
demands but one thing in return—the abdication of

that sinister and barbarous power which took for its arms, not only gun, but whips, and poniards, and which has shed human blood in torrents, and which almost accomplished the ruin of the republic. For the Union to live, slavery must perish, and with it all that still remains of its work both political and social.

CHAPTER XI.

A VISIT TO THE ARMY OF THE POTOMAC.

THE United States have for four years given the lie to most of the prophecies of Europe; the pessimists who announced the final rupture of the Union to-day see its triumph; if they were to be believed a pacific republic could not raise armies, and armies sprung from the earth; a people unaccustomed to taxation would never consent to give up a considerable portion of its revenue to the State, and the American Congress voted an infinite number of new taxes without being able to satisfy quickly enough the impatience of public opinion, preoccupied with placing the resources of the government on a level with the magnitude of the danger, and giving to the world a striking proof of the wealth of the nation. Liberty was to perish in the tumults and disorder of civil war, and liberty has not even received a wound. She no longer protects a privileged race only; she covers also with her newly-tempered shield the race so long oppressed and given over to the most cruel slavery. The imagination of political Cassandras has dwelt with special complacency on magnifying the dangers that would spring from the gigantic armaments of the United States for free institutions and the peace of the world. Would the Executive

have virtue enough not to use the new power placed by
circumstances in its hands for its own interests? Would
not some bold and lucky general be found who would
march his army to the Capitol, and dictate terms of
peace? Hostilities over, these thousands of men, used
to a camp life and the disorder of war, these generals
still intoxicated by the heat of battles and the smoke of
victory, would they consent to return to the silent
obscurity of private life? Feeling all her strength like
a panting wrestler, would not the republic have an
invincible desire to use her new weapons, and punish
the nations that had doubted her courage? It was
natural to ask these questions; it was imprudent to
answer them beforehand. It is not easy to apply historical precedents to a nation where almost everything
is new; until now, wherever a nation has been convulsed
by great civil troubles, armies have outlived revolutions,
and oftentimes it is their sword that has cut the bonds
tightened by discord. In troublous times when everything is shaken, armies bound by discipline, gathered
round a chief who represents the dominant passions of
the moment, easily become the instruments of great
political revolutions. Who does not know the part
played in history by the armies of Cæsar, Cromwell,
and Napoleon? What was not their influence on the
fortunes of Rome, England, France? These disciplined
masses, in which one will is incarnated, at times force all
obstacles to bend before them, and plough a furrow that
can never be effaced. On the other hand, what do we
see in the United States? Immense armies fighting for
four years, practising the great art of war by defeats as

well as by victories, and never for a moment ceasing to be the docile instrument of the executive. These armies were not even composed of professional soldiers, fighting because it was their trade, and long broken in to obedience; they were almost entirely made up of volunteers, who followed all the ins and outs of public life in the camp, who preserved beneath the flag party spirit and the rights of citizenship. Neither on the morrow of the victory nor during the struggle did the American armies throw their sword into the scale; the heroes of so many battles have quietly returned to the shade of domestic life, like those stage kings who wear a crown for a few hours. This force, which had become irresistible, which was so slowly and so laboriously gathered together, was dispersed without an effort: a spectacle as new as strange, that by good right astonishes the world, and that cannot be too closely examined.

It was in the month of January 1865, that I visited Grant's army before Richmond and Petersburg; for some time the battlefields of Virginia have slipped out of sight; also I am less desirous of speaking of military operations than of making known the composition of the American army, its habits, its spirit, and the way in which the mixture of the small regular army, in existence before the war, with so many thousands of raw soldiers, had been accomplished, the share that belongs to the two elements, at once so different and equally necessary. What I saw and what I heard left a triple impression on my mind : the United States, though they have carried on a great war, will never become a military power; they will always retain a permanent army, small but

strongly organised, and under the strictest discipline.
This standing army will not in any way imperil the
liberties of the nation.

I left Washington on the 15th of January for City
Point, the head-quarters of the Federal army, furnished
with a pass given to me by President Lincoln, that I
keep most preciously, for it is all written in his own
hand.   I found the wharf on the Potomac occupied by
a post of soldiers.   I show my pass and go on board
the steamer, with a great number of soldiers, officers
of all ranks, civilians, quarter-masters, pedlars, and
others.   All those who do not wear the uniform are
obliged to place their luggage in a room on the lower
floor of the steamer; this rigorous precaution is taken
against incendiaries, who have several times brought
inflammable matters on board the army transports.
A sentinel is stationed at the door of the luggage-
office, another at the foot of the stairs leading to the
first floor.   Soldiers and non-commissioned officers take
their places on the lower story; the officers occupy the
saloon, a long passage with state-rooms on each side.
The boat starts, and breaks the thin sheets of ice that
edge the shore; we pass before the great buildings of
the arsenal, the vast courts strewed with black silent
cannon of all shapes and calibre, piles of ball, and yawning mortars; farther on the hay-stores, surrounded by a
flotilla of schooners, whose decks are covered with great
hay-stacks.

Seen from a distance Washington presents quite an
imposing aspect.   Above the great river that looks like
a silver ribbon, and the horizontal lines .of the great

public buildings, rises the bold dome of the Capitol, the sun glistening on its shining marble. On the confines of the wide valley the hills of Maryland trace undulating violet lines ; a clear transparent light bathes this picture with a surprising effect. From distance to distance the heights on the Potomac are crowned with forts, so well constructed that they would be hardly seen were it not for the freshly turned up earth and the slopes bare of grass. All round the trees have been cut down, and the woods have only been left on the lower slopes that join the bottom of the valley. Every moment we pass other boats ; every steamer that can float has been pressed into the service, even old wide flat ferry-boats, without stem or stern.

On Arlington heights I see the house of General Lee, surrounded by a fine park. This property once belonged to Mrs. Washington. The house, although abandoned, is still in very much the same state as at the beginning of the century. I had been over it a few days before. In the ante-chambers are the remains of a few bad paintings of episodes of the war of Independence ; the house is out of repair, but the old wooden furniture and the family portraits have not been touched.

The portico that is seen from the river between the pines and cedars is as pretentious as if it covered a great building. Enormous brick columns, covered with white plaster, support a heavy triangular fronton; a palace at a distance—a hovel near to; it is a good symbol of Southern society, half-barbarous, half-civilised.

We stop for a moment at Alexandria, a dirty, dilapidated little town; we take on board convalescent soldiers

returning to the army.   The workmen of the port are
moving in every direction on the quay, almost all blacks,
dressed in old military coats and trowsers, with shapeless
caps or felt hats that have quite lost the regimental shape.
The soldiers unfold the oilcloths that wrap up their
sacks, and that, according to circumstances, serve for
cloaks, tents, or beds.   They spread their woollen
blankets on these oilcloths, and with their heads resting
on their sacks, get ready to go to sleep at an early hour.
The Potomac, rippled by a fresh breeze, assumes the
most beautiful twilight hues.   The water cut by the
prow takes inexpressibly soft violet tones, and on the
troubled and yellowish ground of the river, very high
at this time, the lengthened shadows of a few small boats
throw long spots of azure.   We are off again, and glide
before the heights of Mount Vernon, the favourite retreat
of Washington.   I see for an instant the white walls
behind the branches of the trees that cover the pro·
montory.

Past Alexandria, the clerk goes to his office and
sells tickets for the state-rooms.   Officers are served
first; but I observe that all grades are mixed before the
ticket office.   A lieutenant has no scruple in passing
before a captain or a colonel.   A young colonel from
New York, with whom I made acquaintance, is kind
enough to secure a state-room for me, otherwise I ran
the risk of passing the night in an armchair in the saloon,
in company with a few other civilians.   After four years
of war the officers still retain, when not on service, all
the habits of civil life.   I observe that they never speak
when not already acquainted ; that they introduce each

other just as if they were in a drawing-room. The young colonel who took me under his protection has kept beneath the uniform all the manners of an English gentleman. Nearly all his fellow-travellers, who are returning after leave of absence, are as silent as he is; they belong to such different classes that they do not seek each other's society much. How many different types! Here is a German officer of engineers, with a square head, and thick grey moustache; he was one of the leaders of the revolutionary movement in Hesse Darmstadt in 1848, and since then where has not chance taken him?—to Missouri, to California; to-day in the army. He has already changed his weapons twice. He complains of the jealousy of the Yankees. When they want us, they flatter and make much of us; and when we have done, we are nothing but 'damned Dutchmen!' Why, indeed, is Sigel named general at the outset and his senior officer left a simple lieutenant? A little farther on we recognise a major of the regulars, with the double stripe on his trowsers (volunteers wear only a single stripe). He speaks of the war like a professional man; he laughs at the heaven-born generals, who don't come from Westpoint; he invites me to make an excursion with him to Fort Hell, so called because of the hot firing there at times. Major in an infantry regiment, he tells me that the colonel, the lieutenant-colonel, three majors, and four captains of his regiment, have become generals in the volunteer army. This does not prevent them keeping their rank in the regular army. When a body of volunteers is mustered out, such an officer, who has commanded thousands of men, may find himself at

the head of a company. Among our officers I notice
the pensive countenances of young men who are, doubtless, sadly thinking of their mothers, their sisters, their
sweethearts that they have just left; others, with their
yellow, worn features, wearing their hair and beards
uncombed, are true Yankees—all nerves; indefatigable
people, who live upon nothing, supported by an internal
fire that only shows at times by flashes from their grey
inquisitive eyes.   In all this crowd there is no apparent
hierarchical feeling. At the meal hours everyone crowds
into the dining-saloon, and takes the place that suits
him.   You can only distinguish the grades by studying
the various ornaments on the bands that replace the
epaulettes on the blue coats, all just alike.

Towards night we reach the mouth of the Potomac.
The pilot sees a great fire; everybody runs forward.
A thousand conjectures are made: it is doubtless a
steamer on fire. The boat puts on more steam, but
when we get nearer, it turns out to be an abandoned
fisherman's house. The fire has at once lost all charm,
and I remain alone looking at the far-off spot of flame
and the black plume of smoke that the wind sways and
blows into the river. During the night we go down
Chesapeake Bay, and I only wake at a short distance
from Fortress Monroe, placed like a stone sentinel at
the extreme end of the Virginian peninsula. To the
right I see a long line of sand glistening in the sun;
farther on the undulating line of the pine forests
stretches into the distance. The heavy walls of the
immense fortress—the most important on the coast—
command the entrance to the fine harbour of Hampton

P

Roads: in all the bastions open the black portholes
of the casemates. All along the walls lie the black
fifteen-inch guns. Opposite to Fortress Monroe another
smaller fort is being built, to cover the islet of the
Rip-Raps, and more completely defend the entrance
to Hampton Roads, and the access to the James. A few
vessels only were in the port, and their delicate outlines were gilded by the morning light. Admiral Porter's
fleet had gone to sea a few days before, to return
before Wilmington; there was nothing left but transports, barques, and light vessels. On reaching the quay
we get the news that the second attack on Wilmington
has succeeded. The troops, commanded by General
Terry, made the attack on Fort Fisher, and took it after
a desperate struggle of several hours. Our officers and
soldiers congratulate each other on this great triumph:
a frigate and a government transport run out all their
flags, and the light flames that flicker gaily against the
blue sky are saluted with hurrahs. After stopping
fifteen minutes at Fortress Monroe, we enter the gigantic
harbour of Hampton Roads; all the fleets of the world
could take refuge here and move about at their ease.
Behind the fortress the high white walls of a military
hospital are seen; the houses of the little town seem to
rise out of the water; soon the horizon is shut in between long sand-banks, behind which the pine forests
of the Virginian peninsula on one side, and those of
Norfolk on the other, come in sight. In going up the
harbour I see on the shore the skeleton of the 'Congress'
that the celebrated 'Merrimac' sunk on the eve of her
fight with the 'Monitor.' A little farther on are the

fragments of the 'Cumberland,' worn and rotted by the water, that succumbed in the same struggle. This fine frigate, ripped open by the spur of the 'Merrimac,' went slowly down with all its crew, firing broadsides till its cannon were on a level with the water. Still farther on the masts of the 'Florida,' a Confederate pirate that Captain Collins cut out of the port of Bahia, rise out of the water. Brought into Hampton Roads the 'Florida,' that already had a leak, was struck by a transport, and sunk instantly.

We come opposite Newport-News. There is a small military fort still left here and some wooden buildings. A division of the army was encamped for some time in this place when General Wool was in command at Fortress Monroe : one or two little fights took place in the neighbourhood, but fever killed more men than bullets. The white stones of a cemetery glisten on the sandy shore, sheltered by a few Virginia pines. Though in the month of February the air is soft; the pines of Virginia, with their tall trunks and their thick round tops, recall the beautiful pines of Italy. I get a new impression on the James, wide and lazy, whose yellow muddy waters flow between deserted and wooded banks; the monotony of the great pine forests harmonises with the enormous width of the river. Every other minute we meet some transport going up or down the river; their wooden decks are covered with soldiers; there is not a corner of the boat where you don't see blue coats. On the afterdeck of one transport a regimental band is playing; the steamers pass each other so quickly that we hear only a moment the joyous notes of the instruments mingled with the hurrahs with which the soldiers salute each other. The river has still an air of festivity under the winter sun : the oblique rays play over the little ripple that the wind raises on the orange-coloured waters. The straight columns of the pines seem to spring from the water ; here and there the yellow line of some abandoned entrenchment marks more clearly the edge of the alluvial plains on which the tall forests stand. The lower or more marshy parts are favourable for the cypress ; their roots dip in the water, and sometimes each trunk remains isolated on a little island as on a pedestal. These fine trees are of a very tall growth, and their strong trunks put out thick horizontal branches. From time to time I see the broken piles of some landing in the neighbourhood of an abandoned plantation. At some distance from the great dwelling-houses, mostly whitewashed, are the deserted huts of the negroes. It is plain to be seen that the war has never been very cruel on these banks—houses have not been burned, even when their proprietors were in the rebel army. These isolated plantations, seen from time to time along the river, produced in abundance, before the war, corn of a superior quality ; hardly any cotton was cultivated here. One plantation was pointed out to me where the dwelling-house, situated almost on the river, was built two centuries ago with bricks brought from England. I see an old negress coming out of another house, who descends to the edge of the river to fetch water. She is the only living figure that meets my eye on these beautiful Virginian shores.

All this while the steamer is as lively as a camp.   I mix with the soldiers and listen to their conversations ; with the captain's permission a land-agent comes to make a speech to them, and explains at length the Homestead Bill, a law made by Congress to give lands to soldiers at the end of the war. On giving sixteen dollars of their pay to the State each one has assured to him, at the expiration of his term of service, 150 acres ; in case of death on the field or in hospital this land goes to his heirs. The agent, for a remuneration of four dollars, undertakes to choose the lots for the soldiers, to regulate their title to the property, and to transmit it to their families. On the sight of his commission, signed by the Secretary of War, a few soldiers agree to sign the papers he shows them and pay the sum of twenty dollars. The pay of a common soldier is thirteen dollars a month ; but very few have been seduced by the offer ; most of them have farms already, and send their pay home to their families. In spite of all the explanations a little incredulity still seems to cling to some minds. The law offers such great advantages to volunteers that they are tempted not to believe in them. Besides, is not chance the soldier's only guide ? He who may die any moment does not think willingly of the future.

On a bluff of sandy loam I see the outline of Fort Powhattan, whose interior is turned towards the river. Inside the fort are seen tents, little wooden houses, and a great mast surmounted by the stars and stripes. Round the works, which are in earth, and lined in the

interior with pine trunks, are the abatis, made of rough
branches matted together, that cover all the glacis. Fort
Powhattan completely commands a low plain, situated
on the left bank of the James ; it was on this marshy
ground, covered with rushes and weeds, that Grant's
army came after the campaign of 1864, marked by the
bloody halts of the Wilderness, Spottsylvania, and Cold
Harbour. In his march from the Rapidan to the James
Grant fought nearly every day, and vainly trying to
flank or destroy Lee's forces, protected by the forests
and the configuration of the ground, saw his army di-
minished by at least 70,000 men, in consequence of the
battles and forced marches.   On the edge of the river
the wooden road (the Americans call these routes improvised by putting trunks of trees side by side, ' corduroy roads') that was built for the supplies of the army
is still to be seen.   Bridges were thrown across a little
below Fort Powhattan, and it was from this point that
the various corps were directed on Petersburg.   In
seeing this wide river free from Fortress Monroe to Fort
Darling, situated before Richmond, and incessantly
navigated by the Federal gun-boats, it is impossible
not to ask why General Grant did not transport his
troops direct by water to the south of Petersburg and
Richmond if it was on that side he wished to attack
these towns ? Why not profit at the outset by the
advantages that the uncontested possession of river communication gave to the Federals ? What was the use
of leaving so many needless victims in the forests and
roads of northern Virginia ? To this it can be answered
that a General-in-chief is often forced to guide himself

by political as well as by military considerations. In bending his steps at once to the south of Richmond and the James River, General Grant would have seemed to have recommenced M'Clellan's first Virginian campaign; a campaign the plan of which was excellent, but that had had the fault of ending in a repulse and leaving all the roads of northern Virginia open. If Grant had not dealt blow after blow on his adversary, and rendered it impossible for him to suddenly put himself on the offensive, new anxieties would have arisen in Washington. General Grant, doubtless, hoped that a successful battle would give him Richmond, and he only fell back on the James River to begin the slow operations of a siege, because he had not been able to gain the victory fortune refused to his indomitable energy and the courage of his troops.

Beyond Fort Powhattan I see still a few more abandoned plantations, among them the house of Harrison, that was respected by M'Clellan's army. Harrison's Landing was, during two months, the head-quarters of the commander of the army of the Potomac, after he was obliged to cross the swamps of the Chickahominy, in order to put his army, decimated by operations as fruitless as they were bloody, under the protection of the Federal gunboats. The bare earth still shows traces of the encampments where the army of the Potomac was shut in until it was recalled to Washington to repulse the first invasion of Maryland. Close by a gunboat lay at anchor. I never looked without a sort of respect at these grey gunboats, armed with heavy cannon, that have played so great a part in the war. Thanks to

ı some of these boats, that were, so to speak, the police of
the river, the navigation of the James was as safe as
the Ohio.

Here at last is City Point, situated at the junction of
the James and the Appomatox.   A forest of masts
announces it from a distance ; the steamer slackens,
and comes up through a fleet of schooners, transports,
and tugs.   All along the quays are wooden shops, and
behind them runs the railway built by the Federal
army for more rapid communication.   The war has
given extraordinary animation to a place that used to be
almost uninhabited, though its position at the confluence
of two fine rivers seemed to point it out for an important settlement.   I leave the boat, show my pass, and
direct my steps to head-quarters, which, situated on
the top of a sort of little bluff, overlook the port and
are instantly recognisable by the stars and stripes floating from a tall flag-staff.   I follow a hardly marked
out road, cut up by waggons and horses, and find
myself among the tents and wooden shelters that cover
the plateau.   In the midst of a clump of cedars and
pines I come upon the little parade surrounded by the
huts of the head-quarters.   That of the commander-
in-chief is a plain loghouse, exactly like those I had
seen in the western forests.   It is hardly larger than
those of the officers ; most of these loghouses have no
roofs, and are only covered with canvas.   A soldier
showed me the way to the office, a little square house
containing only one room, where all the staff-officers
stay during the day.   I am received by one of them,
Colonel Bowers, who immediately looks about for

my accommodation, and procures me a lodging in one of the tent houses of the staff. While waiting for the dinner hour I wander wherever chance takes me : behind the small wooden houses is a large dwelling-house that General Grant has given up to the quarter-master. In the wasted garden I still see magnolias and tulip trees in the open air. From the little bluff that overlooks the James, I gaze on all the surrounding country.

The point called Bermuda Hundred juts out like a cape at the junction of the James and the Appomatox. The James flows round it, and its wide sheet is covered with an animated flotilla of steamers and transports. All along the quay I see boxes, barrels, and bags discharged from schooners and taken to the railway, whence they are carried to divers stations as far as the extreme left of the still-called army of the Potomac. The supplies of the army of the James, which occupies Bermuda Hundred and the left bank of the James, are carried by water, and I see boats going all the time in that direction. Just opposite to City Point on the other side of the river, lies low ground covered with pines ; in the evening light their foliage seems greyer between the orange of the river and the pale azure of the sky. The river meanders between this plain and Bermuda Hundred, and the smoke of distant steamers floating above the lines of verdure mark its far-off windings. On the right bank heights rise in the distance that draw faint bluish lines against the horizon. On these hills, close to Richmond, the extreme right of the army is encamped.

City Point is situated on the edge of a great plain, wooded like the rest of the country, slightly undulated and intersected by the marshy windings of a few brooks. Fine cedars, magnificent pines with tall straight trunks and umbrella tops, junipers, shrubs with red berries, looking like gigantic bouquets, still show what this delightful spot must have been before the war brought that devastation that it always drags after it. I walked through the fields for some time; all the regiments had already gone into winter quarters. In summer everybody sleeps in the open air, or under tents. In the winter the soldiers build little loghouses, for which the tent canvas makes roofs. The walls of the huts are built of rough logs; each one has its wooden chimney plastered over with mud; on the top of the chimney a barrel with the bottom knocked out is often placed, which gives it more height and consequently a better draught. The doors are usually made of broken-up biscuit boxes. Four men sleep in the interior on boards raised a little above the ground. A camp is rather a sad sight for any one not a soldier: men sleeping on the ground like animals, in the mud, in the rain dripping through the tents, and in the thick penetrating smoke of wood fires. Camps are savage primitive villages; they bring to mind the tribes without name or history that used to live in the forests; and yet nevertheless it is they who live in camps who write history. This melancholy apparatus —this dirty rotten canvas, these worn muddy clothes, these waggons whose every motion is a jolt, these hollow-flanked mules, these wretched horses, all this is the sordid envelope of organised human force.

The first soldiers I saw at City Point were blacks : their regiment was on parade.* The band was made up solely of young negroes of about fifteen years old, who wore caps with long green tassels. They beat the drum and played the fife with deafening spirit. The regiment went through its exercises with considerable precision, then formed into companies, and filed off to the camp. The officers were all white without exception : the non-commissioned officers were all negroes. I have often heard it said that all blacks look alike ; this illusion is soon lost on seeing a regiment of them. What varying shades and types ! Some heads have still a bestial expression, massive lips, and lengthened

---

* The state of Massachusetts raised the first black regiments ; this example was soon followed by Rhode Island, Pennsylvania, New York, and Ohio ; later the government created several regiments, called United States coloured troops. The officers of these latter regiments, who formed a sort of black regular army, were named after an examination, by the Secretary of War. They were chosen with great care, because the success of the experiment tried in arming the blacks depended in great measure on them. There were ten of these regiments in the army of the James. General Butler, who was for a long time in command of this army, was one of those who most warmly cooperated in the organisation of a black army. On the 20th October 1864, according to the official documents published by the Secretary of War, there were 140 black regiments under arms, comprising 101,950 men, consisting of

12 regiments of artillery	.	12,226
8 batteries of light artillery	.	853
6 cavalry regiments	. .	5,605
121 infantry regiments	. .	83,226
Total	.	101,950 men.

jaws : the ugliness of others is, so to speak, ennobled
by a frank and courageous physiognomy ; others again
possess a true manly beauty, bronzed and peculiar.
The whole plain re-echoed the confused and mingled
murmurs of military bands ; the shadows began to fall,
and the thicker evening smoke spread over all the
camps.   The place inhabited by an army, for only a
short time even, becomes, so to speak, a great *Champ
de Mars*, without cultivation, grass, or flowers, a bare,
unfertile common.   Every other minute a cavalier
rode past wrapped in his blue coat, his horse galloping
heavily over the wide spaces that separated the encampments.   For the first time I felt myself in the
midst of an army, lost in a crowd, where lives and
wills are of no account.   I had just come from Washington, and it seemed as if I had been carried far from
all civilisation.   What had I come to do, a useless
spectator, in the midst of these new scenes ?   Everything appeared like a dream to me ; these blacks armed
and in uniforms ; the *corrals* of the mules, whose light
roofs were covered over with branches torn off the
pines ; all these little nameless villages scattered over
the vast plain ; the long rows of horses picketed ; in
short, this landscape where nature was nothing and
man everything.   I returned slowly on my steps,
and very soon came upon the fine avenue of cedars
partly spared by the axe, which leads to head-quarters.
I dined with the staff-officers.   It was a short, frugal,
silent dinner ; nothing but water was drunk at General
Grant's table, who thus gave a salutary example to an
army where, in the beginning, drunkenness had had a

most pernicious effect. The General even went so far as to forbid whisky to be sold in the camps : any sutler among whose goods a single barrel was found was immediately sent out of camp. The evening was passed in the office, smoking, and reading the latest Richmond papers, that were received regularly every day at head-quarters.

Head-quarters at City Point were situated a little behind the long Federal lines occupied by the armies of the James and the Potomac. General Grant was the Commander-in-chief of both armies ; that of the Potomac was under the immediate command of General Meade, the conqueror of Gettysburg ; that of the James had been under the orders of General Butler since the beginning of the siege ; but at the time of my arrival he had just been replaced by General Ord.

In the spring of 1864, while General Grant led the army of the Potomac from the Rapidan to the James River, giving battle almost daily, the army of the James, about 35,000 strong and commanded by Butler, came up the James, and landed on the point of Bermuda Hundred. This confluence of Appomatox and the James together with Richmond and Petersburg mark the three angles of a nearly equilateral triangle ; the two rivers form two of the sides, and the railway from Richmond to Petersburg the third. General Beauregard hastily collected a few troops, and defended this railway with success against the far superior force of Butler. With a little more audacity and more military experience the latter would have very easily taken possession of Petersburg, which was then the veritable key of Richmond; but he failed to do this, and after a few insignificant demonstrations he shut himself up in his lines at Bermuda Hundred.   From this point as from a centre the Federal lines soon stretched right and left on Richmond and Petersburg. Built from day to day without a plan laid down beforehand, they were very involved, and their direction was frequently modified.   The Virginian soil is eminently adapted to the construction of earthworks : it is a yellow sandy clay, very light and easily moved ; the army had acquired so much experience in the use of the spade in its campaigns that earthworks and rifle-pits rose as by enchantment.

The lines of the army of the Potomac stretched from the Appomatox to a short distance from Petersburg, around the southern side of the town ; at first they were carried as far as the Weldon railroad which runs directly south from Petersburg, and for the possession of which quite a bloody battle was fought : then they had been carried towards the west in the direction of the Petersburg and Danville railroad.   At the same time that the army was at work on its offensive lines, and surrounding Petersburg, it protected its centre and left by a defensive line that from the extreme left swept round and joined Black Water Swamp to the back. The arc of the circle surrounding Petersburg ended, so to speak, in a great loop.

I left City Point very early in the morning to visit the lines of the army of the Potomac with an officer of Grant's staff.   We take our places in a railway car with a few officers.   The soldiers simply climb on top of the great boxes in which ammunition and provisions are transported.   The track, roughly built and very uneven, goes over a wide plain covered with forests : pike-pines and oaks are mixed with the tall Virginia pines, whose needles hang in long tufts.   The great forest has been given over to pitiless woodsmen ; you see them everywhere cutting wood for firing, leaving the great branches for lining the inner side of the entrench- ments.   Round the first station the soil is completely bare, from incessant trampling by men and horses.   I see camps scattered about the clearings ; here and there soldiers are drilling.   We cross the line of the entrench- ments that surround City Point : they are simple rifle- pits, entrenchments lined with horizontal trunks fastened by transversal stakes.   We gain the forest at once : we pass a little country house surrounded by cherry and peach trees ; farther on, by the wooden sheds where the hides of the oxen consumed by the army are piled up ; handfuls of salt are thrown on the still bloody heaps ; the hoofs and horns piled in order near great caldrons where they are boiled.   In a denuded field I see the traces of an abandoned camp ; a forest of little stakes still stand in the ground ; everything else has disappeared.   A little beyond the railway bifur- cates; the right branch, which is in fact the old railway from City Point to Petersburg, goes to Meade's right wing, encamped on the Appomatox ; the left branch has been entirely built by the army ; it runs to the west, and is used to provision the centre and left.   Our old cars entering on this track only advance by jolts ; through an opening of the forest I see the sharp spires of Petersburg for an instant. How near these points seem—inaccessible still to so numerous and tried an army! A new station, called Meade's station: the plain is covered with camps that extend out of sight, as far as the orange-coloured line of the entrenchments surmounted on the horizon by a bluish curtain of pines. The 9th corps encamped near Meade's station belongs to the right of the army: it forms four divisions that contain thirteen brigades, and is commanded by Parke, who, only a captain at the opening of the war in a regiment of regular engineers, was named in 1862 Major-General of the volunteer army. Round Meade station are shops in the open air where newspapers, books, letter-paper, knives, and all sorts of Yankee notions are sold. The railway there runs so close to the enemy's line that a rampart has been raised to protect it from bullets. The track passes at times through thickets that the soldier woodsmen have not yet touched, sometimes through clearings where the little wooden huts of the camp trace vast squares. Every moment you see loghouses and low clouds of smoke circling over them, corrals protected by enormous pine branches; oftentimes the camps themselves are sheltered from the wind by a high wall of branches fastened to light palisades. Here and there a regiment has found the time to surmount these palisades with emblems and figures of evergreen. Beside almost sordid camps you see some, where order and neatness and the green crests of the pines carefully arranged, give quite a festive air. Hancock station is just in front of the 5th corps, formed of three divisions, comprising six brigades; this corps is

commanded by Warren, who, captain of engineers in
1861, was named at the outset of the war Brigadier-
General of the volunteer army.   The two last stations
are used by the 2nd and 6th corps stationed to the left :
in the midst of the 2nd corps is the flag of General
Meade's head-quarters, at the top of a mound that
overlooks an immense plain covered with camps.   A
regiment of Zouaves is on duty at head-quarters : but
this uniform, very much in favour at the beginning
of the war, is but little seen in the army, where
nearly all the regiments have adopted the greyish
blue uniform.   The 2nd corps is under the immediate command of Humphreys, Lieutenant-Colonel of
engineers in 1861, and in 1862 Brigadier-General in
the great volunteer army.   His corps contains three
divisions and eleven brigades.   The 2nd division is commanded by Barlow, the youngest general in the army,
who joined the service as a simple volunteer in 1861,
and has been in all the great battles of the war.   The
6th corps is under the orders of Wright, a ci-devant
major of engineers.

The lines thrown up by this numerous army are
composed of a succession of forts and lunettes, united by
rifle-pits.   From the extreme right, situated on the Appomatox, to the end of the great loop that surrounds
the rear of the left and centre, there are seventeen
forts and forty-one lunettes or batteries, fifty-four twelve-
pound smooth-bore howitzers, fifty-two rifled three-
inch cannon, without counting a few siege-cannon
(thirty-pound Parrott) and four-and-a-half-inch Rod-
man cannon, and a few eight and twelve-inch mortars.

Q

The forts contain magazines and casemates built of logs, covered with a thick layer of earth; the *traverses* are also made of logs. During its long leisure the army has made a sort of luxury of filling the ditches, and covering the glacis with all the obstacles that can be opposed to a besieger—pit-falls, chevaux-de-frise, &c.; trees without number have been cut down for the double line of abatis that bristle on the confines of the glacis all along the entrenchments. In some places they have amused themselves by fixing a net-work of invisible iron wire to little posts, to trip up the assailants. You are no longer astonished at the devastation of the forests when you see the solid lining that protects the inner side of the earth-walls of the rifle-pits and the redoubts.

At the time of my visit to the lines the armies were observing a sort of tacit truce, that was but rarely broken. It was possible to examine the forts and the defences without running the least risk. I even went out of Fort Welsh, situated at the extremity of the line, in company with General Hunt, the commander-in-chief of the artillery, to examine the picquet lines. From the fort itself we see, at a short distance in the plain, the line of the Federal picquets traced by the vaporous curl of smoke from the wood-fires parallel with the defensive lines; farther on a second curl indicates the rebel picquets; on the verge of the horizon the thin yellowish line of the forts of the enemy is only surmounted by a far-off curtain of woods.. We see very clearly, without the aid of a field-glass, a considerable fort rising in front of Fort

Welsh, that is being built with great celerity. We leave
the fort, cross the moat, and going through the forest
bristling with abatis, we come to a great field where a
few stalks of Indian corn still lie on the ground; the
guard there is sheltered by a simple earthen wall; a
little farther on the vidette picquets are hidden to the
middle in holes, and keep behind the shelter of a little
earth and pine branches. Loaded guns are close to
their hands; a few soldiers come out of the holes and
keep guard walking up and down. We are separated
from the enemy on the left by a slight rising, on the
right by a little wood, where soldiers are busy cutting
timber; in front there is nothing between us and the
Confederate picquets. We see them grouped along
from space to space, the sentinels walking slowly up and
down, their guns over their shoulders. I can see with
the naked eye the outline of their grey uniforms; some
of them wear blankets on their backs to keep off the cold.
By raising my voice somewhat I could easily talk with
them. On this extreme frontier, where the armies are
the nearest to each other and death is most imminent
the Yankees and the Johnnies, the blue coats and the
grey coats, are almost friends. The picquets of the two
camps have frequent intercourse that the severest orders
cannot prevent. When there is a favourable opportunity coffee is willingly exchanged for tobacco, and New
York for Richmond papers. A moment before our
arrival some Confederates had come, without ceremony
to ask for wood of the Federal woodmen. I talk for a
minute with a picquet of German soldiers : they do not
complain of their fate, though my words recalled to

their remembrance their native land.   From time to time Confederate deserters—particularly at night—cross the little space that separates the picquets of the armies and take refuge with the Federals, at the risk of being shot by both sides on the way.   In the month of January about a hundred deserters came in a day—not those soldiers that are, unhappily, to be found in every army, who are unworthy to bear arms, but a great many veterans, sick of the war, and without hope for the triumph of the South.   I had the opportunity of seeing several ; they were dressed in coarse grey cloth, sometimes made at the improvised Southern manufactories, but more often of English make.   They did not seem emaciated by privation ; the rations of Lee's army were smaller than those of Grant's, which was treated with prodigality ; but they continued to the end to be sufficient for the health of the soldiers.   I came back from the extreme left to Meade's head-quarters, sometimes over ' corduroy roads,' stretched like long wooden ribbons across the forests and their marshy folds ; sometimes over wide bare spaces, where here and there rose the high wooden scaffolding for the signals.   The heavy waggons, harnessed to eight or ten mules, were moving in every direction.   Smoke curled slowly over the great squares of the camps, and looked like mist through the colonnades of tall pines; the beating of drums, the brazen sounds of military music, the short galop of horses crossing the plain, the neighing of the mules shut into the corrals, the bellowing of the oxen crowded into pens, filled the air with strange confused murmurs.

Beyond Meade's extreme right, the Federal line of

defence, supported on the Appomatox, was continued by the river itself, then by the entrenchments of Bermuda Hundred, that stretched from the Appomatox to the James ; on the northern side of the last-named river the line made an immense curve, the summit of which was close to Richmond, and that turned back to surround the extreme right of the army of the James. This latter army, consisting of three corps, had its left on Bermuda Hundred, its centre and its right on the right bank of the James.   Its lines were supported and protected by twelve forts, without counting the lunettes and the batteries ; Fort Harrison was the most important, situated on an eminence, of which the army of the James only took possession after a bloody struggle. Altogether the lines of the two armies of the James and the Potomac were sixty-seven kilomètres long ; they were placed astride two rivers ; and, from this gigantic entrenched camp, General Grant threatened Richmond and Petersburg at the same time.   General Lee had the advantage of being on the inner lines ; he could move his troops rapidly by the railway that connected Richmond and Petersburg.   Nevertheless Grant, taking advantage of the numerical superiority of his forces, obliged his adversary to strongly fortify a line that was very long, though of a lesser radius than his own : constantly threatening Lee's left or his right, he held in check and neutralised the efforts of the enemy's army, while his lieutenants, Sheridan in the valley of the Shenandoah, and Sherman in the Carolinas, dealt blows to the rebel cause against which it was unable to defend itself.   Very seldom, I believe, have military operations been carried out on so grand a scale over such vast spaces. Everything hung together in Grant's plan : he kept for himself the hardest and most ungrateful part, and held his impatient army in camp, always on the alert, wearing out its ardour in simple skirmishes, while Sheridan's cavalry swept Early's little army out of the valley of Virginia, and Sherman made his astounding marches, took Savannah and Charleston, and showed the extinction of the rebellion to the most incredulous eyes. Mr. Seward once wittily compared the Confederacy to an egg, whose two ends were Richmond and Atlanta: the shell is hard, he said, but once broken you can go through the inside easily enough.   Sherman, when he took Atlanta, undertook in part to demonstrate this proposition ; but Richmond still remained, and that army of veterans commanded by Lee, the most hardened, compact, and numerous army of the South, full of confidence in its old chief, and sustained by the memories of a three years' struggle.   Now that the Union is restored the Americans of the North have no longer any interest in undervaluing their old adversaries ; but it is, perhaps, permissible to say that opinion has been rather too prodigal of eulogiums on the Confederate army at the expense of the Federal troops.   There is nothing that might not have been undertaken with the troops under Grant's orders that were camped before Richmond and Petersburg.   I should ask for no other proofs than the conduct of the regiments detached from this army in the month of January 1865, under the command of General Terry, for the attack of Fort Fisher, that commands the entrance to the port of Wilmington.   General

Butler made the first attack under the protection of Admiral Porter's fleet: he effected a landing, made a reconnaissance, on the result of which an officer of engineers declared the fort could not be taken by assault, and re-embarked his troops. Grant took the command of the army of the James from Butler, and a few days later sent the same regiments against Fort Fisher under the command of Terry. The assault was made; and, after five hours of a hand-to-hand struggle, the assailants were left masters of the fortress. A thousand Federals were killed and wounded on the works, which were disputed inch by inch. Compare these three engagements—Bull Run, where the volunteers disband in a panic; Gettysburg, where, for the first time, the two armies meet on open ground, looking each other, so to speak, in the face; and lastly the attack on Fort Fisher, where the Federals assume the offensive, and carry the works their own officers had declared impregnable. From a military point of view these three trials embody the history of the army of the Potomac—an unregulated force, ignorant, without direction, without unity, embarrassed by its own size, learns first to concentrate itself, to group its elements, to support them against each other—to organise itself, in a word; then, coming to the full possession of itself, it becomes able to deal irresistible blows, while it can, at the same time, resist the most violent shock.

The army of the Potomac contained two elements, numerically very unequal, but perhaps of equal importance, the regulars and the volunteers. The regulars gave the army its military organisation; the voluntee s its patriotic spirit. At the time I saw the army of the Potomac, it had no other chiefs than the old officers of the regular army. All those who by favour of the civil war had been put in high commands at the outset, without passing through the lower grades, the *heaven-born* generals, had somewhat lost the confidence of the army. General Nathaniel Banks, ex-member of Congress and speaker of the House of Representatives was beaten in Virginia in the campaign of 1862. Called to the head of the military department of Louisiana to replace Butler, he had made a disastrous expedition on Red River, and had ended by turning his attention to the political reorganisation of Louisiana. Butler had kept the command of the army of the James for some time, owing to the prestige he had acquired in public opinion by the energy he had displayed at New Orleans, and the important part he had taken in the organisation of black regiments; but after his unlucky expedition against Fort Fisher he also was obliged to return to civil life. Franz Sigel and Carl Schurz, who were made generals at the beginning of the war to flatter the patriotism of the German population, had lost their commands some time before. General Sickles, a brilliant officer, and the only one among the first batch of civilian generals who showed some military talent, had lost a leg at the battle of Gettysburg, and Mr. Seward, to reward his services, had just given him a diplomatic mission to Central America.

Among the volunteers who entered the army as officers, or even as soldiers, several became excellent divisional generals. But they had been tried on the

battle-field, and owed their advancement to their merit.
War brings to light military qualities in people who
never were conscious of them; per contra, it also reveals
their absence in professional soldiers who have been
all their lives preparing for a task that, when the day
comes, they are unable to accomplish.   Nevertheless
it has been seen that General Grant, who was himself
an old West Pointer, had confided to his old associates
the command of all the corps of the army.   He had
not done it so much systematically as by the force of
circumstances themselves.   The regulars had performed
services of every kind; long accustomed to the strictest
discipline, they had set an example to the volunteer
regiments; on all critical occasions, they had been
as firm in defeat as in victory, always well in hand, and
ready to throw themselves on those points where calm,
intelligent, and sustained action would compel uncertain
fortune, knowing how to act as a vanguard as well as
a reserve.   Before the civil war America hardly knew
her regulars; she despised the military profession, and
was ignorant of even the names of her officers, occupied in obscure struggles with Indian tribes.   When
the war broke out, a hundred and eighty officers edu-
cated at West-Point were enrolled under the flag of
the rebellion, and a certain unpopularity clung to the
name of the military school of the United States that
had been the nursery of so many traitors.   But this
impression did not last; Congress recognised the services performed by the regulars who remained faithful
to the Union, and enlarged the number of the standing
army.   The original army of the United States had

only ten infantry regiments of ten companies each, comprising 5,780 men on a war footing ; nine new regiments were raised with twenty-six companies each, comprising 27,996 men.* The whole regular army can be counted at more than 40,000 men. Nearly all the generals who have acquired some renown belonged to the regular army : Grant, Meade, Sheridan, M'Clellan, Rosencranz, Hooker, Hancock, Buell, Humphreys, Wright, Gillmore, Park, Warren, Abbot, Pleasanton, Sedgwick, Stoneman, Thomas, Custer, Schofield, Ord, Barry, Hunt, Franklin, Reynolds, Heintzelmann, Sumner, Mansfield. These officers brought military habits and ways of thinking among the volunteers, accustomed them to discipline, and corrected as far as depended upon them all that was defective in their primitive organisation. On the other hand, their personal feelings, which it must be confessed were not very favourable to the abolitionists at the outset, were by degrees overwhelmed by the enthusiasm and the ardent patriotism of the volunteers. The spirit of

* According to official documents, the army was constituted thus at the end of the war :—

6 cavalry regiments	7512 men
1st, 2nd, 3rd and 4th artillery regiments .	3805 ,,
5th artillery regiment	1867 ,,
10 infantry regiments, (the old army) .	5780 ,,
9 ,, ,, (new formation)	21,996 ,,
ordnance department	984 ,,
engineer corps	805 ,,
medical corps	849 ,,

The total, counting the general officers, aides-de-camps, the signal corps, the provost-marshals, the quartermasters, &c., amounted to 43,330 men. This army was commanded by five major-generals and nine brigadier-generals.

West Point, at all times subject to the Southern oligarchy, was forced to abdicate before the national spirit.
An army sprung so to speak from the soil, without
traditions, without past, could have no other feelings
than those of the nation.   Under General M'Clellan's
command, it was seen to hesitate like the country itself
between its love of the Union, and the fear of giving
an emancipation colouring to the war, and thus making
reconciliation with the South impossible.   These scru-
ples and hesitations deprived the military operations of
promptitude and vigour ; the enthusiasm of the early
days was worn out by degrees, and expired at last in
the swamps of the Chickahominy.

Never was an army put to such trials : its commanders were changed six times in four years ;
always beaten in Virginia, it seemed only to regain
its strength in touching Northern soil ; defeated at
Bull Run under M'Dowell, in the Virginian peninsula
under M'Clellan, before Fredericksburg under Burnside, at Chancellorsville under Hooker, it was victorious at Antietam and Gettysburg.   At times everything seemed to turn against it ; the faults of its chiefs,
their divisions, the hostility of the civil and military
power, the defects of its organisation, the necessity of
taking the offensive under the most unfavourable
circumstances and on a ground that seemed formed
by nature for defence.   In the midst of its misfor-
tunes, nevertheless, the army never doubted itself ; it
was borne up by its own patriotism.   Mercenary
legions would never have shown this courage and
constancy ; it can even be questioned if professional

soldiers, better drilled, more familiar with the art of war, would have been willing to undertake afresh, so many times, a plan always broken up, under so many different leaders, and in face of so many difficulties. I think that which especially characterises the army of the Potomac, was its constant readiness to act ; it was always ready to march ; the volunteers, who had left their wives and families and farms, wanted to see the end. They only asked to fight ; nothing is so fatal to such an army as inaction, which brings with it, per force, desertion, drunkenness, and demoralisation. You cannot expect from volunteers either the soldier-like bearing, or the precision of drill and manœuvring, that is always exacted from professional soldiers. By the end of two months they have learned all they want to know, and after that, they can only gain by making a campaign. It was a very great mistake, at the opening of the war, to keep the army of the Potomac encamped for months round Washington. As soon as a volunteer has learned the use of fire-arms, of a gun or a cannon, he should not be sent to a review, but into a battle. In an army where nearly all the soldiers were good, but where subaltern officers were wanting, war was the only means of creating a good body of officers ; the soldier could not respect leaders as ignorant as himself, and who only owed their brevets to political patronage. Later officers owed their advancement to courage, and the presence of mind displayed on the field of battle ; then there was no difficulty in obtaining obedience. The governors kept all through the war the right of making all promotions in the regiments of their respective states; this power is granted to them by the constitution, taking it away from them was not to be dreamed of. But practically, when once the war had begun, they only gave advancement on the special recommendation of the corps commanders, and the Secretary of War. There is not one who did not make political considerations bend to the necessity of giving a strongly organised army to the republic. Sickness, death, and above all resignations, very rapidly cleared the ranks of a host of officers who had been named at first by chance or favour. Advancement was owing to courage and desert; and if the general-in-chief did not possess the right of making promotions on the battle-field, a recommendation from him to the Secretary of War always met with consideration. I saw in the army of the Potomac several officers from the State of New York, violent abolitionists, and devoted to the administration, who held their commissions from a democratic governor; in spite of all that the detractors of the United States have said, the armies recruited from 1860 to 1864 have always preserved a national character: the foreign elements that entered into them were absorbed and, as it were, overwhelmed by the American element: the Irish and Germans, attracted by the great bounties, never got beyond the lowest ranks, and in no way altered either their character or sentiments. The corps of officers, with very few exceptions, was exclusively recruited from the citizens of the United States. Voluntary enlistments, till the very last, filled nearly all the vacancies made by war and sickness. On the 1st of January

1863, the Northern States had already furnished more than a million of volunteers. The repeated calls of the President had raised the figure of the State and town bounties to an extraordinary degree; and in 1863, Congress voted a conscription law to keep up the effective force on a sufficient scale. This by no means popular law met with many difficulties in the execution; most of the townships preferred to vote large sums of money, in order to obtain volunteers enough to fill their quota. The last official report of the Secretary of War shows, that from the 1st of November 1863, to the 31st of October 1864, the draught only furnished 42,727 soldiers; while during the same period 366,459 volunteer recruits were obtained for the one, two, or three year regiments. (Regiments were raised all through the war, some for one, others for two or three years; at the opening of the war, when it was hoped the rebellion would be speedily vanquished, there were a great many regiments enlisted for one year; later they were generally enlisted for three years.) The conscription therefore played a rather insignificant part in the recruiting of the armies; it was ill carried out, and for too short a time to enter into the customs of the country. At all times the regular army has been made up by enlistment; from the 1st of January 1864, to the 31st of October of the same year, 13,019 men entered it.

Could a volunteer army be anything but a national army? In constant communication with the country, it partook of all its passions and emotions. You always found the citizen beneath the uniform. The postal service was performed with the utmost regularity in the army of the Potomac, as well as at all the stations of the Federal troops, and letters left the camp by thousands. The newspapers were read there as eagerly as in Boston or New York : the army felt itself to be under the eyes of the country ; every day it could read what it had done the day before; encouragement and applause followed its steps wherever it went. More than once I saw newspaper reporters come into the tent of General Grant's head-quarters, familiar with all the officers, always in search of news, and often ready to run into real danger to procure them.

The army was fully aware of the sacrifices the nation made for it : the soldiers were the pets of the people. I never heard them called anything but *our soldiers.* How often in a railway train have I not seen charming young women get up to make room for a sick man, a convalescent wearing a blue coat? I remember one day seeing one get out at the station of his little town ; he was pale, emaciated, and walked with difficulty. A barouche, with two horses, was waiting for a lady at the same station : she insisted on the soldier's getting in, and on carrying him to his house before she went home herself. Never was an army treated with such liberality by a nation : the pay of a common soldier was thirteen dollars a month; the rations were enormous; fresh meat was distributed every five days to the regiments of the army of the Potomac. But even that was not enough ; the Sanitary Commission, the Christian Commission, had their agents in the camps and hospitals, who devoted themselves to satisfying the wants and wishes of the soldiers ; soldiers on furlough found at nearly every halt a soldiers' home, improvised establishments, where, on showing their papers, they were fed; beds were given them, and their money and knapsacks taken care of during their stay.

An army in constant communication with the people remained open to all the emotions and passions that agitated the country: it was never isolated by an exclusive party spirit, either in its own opinions, or in an excessive attachment for any of its Generals. It saw M'Clellan withdraw with some regret, when Mr. Lincoln took the command from him; but the idea of resisting the decision of the Executive passed through very few minds, and never even dared to openly show itself. When, in November 1864, it was called upon to choose between Mr. Lincoln and its old leader, many more votes were given to the first than to the second; neither the soldiers nor the generals were deceived as to the importance of this great electoral struggle, the issue of which was to decide the very fate of the United States. Before so many solemn problems submitted to the nation, all individual pretensions, all preferences, all prejudices gave way without regret.

There were hardly any traces left at this epoch of what might be called the old spirit of West Point; I mean that small jealous professional spirit, despising the great struggles of civil life, affecting contempt for lawyers, politicians, abolitionists, and for the eloquent leaders of opinion. The regulars, nearly all of them in high commands, had become quietly reconciled to an administration that had done so much for them, with a war that had given their names to popular admiration. Their contempt for volunteers had changed into esteem, in the midst of so many common dangers, and on so many battle-fields. In the regular army all the nominations, and in the volunteer army all the promotions above the rank of Colonel, were discretionary with the Secretary of War, and must be confirmed by the Senate. The superior officers had therefore no interest in being hostile to the Administration.

Congress, to confine them within a narrow independence, and to subject them to a sort of perpetual *surveillance*, had named, at the very outset of the war, a Committee on the Conduct of the War, which after every campaign, above all after every defeat, subjected officers of every rank to an interrogatory. Without fear of compromising discipline, it received the depositions of inferiors against superiors, and no one escaped its jealous and exacting inquisition. The reports of this Committee fill whole volumes, and though there are doubtless many omissions and many contradictions, they will certainly remain among the most important materials that will one day be used to write the history of the civil war of the United States. Forced to make friends for themselves in the Senate, almost entirely made up of Republicans; to keep aloof from the anger of the irritable Secretary of War, Mr. Stanton; and the suspicions of the Committee of Congress, the Generals kept strictly within the limits of their military duty. The Commander-in-chief gave an example to all. General Grant did not allow political discussions among the officers of his staff; very reserved himself and very silent, he exacted a like reserve from all around him. Whenever Mr. Lincoln visited his camp, he treated him with a deference that was not alone inspired by his personal sympathy for the President. He had contemptuously thrust aside the tempters who came to offer him the presidency in 1864, when the electoral campaign opened. The conqueror of Fort Donelson, of Vicksburg, the rough captain of the West, the indefatigable wrestler of Virginia, face to face with Mr. Lincoln, bent before the man who was proclaimed Commander-in-chief of the army and navy of the Union by the Constitution. By his firm and upright attitude General Grant had inspired with an equal confidence Mr. Lincoln and the army; the administration of the war interfered with none of his plans, and did not even try to raise the veil that he liked to throw over his mute solitary will. The soldiers also, though he was a severe commander, could refuse him nothing; without attempting to understand his plans, they followed him everywhere, confiding in his tenacity, his bold or patient combinations, in that iron will that slowly crushed all it could not break at the first blow.

Unity was thus established in the army; its leaders had espoused the great cause for which so many thousand volunteers had shed their blood. In the midst of events of an almost epic grandeur characters had been formed. After so many bloody campaigns, soldiers and generals had nothing more to learn; they knew and had mutually tried each other. One spirit and one will moved this great mass, become a formidable and almost perfect instrument. The army had no doubt as to the final result of the campaign; it was intelligent enough to understand that the lines behind which it chafed were slowly stifling the rebellion; it waited with impatience for the moment when it would be called on to cross them and deal the last blow.

With what promptitude and energy this blow was dealt, everyone knows. Europe, that for several years had witnessed with emotion the events of a struggle where, for a long time, chances seemed almost equally balanced, remained confounded at the results of this ten days' campaign, that gave Petersburg, Richmond, and the two still imposing armies of Lee and Johnston, to the North. Modest as he was, General Grant had stated many times that the spring campaign of 1865 would be short and decisive: he had often publicly declared that the evacuation of Richmond was only a question of time. When all was ready, when Sheridan's magnificent body of cavalry had destroyed the last Confederate forces in the valley of the Shenandoah, and was able to rejoin the main army—when Sherman, advancing rapidly with his magnificent Western regiments, forced Lee to weaken himself by sending reinforcements to Johnston—the signal was given. Leaving only a *rideau* of troops on the left bank of the James, Grant sent Sheridan and the greater part of the army of the Potomac to his extreme left to overwhelm the enemy, at the same time that he seized the Danville railroad, the last great line of communication between Richmond and Petersburg. The sixth and ninth corps, left within the lines of the army of the Potomac, attacked the Confederate entrenchments on two points at once, and succeeded in breaking them, in spite of so many obstacles, accumulated for very nearly a year; and there remained no resource for Lee but to precipitately evacuate the capital that he had defended with such determination for so long.   All the movements were executed as they were conceived, with almost mathematical precision. The consequences have been seen: the successive capitulations of Lee and Johnston, and lastly of those remaining troops who on the distant battle-fields no longer sought to prolong, in useless combats, a struggle without an object.

Of this army that accomplished such great things nothing is left but the remembrance.   It was seen once more, after the taking of Richmond, defiling, in the midst of the applause of the people, down that magnificent avenue in Washington that leads from the Capitol to the White House.   Then all the corps were mustered out one after the other.   The volunteers set off at once for their respective States, and returned to civil life immediately.   It doubtless required some virtue in the American people itself to consent to break an instrument that had cost so dear, at the very moment when it had become perfect, and when it seemed that everything might be expected of it.   Leaving all political questions on one side for a moment, whoever loves the great art of war will also feel a sort of regret at the thought that an army tempered by so many combats and struggles, and which, in spite of all the vices inherent in its first organization, had become so homogeneous, so malleable, so sure of itself, should disappear thus in a

day. Born in the thunder of the cannon fired against
Fort Sumter by the Charleston rebels, it abdicated
shortly after the national flag was once more raised over
the ruined walls of the insolent fortress. Like the soldiers
of Cromwell's revolutionary army, their work accomplished, the volunteers of the army of the Potomac
retired noiselessly to the shades of private life. In my
conversations with officers and soldiers I have, however,
never seen the least trace of that purely military spirit
which—nurtured on glory, pride and thoughtlessness,
hardened by discipline and routine, loving either strong
emotions or untroubled leisure—ends, with those who
make war a profession, in becoming a second nature. I
can still recall the confidences of a young captain from
Vermont, a Green-Mountain boy, who came back with
me from City Point to Washington. He was twenty-three
years old, and thought the boat that was taking him
home to his family went very slowly. For three years
he had followed the fortunes of the army of the Potomac; he had been in I don't know how many battles,
and had seen death face to face a hundred times. I
asked him if he had any fancy for military life. 'No,
sir,' he told me; 'I think I have done my duty as
well as any other, but what I have done I only did as a
duty, and often I found it very hard to do. I can
hardly wait to be with my own family, to be among my
friends and equals, and choose a profession. What I
have done, I would do over again if the country needed
it; but what has been a pleasure to some people has
been a sacrifice to me.' All this was said with a

sort of proud modesty, without embarrassment or arti-
fice, a great deal better than I can repeat it. I very
often heard like language. Is it because of such feelings that the American soldiers very rarely have that
indescribable military look that makes a soldier recognisable in any part of Europe? I don't know; but one
would think that, so long as it is natural for an American officer to say he does not like the military profession, there is no reason to fear that the nation will be
run away with by a love of military glory. It will
always keep up a regular army as a necessity. This army
will be more numerous than before the war. The regulars will be useful in the future, as they have been
for the past four years, as the instructors of the volunteer
armies, if new circumstances should require it. They
will never, however, be a danger to the liberties of the
country. Disseminated in various garrisons, they will
occupy for a long time the principal strategic points of
the vast reconquered territory—the seaports, and the
junctions of the important railways. Sentinels of the
North, they will always be far from the capital of the
United States, from the President and Congress. It is
hardly worth while to be preoccupied by the dangers
to which democratic institutions might be exposed by a
few corps isolated from each other, and far from the
theatre of political conflicts. It would be hardly necessary even if, during the last few years, unscrupulous
ambition had shown itself in the ranks of the army,
disobeying law, and ready to turn to its own advantage
the occasions that offer during the disorders of a civil

war. But, in the midst of so many bitter trials, this humiliation and this danger have been spared to the United States. In the hour of the greatest peril, Democracy remained faithful to Liberty ; and, as they have fought side by side, they can triumph together to-day.

CHAPTER XII.

ABRAHAM LINCOLN.

HIGH above all men whom the American civil war has placed in view and given to fame, Abraham Lincoln stands henceforth as the purest and the greatest. After some years of struggle and anxiety, after having so long hoped against hope, and seen so much precious blood shed in vain upon the soil of Virginia, the twice-elected President believed he was about to reach his aim. He had almost accomplished the formidable task imposed upon him by events and by the popular will ; and at the very moment when it seemed as if Fortune could refuse him nothing, when he was about to reach the late fruit of so much labour, death—a death cowardly and trai-torous—snatched him away. A succession of brilliant victories had at length opened the gates of Richmond, and the remains of that army which had so long defied the North were obliged to lay down their arms. Sur-rounded by almost delirious transports of joy, no words but of gentle kindness were heard from Mr. Lin-coln. Never was victor more modest, one might almost say more humble. He had been to Richmond, he had entered for a moment the house of Jefferson Davis, some black regiments had passed in review before him, he had shown to Virginia the President of the United States; but amid the smoke of the burning city, the gleam of bayonets, and the noise and confusion of war, he himself thought only of peace. He had not hastened to Richmond to sign lists of proscription; no gust of pride or hatred could enter that soul, so naturally humane, filled with the tenderness of such a multitude of emotions during so many years. How many times, in journeying from Washington to the camp, and from the camp to Washington, had he gone up and down the sluggish Virginia rivers a sombre, careworn visitor, seen oftener by the army on the morrow of a defeat than on the eve of victory! This time, all was done. Grant and Sherman now overran at will those provinces where every inch of ground had been so long contested. For the first time, Mr. Lincoln might return lighthearted to the capital. Wisdom forbade his joy to be of long duration, and hardly had he arrived when he convoked his ministers, to consult with them upon the recent events, and the pacification of the South. He spoke of Lee with kindness, ready to extend his loyal hand to a captain who had been upon the field of battle a loyal enemy. This is the language he used on the morning of the 14th of April; that very evening he was assassinated. History shows us a few great sovereigns thus struck down in the midst of great designs, on the eve of important decisions, on the morrow of memorable actions; but, if they paid so dear for greatness and for glory, they at least bought them for their whole lives, for their children, and for their entire posterity. Democracy draws from the shades of private life her favourite

of a day, and having laid upon him for a time the ac-
complishment of tasks almost regal, she commands his
abdication.   Is it now her will that a few years of pre-
carious authority without futurity shall cost as dear as
crowns and empires?   Must her chiefs, too, be victims
devoted to be sacrificed?   Shall assassination, which
hitherto has only stalked round palaces, now lie in wait
for those popular magistrates that are here to-day and
gone to-morrow?   Must they, too, pass on through
snares and swords?

Henceforth the life of Mr. Lincoln belongs to History:
and she will recall his humble beginning only to contrast it with the grandeur of his end.   She will not
follow him step by step as he climbed from the most
obscure ranks to the great theatre of public life, by dint
of patience, intellect, and will. The life of the fields and
the open air of the Western plains formed this robust
nature for the struggles it was to undergo.   Like almost
all the Western people, he did a little of everything.
He commanded a flat boat on the Mississippi, and was
a rail-splitter, cutting and sawing wood for the fencing
of farms in Illinois.   The great rivers and the prairies
taught him more than books.   He tells us himself that
it was during his trips on the Mississippi that he began
to hate slavery, as he remarked the contrast between
the States that had preserved this institution and those
that had never known it.   It is from the wilderness,
among the woods, the wild flowers, and newly-planted
fields, that he took that love of independence, that contempt of etiquette, that respect for labour. He began late
to study law ; but his originality was already in flower,

and under the forms and skilful circumlocution of the civilian there was something frank and ingenuous, as it were a perfume of the soil. From law to politics there is in the United States but a single step; every lawyer covers a politician.

The political career of Mr. Lincoln was not long. At the outset, he found himself face to face with an adversary who would have been formidable to any other man. For several years Mr. Lincoln struggled in Illinois against the preponderating influence of that Douglas whom men called 'the little giant of the West.' Gifted with wonderful eloquence, knowing how to flatter and excite to madness the democratic passions of that Western population, so lively, so enthusiastic, and so easily led away, Douglas was astonished to find a competitor worthy of him in this somewhat awkward man, without oratorical ability, who had hardly time to read anything but the Bible, Shakespeare, and a few law-books. The skilful rhetoric of the Democratic agitator was turned aside by that acute logic, that robust good sense, that familiar speech, sometimes serious, sometimes jesting, always manly and honest. It has been too often said, that in the Convention of the Republican party which met in Chicago in 1860, Mr. Lincoln was chosen as a candidate for the Presidency merely because he gave umbrage to no one; and that his very obscurity was considered as his principal claim. It is true that for a time it was expected that Mr. Seward would be chosen: the nomination of Mr. Lincoln was made to propitiate the West, of which the political importance had so greatly increased as to weigh down the scale into which it should be cast. But there would have been no sense in such a propitiation if Mr. Lincoln had not at the time been in high credit among the people of the West. He was not, then, a mere chance candidate. His great oratorical tourneys with Douglas had brought him before the whole public. He was known as a formidable debater and an able lawyer; but his two great claims were his spotless integrity, and his constant opposition to the encroachments of slavery.

It must, however, be confessed, that Mr. Lincoln had not, in the eyes of the whole Union, when he came into power, the prestige of a Madison, a Jefferson, or an Adams. He knew it better than any one else; and his first act was to offer the Secretaryship of State to his rival, Mr. Seward, fully appreciating his vast acquirements, his elastic intellect, so ingenious and fertile in resources, and the high authority of his long parliamentary experience. We know what followed : when once the Union had been rent, and the war begun, Mr. Lincoln appeared fitter than any other man, by temperament, by character, and even by the circumstances of his elevation, to represent the American people in the great crisis through which it was about to pass. His ruling passion, and, so to speak, his only one, was found to be that of the nation. The word passion ought not, perhaps, to be used to express a resolute, calm, inflexible conviction, a sort of inborn, inbred faith in the destiny of the American people. I have before had occasion to remark, in speaking of the West, that nowhere has the national sentiment penetrated the souls of men so deeply as among the people beyond the Alleghanies. The inhabitant of Massachusetts may take pride in the history of his little State. The greater part of the States washed by the Atlantic have traditions and memories ; but Indiana, Ohio, Illinois have as yet no history. The inhabitant of those vast regions who feels himself irresistibly called to such high destinies is, above all, an American. He is, and is determined to be, the citizen of a great country. He is determined to measure the power by the immensity of its provinces, and his patriotism literally knows no bounds. During the long years of peace and prosperity of the first half of the present century, this national passion of the American people was almost unknown to itself. It had merely burst out in eruptions few and far between, seeming to superficial observers to wear itself out in the endless strifes of hostile interests. The civil war brought it out in all its strength. Europe might think the United States had become a simple agglomeration of provinces, and even in America some minds had reached a mistaken conclusion as to the true characteristics of the Confederation. But when its flag was insulted, the American people stood revealed to itself. It vowed to remain a people. It saw on one side the principle of Union—the great native land ; and on the other, State sovereignty—the little native land. It did not hesitate an instant, but chose the great country, and made ready for every sacrifice. Who better than the former deputy of Illinois could represent the wishes and the popular instincts, and become the living image of that patriotism without alloy, proud of the past, but prouder still of the promise of the future ?

Faith in the Union has been the dominant feature

of Mr. Lincoln's policy. His whole conduct is easily explained when one seeks, amid the confusion of events, words and deeds, for this clue, so strong and tightly drawn. At the first glance, he understood the character of the war. He knew well his enemies, and knew them to be formidable. We do not find in his speeches a word which indicates that he was ever self-deceived as to the difficulties of his task. He had already foreseen them when he took leave of his neighbours and friends at Springfield in these touching words, where it seems to me we can read his whole character, such as after-days were to reveal it to his country :—

'No one not in my position can appreciate the sadness I feel at this parting. To this people I owe all that I am. Here I have lived more than a quarter of a century, here my children were born, and here one of them lies buried. I know not how soon I shall see you again. A duty devolves upon me which is, perhaps, greater than that which has devolved upon any other man since the days of Washington. He never would have succeeded except for the aid of Divine Providence, upon which he at all times relied. I feel that I cannot succeed without the same Divine aid which sustained him, and on the same Almighty Being I place my reliance for support; and I hope you, my friends, will all pray that I may receive that Divine assistance without which I cannot succeed, but with which success is certain. Again I bid you all an affectionate farewell.'

It was not pride that made him find his place in history by the side of Washington; there is nothing in his tone but gentleness, modesty, and goodness. But he understands the present danger, and already is futurity revealed to that soul gifted with the foresight that belongs to the poor and disinterested. With these thoughts he quitted the State he loved so much, and that he was never more to behold. Let us recall the circumstances in the midst of which he received the presidential power from the hands of his feeble predecessor. Washington, and even the Capitol itself, were full of traitors. The treasury was empty; no navy, no army; a few officers, all personal friends of the rebels; the houses of Congress profoundly divided; public opinion almost as warmly roused against the abolitionists as against the secessionists, confusing them together in its thoughtless rage; a disposition, tacit or avowed, to avoid all immediate, direct struggle with slavery, with the idea of bringing back, if it were possible, those whom it still considered as erring brothers; the national sentiment taking shelter under the formula of 'the Union as it was,' but in reality disposed in its blind fervour to restore to the South more than its old privileges;—this was what surrounded Mr. Lincoln on his accession to office. In the tide of opinions, passions, and conflicting projects, he perceived but one immovable point, and on that he planted himself. All else might change, but one thing must remain standing,—the Union. The great sagacity of Mr. Lincoln quickly discriminated between what was false, artificial, and perishable in the sentiments of the American people, and what was stable and fundamental. The eye does not perceive the tenacious root which almost forms a part of the rock beneath the soil ; it only takes cognizance of the branches, leaves, and flowers that are the sport of the sun and the air : but when the tempest has swept away all these, life still takes refuge in the root.

The prudent and almost timid attitude of Mr. Lincoln at the beginning of his presidential term is explained by his great deference for public opinion : great reserve, too, was imposed upon him by the very circumstances of his elevation to power. For long years the Democratic party had reigned paramount at Washington. The Republican party had neither the traditions nor the prestige which are acquired by the long exercise of authority. It even owed its triumph in the elections to the division of its adversaries. Mr. Lincoln was regarded as an intruder at that Capitol where men like Sumner, Seward, and Chase had been so long looked upon as strangers. I am, for my own part, convinced that on the day when Mr. Lincoln entered the White House, he said to himself, in the solemn stillness of his conscience—' I will be the Liberator of four millions of slaves. Mine has been the hand chosen to strike the death-blow of the servile institution.' Ought he, could he say it aloud from the balcony of the Capitol ? If he had done so, he must have passed for a fool and a fanatic. Such a declaration would perhaps have provoked a civil war at the North. It would at least have aroused such resistance that all might have made shipwreck in the division of parties, —the Constitution, the laws, the principle of the Union itself. Mr. Lincoln had but one mission, to save that principle; and how could he fulfil it, if he audaciously separated himself from public opinion? He must, then, wait patiently until the whole country, man after man, should have received the rude, sharp lessons of war, till the public conscience, stirred to its depths, should yield to heroic inspirations and great and generous emotions. Mr. Lincoln was like the physician who knows the remedy, but may not use it till the supreme crisis has passed. They have been most unjust to Mr. Lincoln, and to the North itself, who accuse them of not having seized the arm of emancipation till the last hour, in a fit of despair, and out of hatred to their enemies. That hatred was felt neither by President nor people; and it should moreover be understood that how great soever may be the cause of emancipation—and it is not we who could ever strive to lessen its claim—it comes to the American people but after the national cause itself. While the maintenance of the Union seemed in a sort bound up with this institution of the South and the guarantees the Constitution had given it, we may understand the trouble and embarrassment of statesmen placed between their love of their country and their hatred of slavery.

Mr. Lincoln did not entirely escape from these uncertainties. During his whole life, he had sincerely detested slavery, and he had a hundred times foretold its dangers. He could never believe with Mr. Douglas that the slave-laws were of the same nature as the Virginian oyster-laws, or any other local laws of the States. He said publicly, on June 17, 1858, at Springfield, in Illinois, 'A house divided against

S

itself cannot stand.   I believe that this government
cannot be maintained, upheld on one side by liberty,
and on the other by slavery.   I do not believe that
this Union will be dissolved, or that this house will
fall; but it will cease to be divided.'   At Chicago,
on July 12, 1858, he said: 'I have always hated
slavery—as much, I believe, as any abolitionist.   The
American people regard slavery as a great social evil.'
And in one of his public debates at Ottowa, with
Douglas, in 1858, he repeated—' I cannot but hate
slavery.   I hate it because of its monstrous injustice.'
On this point he never varied.   Before, as after his
presidency, he often repeated this maxim : 'If slavery
is not wrong, nothing is wrong.'   Such was the language of the moralist.   The President of the United
States was restrained by all possible obstacles.   He
could advance only step by step in his emancipation
policy.   He could not go faster than the people ; but
he constantly urged his friends to act upon public
opinion.   He had nothing to fear from publicity, and
he appealed to the thousand voices of pulpit, tribune,
and press.

The constitution formally forbade him all inter-
ference in the interior governments of the loyal states,
and his first thought was, besides, to retain in the
Union the frontier states of Maryland, Kentucky,
Tennessee, and Missouri, where slavery still existed
at the outbreak of the war.   He must not dream of
imposing its abolition upon them, but he urged upon
them to amend their constitutions, and generously
offered them the support of the whole Union, to faci-

litate the transition from the old to the new order of things. He had at the same time an idea of peopling distant colonies with the black race, but he abandoned it when it was proved to him that the plan was impracticable. When he was urged for the first time to issue a proclamation emancipating the slaves in the rebel states, he at once placed himself in a completely practical point of view. 'A proclamation,' said he, ' will emancipate nobody. A bull might as well try his horns against the tail of a comet.' He allowed himself to be persuaded, however, and he soon understood that, if the proclamation of liberty was without material effect, its moral effect would be immense in the North, at the South, and throughout the world; that if it did not act upon the present, it would not fail to do so upon the future; and he foresaw so clearly the indirect and distant consequences, that he solemnly announced it beforehand to the Southern States, and held them three months under the expectation of it. On January 1, 1862, the proclamation was issued, and from that day we may date the abolition of slavery in the United States.

The President was at times, notwithstanding, full of anxiety, and disturbed by doubt as to the future consequences of this great act. It was to be feared that the Supreme Court might some day decide the proclamation to be a dead letter by declaring it to be unconstitutional. Mr. Lincoln took advantage of the death of Chief Justice Taney, who had for thirty years been the docile tool of the Southern oligarchy, to offer the highest judicial function of the country to a decided enemy of slavery, Mr. Chase, although Mr. Chase had just retired from the cabinet and taken a discontented, if not a hostile attitude, to the administration. Whenever the abolitionists expressed fears with respect to the proclamation, he reassured them ; and he took every occasion to make the American people understand that, so far as he was concerned, the character of the act was irrevocable. He said in his message of December 8, 1863 : ' I shall never retract or modify my emancipation proclamation, and I will never return to slavery a single person who has been made free by its terms, or by any act of Congress.' A year after, in view of the coming presidential election, he repeated the same declaration, and added : ' If by any way or by any means the people ever should lay upon the executive the obligation of returning to slavery those whom my proclamation has made free, it must choose another, not myself, as the instrument of its will.'

He pursued the emancipation policy with as much tenacity as he did the principle of union itself from the moment that the nation blended these two causes into one. It will be remembered that, during the last summer, commissioners from the South entered into non-official conferences in Canada, near Niagara, with some of the political men of the North. Mr. Lincoln, not choosing to treat with them directly, contented himself with giving to those about to represent the North in this conference a note in the following terms, in which we find something of· the keenness of the lawyer, combined with the sagacity of the statesman : ' To all whom it may concern : any proposition embracing the re-establishment of peace, the integrity of the Union, and the abandonment of slavery, which shall be presented with and by the consent of those who control the armies now in the field against the United States, will be received and examined by the executive power of the United States, and will be replied to in liberal terms as to all secondary and collateral points.' In the spring of 1865, the Vice-President of the Confederacy, Mr. Stephens, having demanded a personal conference with Mr. Lincoln, the President consented to meet him in the harbour of Fortress Monroe ; and there again he insisted as energetically upon the abolition of slavery as upon immediate submission to the Union; and while testifying the most conciliating intentions, he refused to be drawn into compromises dangerous to the great principles he was set to defend.

During this long conference held under the guns of Fortress Monroe, he did not for a single moment lose sight of his main object. In vain did Mr. Stephens intimate to him that the armies of the North and of the South would quickly become reconciled on new battle-fields, beneath the banners of all the states, while in the intoxication of great victories over a foreign foe, the passions excited by civil war would give place to new ones; that the military honour of the South once saved, the political sacrifices would be less galling to its pride; Mr. Lincoln remained inflexible. He would neither buy the triumph of the Union at the cost of a foreign war, nor sacrifice the coloured race to the ambition of his own people.

Mr. Lincoln always realised that the abolition of slavery ought not to retain the character of a mere measure of public safety, defensive and military. So, when the great Baltimore Convention, which bore him for the second time to the presidency, demanded that he should submit first to Congress and then to the states an amendmènt of the constitution, he hastened to do so, in order to efface from the laws of the country the last trace of that fatal institution which had almost been its ruin. I was at Washington while the proposition for the amendment was discussed, and I know with what interest the President followed all the phases of that memorable debate. His tone had for some time been touched with a singular solemnity, whenever he spoke of slavery. One delights to repeat the words he addressed to Congress in his message of December 1, 1862 :—

' Fellow-citizens, we cannot escape from history. We all make a part of this Congress and this administration, and we shall be remembered in spite of ourselves. Neither our insignificance nor our personal worth can guarantee any of us. The trial through which we are passing will leave around our names a memory of honour or of infamy to the remotest generation. We say that we are defending the Union. The world will not forget it. We profess to be able to save it : the world takes note of the same. In freeing the slave, we secure all liberties. Other means might possibly succeed, but this is infallible.'

This tone, already so noble, did but rise till it became religious in the discourse which he pronounced

on March 4, 1865 —the day of his second inauguration :—

'The Almighty has His own purposes. " Woe unto
the world because of offences, for it must needs be that
offence cometh." If we shall suppose that American
slavery is one of these offences which, in the providence
of God, must needs come, but which, having continued
through His appointed time, He now wills to remove,
and that He gives to both North and South this terrible
war as the woe due to those by whom the offence
came, shall we discern therein any departure from those
divine attributes which the believers in a living God
always ascribe to Him? Fondly do we hope, fer-
vently do we pray, that this mighty scourge of war
may speedily pass away.

'Yet, if God wills that it continue until all the wealth
piled by the bondmen in two hundred and fifty years of
unrequited toil shall be sunk, and until every drop of
blood drawn with the lash shall be paid by another
drawn with the sword—as was said three thousand years
ago, so still it must be said, that the judgments of the
Lord are true and righteous altogether.

'With malice toward none, with charity for all, with
firmness in the right, as God gives us to see the right, let
us strive on to finish the work we are in, to bind up the
nation's wounds, to care for him who shall have borne
the battle, and for his widow and his orphans ; to do
all which may achieve and cherish a just and lasting
peace among ourselves and with all nations.'

After such words, is it possible to accuse Mr. Lincoln
of having entered with reluctance upon the path to

which the abolitionists had urged him from the beginning? If he advanced slowly, it was because he knew he must not separate himself from the nation. Patience and moderation were not merely his natural qualities; he esteemed them to be the duties of his high position. While all around him might abandon themselves unreservedly to their emotions of patriotism, indignation, or wrath, he alone must be calm, for he was the President of all the states, rebel as well as loyal. While the Union was receiving such cruel blows, he would not himself be one to deal them. Never did an irritating expression or a word of bitterness escape from his lips. During my visit to Washington, at the beginning of the present year, it chanced to me to converse with him of President Davis. One may judge of the moderation and the modesty of his language by these words, which I report literally : 'Our adversaries have been more fortunate than we; for it has been their good luck to have for their chief one of the ablest of men,—very capable of conducting at the same time both civil and military affairs. As minister of war, Mr. Davis had known all the officers of the regular army. I had never seen but three of them before I came to Washington as President.' Long did his merciful heart recoil before the most imperious necessities. There was great difficulty in obtaining his consent to shoot deserters. He was always ready to pardon. He had no need to pardon attacks and injuries against his own person ;— he ignored them. This goodness was not weakness. There was no place for that in a man so robust, so severe towards himself, and who had all his life breathed the air of liberty and undergone the collisions of democratic life.

But with all that loftiness of soul, which from time to time took refuge in thoughts far above vulgar politics, Mr. Lincoln was nothing of a *doctrinaire.* He had been brought up in the rude school of experience, and she always remained his sole guide. He did not pique himself upon an inflexible logic, and his strong will dispersed the array of useless formulas. Books had taught him less than men, and he thought no better of himself than of humanity at large. A man of the people, he did not think it possible to save a people in spite of itself. 'Such as it is, I will run the machine,' he said, on attaining power. We have seen him on the question of slavery varying his language, and following with docility the pressure of necessity; at first insisting only on preventing the extension of the servile institution in new territories; declaring himself, later, for gradual emancipation, then for immediate freedom; and finally, after two years of civil war, arriving at the supreme resolution of freeing three millions of slaves at a stroke of the pen; and not hesitating at length to demand of the nation the modification of its fundamental charter, so as to establish unity and harmony between the facts and the laws.

The question of reorganisation, or, as they call it in the United States, the reconstruction of the Southern States reconquered by the Federal arms, pre-occupied Mr. Lincoln from the very beginning of the war. On this point again it cannot be affirmed that he had a really decided plan. It was always repugnant to his mind not to treat the Southern States reconquered by the Federal arms as still constituting real states. He did not like to regard them as simple territories fallen from their ancient dignity, and making a part of that domain outside of the confederation properly so called which the arms or the diplomacy of the Union might at any time acquire. He was disposed to recognise in states brought to terms, any substitute or platform of a government, provided it declared itself faithful to the Union. He allowed, somewhat arbitrarily, it must be confessed, to a tenth part of the inhabitants of a state to reform the political frame-work, and to summon conventions, legislatures, governors. He was always impatient to replace a civil power, however fragile or ephemeral it might be, by the side of the military power, in order to remove from the occupation the character, or at least the appearance of conquest. This prepossession may have drawn him into some mistakes, but it seems to us to do honour to his liberality. Moreover, as he himself said in his proclamation of July 9, 1864, he would not bind himself inflexibly to any definitive plan of reconstruction. This he repeated on April 11, in his last public discourse. 'We are all of one mind,' he said, ' on this point, that the seceded states are not in their normal situation with respect to the Union ; and the object of the Government is, to place them in a regular position. What I say of Louisiana applies to the other states, and yet so great peculiarities apply to each, and so new and unprecedented is the whole case, that an inflexible plan would become a new entanglement; and I may perhaps make a new proposition to the South when the time comes for it.'

Mr. Lincoln held no more tenaciously to men than to measures. All were good in his eyes who could serve his great national object. As soon as they became obstacles, all were rejected. He never sacrificed the slightest duty to his personal friendships. The Democrats had as easy access to him as the men of his own party. He had never any favourites, and always withdrew from influences too encroaching. Singly responsible, and at a time when responsibility was a weight almost crushing, he was able to preserve his independence entire. He used his prerogatives with a firmness that may have sometimes seemed audacious, but he never made the interests of the Union subordinate to the mere satisfaction of his own pride. He surrendered to England the Confederate Commissioners taken on board the Trent, without consulting Congress, the Senate or the Cabinet, and without allowing himself to be troubled by the murmurs of the national self-esteem. He took from General M'Clellan the command of the army of the Potomac on the morrow as it were of the victory of Antietam, because the sentiments of that general were not in harmony with those of the country, and because he wished to spare the republic conflicts between the military and civil power. He at once relieved General Fremont at St. Louis, and General Hunter in North Carolina, because their emancipation proclamations went beyond, and anticipated the action of, the Government. He removed General Butler, once from New Orleans, and again from the army of the

James, when that energetic auxiliary became trouble-some and ceased to yield to discipline. He tried suc-cessively M'Clellan, Burnside, Hooker, Grant, till he found in this last a general capable of conducting the operations of the war on a consistent plan, with energy and success. He interfered as little as possible with details, especially towards the last of the war. He laid but one absolute obligation upon his generals,—to save to the Union at any cost its Capitol.

The feature of Mr. Lincoln's character which has probably been the most misunderstood is his firm, in-flexible will; because, having none of the little vanity of power, he was solicitous to veil rather than to display the signs of it. And, besides, this will was bent only upon certain capital points. It gave place, in all details or questions of a secondary order, to affable and indif-ferent complaisance. It was also, if I may so speak, defensive rather than aggressive, avoiding useless con-flicts and barren victories. One would never have sus-pected such a fund of tenacity in a man who listened to everybody; a man of so much kindness in conversa-tion, who received with the same cordiality deputations from all parties. He was more accessible than any of his ministers: more so than Mr. Seward, shut up in his cabinet of state, holding the tangled threads of American diplomacy : than Mr. Stanton, the Minister of War, indefatigable in labour, desirous to merit the name of the American Carnot, given him one day by Mr. Seward. To whoever knows anything of Washington, it will seem wonderful that Mr. Lincoln should have succeeded in preserving this integrity and independence of personal

will, and yet have remained so affable and accessible.
Washington is in reality a purely political city. Take
away the White House and the Capitol, and nothing
remains. The hotels and private houses are but ante-
chambers to Congress. There, one constantly elbows
senators, deputies, envoys, governors of states, from all
parts of the Union. No lasting influence, whether social,
political, or merely worldly, there interferes with the
exercise of the rights and the fulfilment of the duties of
public life. The representatives from Nevada or California have none but general questions to debate with
those of Massachusetts and Maine. One is ever upon
the forum ; and in such a medium, where party spirit
is constantly being sharpened and exalted, it is difficult
to preserve that measure and coolness which are the
defences of individual will. During the four years of
his presidency, perhaps not a day passed without sub-
jecting Mr. Lincoln to the pressure of various ambitions,
rancour, and personal claims. He defended himself by
his discretion, evaded attack by his inflexibility, and in
the midst of universal agitation, preserved his calmness
by his resolute moderation.

He never had a real cabinet, though he sometimes
called a ministerial council. Isolating himself in his
responsibility, he confined the ministry to their respective functions, in foreign affairs, finance, or war, leaving
each in his own sphere an almost complete authority.
If he thus isolated himself too much, as his detractors
said, it was attributable neither to pride nor ambition.
The interests of the country obliged him to keep at
work at the same time ministers who were sometimes

divided from each other by personal dislike or distrust. On almost all the subjects he lacked their special information; but his great science was the knowledge of men, and he knew how to make use of them, and to find the best, for the fulfilment of the special tasks that he felt himself incapable of accomplishing. As ignorant of the affairs of Europe, of its dynasties, of its statesmen, and its entangled politics, as he was well informed respecting his own country, he had the good sense to leave the diplomatic work entirely with Mr. Seward, who was abler than any other to cause the rights and dignity of the United States to be respected, without leading them into foreign embarrassments. On one point only did he take ground with Mr. Seward: he was determined by every honourable means to save his country from a war with European powers while it was torn by a civil war. In spite of much provocation, he never employed, with respect to these powers, any but the most kindly and cautious expressions. He thereby showed himself to be not only a skilful politician—he obeyed a secret instinct of his heart. A man of the West, he did not experience in regard to Europe, its appreciations, its criticisms, the lively susceptibility of the inhabitants of the Atlantic States. There was at the bottom a little indifference, perhaps a touch of disdain, in the uniform tranquillity of his language.

His great love, his great respect, were for the American people. The spokesman of the nation, he aspired neither to guide nor to resist it. He chose to walk by its side. He excelled in leading the politicians, who were sometimes simple enough to think they were leading him. He never aimed at leading the people. He had entire and absolute faith in the wisdom, the good sense, the courage, and the disinterestedness of his nation. That faith remained as pure at Washington as in the wilderness of Illinois. His mind was not imprisoned in that strange Capitol, half city, half village, where, as its marble palaces are built among meaner dwellings, so the lofty purposes of statesmen are stifled and obscured by the baseness of political beggary, shameless covetousness, and the falsehoods and intrigues of low ambition. His eyes overlooked them all, and were continually turned from Massachusetts to Missouri, from Illinois to Pennsylvania. He knew how to rid himself of the troublesome by a witticism, and he replied to pretentious exhortations by parables or piquant anecdotes. His firm, elastic nature resisted the most unexpected blows of fortune, and he often sustained the courage of his friends by his stoical good humour. Under his odd and sometimes trivial language, lay a profound good sense. His words went straight to the hearts of the people, and engraved themselves on every mind. What discourse, pronounced during the Presidential campaign of 1864, is worth this simple touch of Mr. Lincoln,—' It is not the place to change horses, in the midst of the stream.'

Mr. Lincoln's causticity not only covered great wisdom ; it concealed also a soul somewhat striking and sensitive, and endowed with almost feminine gentleness. His comic vein, was, if I may so speak, a sort of modesty. The purity of his life had given to his feelings a delicacy very touching in so robust a nature, concealed

as it was under a rude exterior. 'Come and see Saint
Louis under the oak of Vincennes,' said my friend Charles
Sumner to me one day. Then he informed me that once
a week, however pressing the President's avocations
might be, he opened his cabinet to all who had a request
to prefer, or a complaint to make. We set out for the
White House, and penetrated to Mr. Lincoln's cabinet,
where we took our places unannounced, with a dozen
others, each waiting his turn. The walls were hung
with immense maps of the theatre of war. Over the
chimney hung the portrait of President Jackson—his
hard, dry face bearing the impress of vast energy. On
the marble there was nothing but a beautiful photograph
of John Bright, the eloquent defender of the American
Union in the English Parliament. Through two great
windows I could see the silver lines of the Potomac, the
hills of Maryland and the unfinished obelisk of Washington, rising against the blue sky. The President was
seated at an immense writing table which stood across
the space between the two windows. He did not remark Mr. Sumner, being engaged in conversation with
a petitioner, whom he sent away almost immediately
after our arrival. The door-keeper, in ordinary citizen's
dress, like the rest of the world, led forward a woman.
She was in great trouble, and had some difficulty in ex-
plaining that her husband was a soldier of the regular
army who had been long in the service, and wished to
be authorized to quit his regiment on account of his
family. She was every moment more and more embarrassed. 'Let me help you,' said Mr. Lincoln kindly,
and he began to question her with the method and clear-

ness of a lawyer. His profile showed dark against the bright square of the window, illuminated by a flood of sunlight. His right hand was often passed through his hair, which it left in bristling disordered locks. While . he spoke, all the muscles of his face in movement gave an odd, unharmonious expression to his head, somewhat like the sketches of Mephistophiles; but his voice had an almost paternal gentleness. After having questioned the poor woman, 'I have no power,' he said, 'to grant your request. I have the right to disband all the armies of the Union, but I cannot dismiss a single soldier. Only the colonel of your husband's regiment can do that.' The woman complained of her poverty. Never before, she said, had she suffered so much. 'Madam,' said Mr. Lincoln, his voice changing to a tone of slow and touching solemnity, 'I share your sorrow. But remember that so it is with all of us, whoever we are: we have never before suffered what we suffer to-day. We all have our burden to bear.' Then he leaned toward her, and for some time we only heard the murmur of the two voices. I saw him write a few words upon a paper, which he gave to the supplicant, and then dismissed her with all the forms of the most scrupulous politeness. The moment after, a young man entered, and stretching out his hands as he advanced toward the President, exclaimed, in a ringing voice, 'As for me, I have come to shake hands with Abraham Lincoln.' 'Much obliged,' said the President, offering his large hand, 'this is the business-day.'

This respect for the people is to be found in all his speeches to the army. At the inauguration of the

T

National Cemetery at Gettysburg, Mr. Everett, facing the battle-field where the destinies of the American republic were decided, made a long discourse, in which he exhausted all the resources of his marvellous eloquence. How much should I, notwithstanding, have preferred to listen to these simple words uttered by Mr. Lincoln, in view of all those graves :—

'Fourscore and seven years ago, our fathers brought forth upon this continent a new nation, conceived in liberty, and dedicated to the proposition that all men are created equal. Now we are engaged in a great civil war, testing whether that nation or any other nation so conceived and so dedicated can long endure. We are met on a great battle-field of that war; we are met to dedicate a portion of that field as the final resting-place of these who here gave their lives that that nation might live. It is altogether fitting and proper that we should do this. But, in a larger sense, we cannot dedicate, we cannot consecrate, we cannot hallow this ground. The brave men, living and dead, who struggled here, have consecrated it far above our poor power to add or to detract. The world will little note nor long remember what we may say here; but it can never forget what they did here.

'It is for us, the living, rather to be dedicated here to the unfinished work that they have thus far so nobly carried on. It is rather for us here to be dedicated to the great task remaining before us; that from these honoured dead we take increased devotion to that cause for which they here gave the last full measure of devotion; that we here highly resolve that those dead shall not have died in vain, that the nation shall, under God, have a new birth of freedom; and that governments of the people, by the people, and for the people, shall not perish from the earth.'

Is not that the true eloquence which the orator does not seek, and finds without thinking of it? Under the pressure of a powerful emotion, he cast aside vain ornament, and attained the purity, the conciseness, the nobility of the great classic models. Does not the listener also feel in these accents, so pathetic and self-controlled, something of that tenderness of which I have spoken? One would have said at times, on beholding Mr. Lincoln, that his heart was in mourning for all the dead of those four terrible presidential years. An almost superhuman sadness passed sometimes over that forehead whose wrinkles had become furrows; over that strange countenance, where the laugh of old times was changed into a sad contortion. I recollect, as if it were yesterday, to have met the President at night-fall. He had left the White House according to his wont to get the news at the War Department. No one accompanied him, though he had often been besought not to risk himself alone. He despised the danger and detested all restraint. Wrapped in a plaid for protection against the cold, he walked slowly, lost in thought, like a tall phantom. I was struck with the pensive, suffering expression of his face. Agitation, anxiety, emotion, had slowly bowed and at length broken that strong rustic frame, had worn out the giant's nerves of steel. For four years he had not had an hour of rest. Even his holidays were dreadfully suffering seasons. When the saloons of the White

House were opened, the tide of visitors passed before him without stopping, and his broad loyal hand shook every hand that presented itself. The servant of the American people, he was condemned to remain at Washington, when the rest of the world fled away from its heat and dust. He could only escape for a little verdure to the smiling hills that surround the presidential country-seat by the side of the soldier's home, the state asylum for the invalid soldiers of the Mexican war. In his walks, he saw the beautiful woods cut down, to make room for the parapets and the glacis of the forts. At a little distance, he passed the great cemetery where ten thousand fresh graves are dug in rows. I have seen in the middle of these woods that city of the dead, where rise ten thousand white stones, all alike, each one bearing the name of a soldier. One seems to pass a review in stretching along these interminable files. Their monotony is something terrible. Mr. Lincoln had beheld them young, strong, and full of health—those soldiers who sleep there now in untroubled order for evermore.

His country retreat was not always safe from the incursions of the enemy, and Mr. Lincoln once saw from his window Breckinridge's cavalry venture to the very foot of the neighbouring forts and set fire to the house of his friend Mr. Blair. At a musket shot from this country-seat is the dwelling of a partisan of the South, who at the outset of the war made nightly signals to the rebel posts on the other side of the Potomac. He was arrested and thrown into prison, but Mr. Lincoln caused him to be set at liberty. Everywhere around him he saw the signs of war; the starry streamers floating against the sky above the red lines that dress the summits of the charming hills round Washington; the black-mouthed cannon asleep upon their stands; the cannoniers, the heavy smoke, the transports sailing up or down the Potomac. On this road between the wooded heights of Meridian Hill, he had to cross a barren devastated plain, where nothing was to be seen but vast wooden hospitals, built up hastily at the beginning of the war. He lived, it may be asserted, in a camp. Everywhere blue coats, troops of horsemen on the gallop, detachments on the march. Mounted generals —each followed by his staff, ambulances, train waggons driven by negroes and drawn by mules—all the confusion of war, without any of its grand emotions. This busy, anxious life had neither leisure nor pleasure. Mr. Lincoln's moderate fortune did not permit him to offer to many the hospitalities of the White House. He had refused to receive his salary except in paper money, though Congress would willingly have authorised its being paid in gold. He impoverished rather than enriched himself in the four years during which he had held the reins of government, while the budget of the United States reached, at a bound, a sum to be compared only with that of the oldest and the wealthiest European States. He did not take a single instant from State affairs. He entered but a single time the beautiful conservatory of the presidential mansion during that whole four years. His only relaxation was when Mrs. Lincoln on rare occasions took him, almost in spite of himself, to the theatre. He was passionately fond of Shakspeare. 'It matters little to me,' he one day said to me, 'whether Shakspeare be ill or well played. The *thoughts* are enough.'

I had one day, in the month of January, the honour of being invited to accompany him to the representation of King Lear. I went with him to that same Ford's Theatre, and to the same box where he was afterwards so cowardly assassinated. The Washington theatre is small and out of repair. You reached the Presidential box by a passage left open behind the spectators in the galleries, and to gain entrance, there was only a door to be opened and a curtain to be raised. The back of the box was hung with a piece of red velvet, but they had not even taken pains to cover, either with velvet or cloth on the inside, the pine boards that formed the front. It will be easily imagined that I was more occupied by the President than by the piece. He listened attentively, although he knew the play by heart. He followed with attention all the incidents, and talked with Mr. Sumner and myself only between the acts. His second son, a boy eleven years old, was close to him. Mr. Lincoln held him almost all the time in his arms, often pressing the child's smiling or astonished head to his broad breast, and replying to his numerous questions with the greatest patience. Certain allusions made by King Lear to parental grief brought a cloud over the President's forehead. He had lost a young child at the White House, and was inconsolable for its death. I may be pardoned for awakening such personal recollections, that in other circumstances I should never have dreamt of imparting except to a few friends, for it was on that very spot where I saw him surrounded by his family that death struck this man so full of kindness, gentler than a woman, simple as a child. There it was that he received the Parthian arrow of vanquished slavery, and fell never to rise again—the noble victim of the noblest cause.

Even by his death, Mr. Lincoln served the cause to which he had already given so much; for there are emotions so powerful that they weld all souls together. They elevate the hearts of nations. They impose silence on brawling opposition, they fling a veil of forgetfulness over the past, and harmonise all wills to one desire. We need not, then, too greatly pity the United States, for having lost this chief in whom they had placed their confidence. He will remain at the Presidential mansion, invisible, but inspiring for years to come the counsels of the nation. And it is the prerogative of a free government to form men enough for its service to prevent the absolute necessity of any one of them. The destinies of the nation are never suspended by the fragile thread of a single life. Those who find themselves raised to the highest functions of the state, adapt themselves with wonderful facility to the new circumstances in which they are placed. Liberty began their education—responsibility finishes it. Compare the judgments of Europe respecting Mr. Lincoln four years ago with the testimonies of respect lavished to-day upon his memory! Doubtless the exercise of power in the most critical circumstances enlarged his capacities, but he was essentially the same man when he accepted, with modest resolution, the burden of authority, and when his first words woke no other echoes than those of vain and frivolous criticism.

But if there is no need to offer to the American Republic, stricken in the elect of its choice, yet soon grouped around a new chief, the testimony of anxious compassion, which its pride would reject, one may at least pity that hard-wrought labourer who did not live to receive the payment of his work, and who during all his life knew no rest. His loss was mourned in the United States, no less as a private grief than as a national calamity. Black crape waved not over the palaces of the public administration only; it hung sadly from the humblest dwellings—a people in tears followed mournfully the coffin that was borne slowly from Washington to Illinois. As always is the case with a people suddenly seized upon by sorrow, it knows not at once the full worth of what it had lost. Condemned by events to become a great man, Mr. Lincoln has obtained the glory that he never courted. How earnestly and how joyfully would he have repelled it, could he at that price have spared his country the sad trials amid which his name has been slowly lifted! That glory will survive how much noisy and deceitful renown! It will add new features to that pure ideal which finds greatness in simplicity, which bends power before the law, and which never separates heroism from self-abnegation. I shall have said all, in calling Mr. Lincoln a Christian statesman, taking that word in its most sublime sense. He thought not of himself, and therefore his country and the world will remember him for ever.

CHAPTER XIII.

THE FINANCES OF THE WAR.

In the history of the civil war, financial questions form perhaps the driest, though not the least interesting chapter. Europe has beheld with stupefaction the debt of the United States, so insignificant before the war, attain by prodigious strides the level of the debts of the richest and most long-established nations of the old world. Everybody knows that the American nation has made the greatest sacrifices to maintain the principles of its government, and its imperilled national existence; but the financial history of the last few years deserves a close study: it is rich in lessons of many kinds. So many laws have been passed in four years, so many different stocks thrown into the market, so many loans taken up under various names, that it is rather difficult to find one's way in the present labyrinth of American finances. I therefore propose to review the series of acts by which Congress met the expenses of the war, and upheld the credit of the nation, in the midst of a frightful crisis, the end of which was unseen for a long time.

We must go back to the year 1860, when Mr. Buchanan was still President, but was, so to speak, scarcely doing more than occupying the seat of his successor. The Southern States at that time separated themselves from the Union, one after another, by what was called an ordinance of secession. On December 17, 1860, Mr. Buchanan approved the Act of the thirty-sixth Congress, entitled : *An Act to authorise the issue of Treasury Notes, and for other purposes.* This act allowed the President to issue Treasury notes to the extent of 10 millions of dollars. These notes were to be for not less than 50 dollars; they were redeemable one year after issue, and bore an interest of 6 per cent.

At the beginning of 1861, the first loan was raised. The Act of February 8, 1861, authorises the President to borrow, before July 1, the sum of 25 millions of dollars, to meet the demands on the Treasury, and to redeem outstanding Treasury notes. The issue was to be made by certificates of $1,000 each, bearing an interest of 6 per cent. maximum, and to be reimbursed within a period not beyond twenty years and not less than ten years.

Before July 1, a new loan was voted of 21 millions of dollars, at the same rates as the preceding, with which it was blended. At the outset the only thought was to fill the empty vaults of the Treasury: but soon it became necessary to think of creating permanent resources. Before asking them from taxation, the customs were first applied to; the tariff was revised, and the Act modifying it was approved by the President, March 2, 1861. The import duties were somewhat raised, and in many cases specific duties were substituted for the *ad valorem* duties established by the previous laws. The Act of

March 2, 1861, authorised also a new loan. It gave
the President the power to borrow 10 millions, in the
space of twelve months, to meet the necessities of the
public service. The certificates of the loan, which
were to be for sums not less than $1,000, bore an
interest of 6 per cent. The Government reserved the
right of reimbursing these certificates, at whatever epoch
was convenient, after the lapse of ten years, to begin
from July 1, 1861, the public having had three
months' warning. The payment was to be made at the
end of twenty years at farthest. In case the banks
should not make sufficiently advantageous proposals to
the state, instead of loan certificates, the President could
issue Treasury notes (of 50 dollars at least) bearing an
interest of 6 per cent. These notes, redeemable within
two years, were to be received in payment of all debts
to or from the United States; they were receivable for
duties on imports, and for awhile they were put to
this use. Great quantities of the notes were paid out
to the quartermasters and army contractors, which returned afterwards to the Treasury in payment of import
duties.

However, the spirit of revolt had overstepped the
bounds of political agitation. The attack, and the taking
of Fort Sumter, had caused a thrill of anger and indignation to run through the whole North; blood had run
in the streets of Baltimore, where the Massachusetts
soldiers, who had hurried to the defence of Washington,
had been attacked by a furious mob devoted to Southern
interests. The people having long refused to believe in
the civil war, saw the last hopes of peace and settlement

vanish. Congress was at last obliged to resolve on
vigorous measures to put down the rebellion. I shall
here only inquire into those relating to finance. On
July 11, 1861, was passed '*An Act to authorise a
loan.*' We leave all of a sudden the modest figures of
the preceding Acts; this time the Secretary of the
Treasury is authorised to raise a loan of 250 millions
of dollars, either in the shape of coupons, of bonds,
or Treasury notes. The bonds are to bear interest not
exceeding 7 per cent., and are irredeemable during
twenty years. The Treasury notes, so well known
later as *seven-thirties*, are to be of 50 dollars at least,
and are payable three years after date, with interest
at the rate of 7,30 per cent. a year. The Act also
authorised the issue of the *demand-notes* of smaller
denomination than 50 dollars, that bear no interest,
but are payable on demand, as well as the issue of
Treasury notes payable one year after date, and bearing 6 per cent. interest. The demand-notes were not
to exceed 50 millions.

The loan of 250 millions of dollars was the first step
made on the high road of great popular loans. Sub-
scription-lists were opened, where sums of 50 dollars
even were taken. The American people responded to
the call of the Government.

It would not have been possible to issue so large a
mass of paper, let the patriotism of the country be ever
so great, if at the same time means had not been taken
to secure the payment of the interest of the new national debt. It was with an eye to this that Congress
voted an act imposing a war tariff, and levying a direct

tax on the people of the several states. The Act was approved August 5, 1861, its title being : ' *An Act to provide increased revenue from imports to pay interest on the public debt, and for other purposes.*'

The new tariff raised in a very high proportion all the import duties, especially those on articles of luxury. All articles of consumption that were not of absolute necessity, even sugar, spices, and spirits, were made to come under this category.

The Act levied a direct annual tax of 20 millions of dollars, apportioned among the Northern as well as the Southern States. This direct tax was to be assessed on the value of all lands with their improvements. Assessors and collectors of the United States were to fix and collect the amount. Each state, however, had the right to pay and collect its quota in its own way, in in which case it was allowed a discount of 15 per cent.

The same Act created an income-tax. From January 1, 1862, a tax of 3 per cent. was to be raised on the excess of incomes over 800 dollars. In the cases where this income was derived from the federal securities, the tax was reduced to $1\frac{1}{2}$ per cent. This income-tax was modified later by the Internal Revenue Act of July 1, 1862.

While such efforts were made to increase the receipts, new loans were raised. An Act of August 5, 1861, authorises the Secretary of the Treasury to issue bonds bearing 6 per cent. interest, and payable after twenty years from date. He was authorised, either at the time of maturity or before, to exchange these bonds for seven-thirties ; the bonds were to be nominally worth at least 500 dollars, and the sum total was not to exceed the sum total of the seven-thirties. The same law authorised the issue of five-dollar demand notes, and made the notes of a less denomination than 50 dollars receivable for public dues.

This Act closes the series of the financial measures of the first session of the thirty-seventh Congress, that sat from July 4, 1861, till August 6, 1861. The second session of this same Congress opened on December 2, 1861, and ended July 17, 1862: during this period financial questions yielded nothing in importance to political ones. The system of taxation was completely modified, and though it may since then have been subjected to some further modifications, its main features were traced at that time. The war had become a gigantic struggle; armies sprung from the soil, and the navy was being formidably developed. The current expenses were enormous; it was necessary to attend to the most pressing first, and to create resources, without having much choice as to the methods or thought for the future.

Hardly had Congress come together, when it revised the tariff, and by the Act of December 24, 1861, raised the duties on tea, coffee, and sugar.

The 12th of February, 1862, it authorised a new issue of United States notes. Besides the 50 millions of demand-notes, bearing no interest, issued under the Act of June 17, 1861, the Government was authorised to issue 100 million dollars worth of like notes, that at the same time were to form a part of the loan of 250 millions allowed by that Act.

At that time the Treasury had been gradually emptied, in consequence of incessant demands. Projects were springing up on every side to procure resources for the state; the most absurd and chimerical ideas were discussed by the people. Congress, in alarm, saw the growing danger, and found in its own bosom no financier able to guide it through the ever-increasing difficulties, and to strengthen the public credit. This session was perhaps the most sombre era of the great drama of the civil war. After long and wordy discussions, when the darkest predictions were not spared to the republic, Congress at last decided to leave expedients on one side, and boldly enter on the path of extreme measures. The revolutionary era for finances opened.

Until then, only 50 millions of demand-notes of real paper money had been issued. The law of February 1862, inaugurated the reign of the famous *greenbacks*. By this law the Treasury was authorised to issue 150 millions of United States notes, 'bearing no interest, payable to bearer,' and of every decimal denomination, down to the minimum figure of 5 dollars. The issue was in reality of but 100 millions, for the other 50 millions were to replace the demand-notes that were to be withdrawn from circulation as quickly as possible. The new notes were declared *legal tender*, and would be used to pay all public or private debts.

The same law authorised the issue of *five-twenty* bonds (payable at the end of five years, of twenty at the maximum), which became the favourite popular investment, and spread rapidly to all parts of the Union. The issue of paper money was connected with the last-named notes, for, according to the spirit of the law, they were to be used for the withdrawal of the paper.

The sum total of the five-twenties, placed at the disposal of the Government, was 500 millions : the interest of 6 per cent. was *payable in gold.*   These bonds were exempt from all local or state tax, and thus became a privileged investment.

But how was the payment of the interest of so considerable a sum to be secured?   There was no other way discovered than to oblige all importers to pay their import duties in specie.   The receipts of the customs thus became the security of the loan; indirectly, the tariff was thus greatly raised, for gold was already very high, and trade, obliged to resort to it, could only get it in the market at a great sacrifice.   The connection between the payment in gold of the interest of the debt, and that of the payment of duties, was the fundamental idea of Mr. Chase's administration ; the latter also had turned his attention to a sinking fund ; the law that specifies that the custom duties should be payable in specie, also says that gold so obtained should be employed in the ' purchase of 1 per cent. of the entire debt of the United States, to be made within each fiscal year, after the first day of July 1862.'   •

Congress was well aware that indefinite supplies were not to be expected from loans; the present was to bear a part at least of the burden of the war, and not to leave it all to the future.   During nearly the whole session therefore the chapters and articles of a law, creating a completely new system of taxation, was discussed. Never before was seen such a spectacle; usually parliaments struggle against old taxes, try to do away with them, or to lighten their weight; the American parliament was seen, on the contrary, endeavouring to invent taxes, sparing nothing that could be subjected to taxation, and organising a species of financial procedure as minute as it was pitiless.

The Act of July 1, 1862, 'the Internal Revenue Law,' is a whole volume. You can hardly find the trace of a general idea or system in this heap of rules and stipulations. It would appear, however, as if the object had been to reach all manufactured products, all trades, and all articles of luxury. A stamp tax was made to weigh upon all sales; in each electoral district two United States officials, an assessor and a collector, were to apportion and collect the new taxes.

The 11th of July, 1862, a new loan was authorised, and a new issue of 150 millions of dollars of United States notes voted, payable to bearer without interest, and of whatever denominations the Treasury saw fit to allow. It was under the sanction of this law that two and one dollar notes came into circulation. The circulation of notes of less than five dollars was, nevertheless, limited to 35 millions. These notes were declared legal tender, which assured their forced circulation. The limit of temporary deposits in the State Treasury, which had already been raised from 25 to 50 millions, was extended to 100 millions of dollars.

Soon after, July 14, 1862, was approved a new 'Act increasing temporarily the duties on imports.' The tariff was once more completely revised, and its demands

U

rendered still more imperative ; it was necessary to in-crease the receipts in gold at any price, in order to meet the interest of.the public debt.

I now come to one of the most important acts of the financial administration of Mr. Chase—his law rela-tive to banks.   Mr. Chase's secret wish was to create a Federal bank that would destroy all the private banks, independent of the state ; a political idea that was connected by visible links with the doctrines of the party called to contend with the principle of state rights.   It was, however, impossible to suppress all the old banks at one blow ; to replace them by a United States bank, like that of France or England, was no easier ; the memory of President Jackson's victorious struggle against the United States bank was not yet forgotten ; the Democratic party had always repulsed all projects for the establishment of a Federal united bank as unconstitutional.   Mr. Chase, not being able to reach his ends directly, was obliged to look for indirect means to gradually weaken the influence of the old banks, and to bind the credit of the new banks as firmly as possible to the national credit.   He gave up the idea of creating a single bank, placed under the immediate control of the Central Government, but he established a close solidarity between the new banks, and compelled them to be the numerous agents of one financial policy.

The very title of the banking law, passed Feb-ruary 2, 1863, shows its spirit.   It is ' an Act to pro-vide a *national* currency, secured by a pledge of United States stock.'   According to the terms of the law, each national bank should possess a capital of at least $50,000 ; one-third to be paid in on the opening of the bank, the remainder payable by tenths; the payments to be made at intervals of not more than two months. As security for its issues, the bank is under obligation to deposit United States bonds in the Treasury of the United States at Washington. The bank notes are furnished to the banks by the administration itself. The total issue of bills is limited to $300,000,000. National banks can only issue bills up to 90 per cent. of the value of the Federal bonds constituting their deposit. The law clothes them with one important privilege, for the states cannot tax their capital, whereas the old banks were subject to a variable local tax that was equal to about 1 per cent. of their capital. In a very short time, therefore, the old banks underwent a transformation, and constituted themselves national banks. This tendency to transformation will find its natural limit when the issues of the new banks will have attained $300,000,000. It will then be impossible to increase the number of national banks; those already established will enjoy a real privilege as regards taxation ; they will be so many branches of a vast financial establishment that will not, it is true, have an apparent or nominal centre, but whose operations will be necessarily guided by a single and purely national interest. The bills of the new national banks were already in general circulation when I left the United States, in March 1865; in all the great towns I went through I read on the signs: *First National Bank, Second National Bank, Third National Bank*, &c.

The 3rd of March, 1863, Congress authorised a new loan of $300,000,000 for the current fiscal year, and of $600,000,000 for the coming fiscal year. The issue was to be made in the shape of bonds payable at the will of the Government, after a minimum term of ten, or a maximum term of fifty years, whence their name of *ten-forties*. These bonds bear 6 per cent. interest, payable in coin. This act also authorised the issue of $400,000,000 in the shape of Treasury notes, payable after a lapse of time not to exceed three years, bearing an interest of 6 per cent., payable in legal currency, consequently in paper. These notes themselves were declared legal tender for their full value. In order to secure prompt exchanges of United States notes for Treasury notes, the Secretary was authorised to issue notes to the amount of $50,000,000 to be used for such exchanges. He was also empowered, if necessary, to issue $150,000,000 of legal tender notes, bearing no interest, for the payment of the army and navy. Previous to this, January 17, 1863, a joint resolution of the two houses had allowed the issue of $100,000,000 of paper money for the same object. The $100,000,000 were to be included in the $150,000,000 authorised by the Act of March 3. Divers articles settled the terms of the exchange of the new bonds, and those created by the laws of February 25, 1862 and July 11, 1862. The administration was thus empowered to create $850,000,000 of paper money, under the designation of United States notes and Treasury notes; the first bearing no interest, amounting to $450,000,000, and designed for current circulation; the second bearing interest, and which it was hoped would be withdrawn from circulation, as they were estimated legal tender only at their nominal value, without taking the interest into account.

Gold certificates were authorised in return for deposits of gold and declared receivable for interest on the debt and for duties. The law allowed the Government to issue $50,000,000 of paper, to be used as small change, to prevent the use of postage and trade stamps, of which the public bitterly complained. Finally, the law laid a tax on the circulation of banks from April 1, 1863.

On the same day the Internal Revenue Act was amended, in order to obtain larger receipts. The duties on a great many articles were raised.

The thirty-seventh Congress met on December 7, 1863, and adjourned on July 4, 1864. Like those of the preceding congresses, its history was marked by important financial measures. The first, dated March 3, 1864, was a mere supplement to the law of March 3 of the preceding year, which has been already noticed. The administration was notified not to borrow more than $200,000,000 during the fiscal year (instead of 300,000,000), and that in the shape of five-forties, redeemable in specie, bearing 6 per cent. interest, and free from all taxation, like all the other United States bonds.

At a later period of the session June 30, 1864, Congress came back again upon the law of March 3, 1863, and decided that its terms were only good for the 75,000,000 that the administration had already publicly announced were about to be issued. The Secretary was authorised to issue 400,000,000 of 5·40 bonds. He was also empowered to issue instead of one half these bonds 200,000,000 of Treasury notes, that were declared legal tender, with interest of 7·30 maximum, payable in legal tender after three years from date and convertible at the will of the Government into 5·40 bonds. The Secretary of the Treasury was authorised to substitute an equivalent amount of new notes to all the Treasury notes already issued ; but the maximum figure of bonds and notes was fixed at 400 millions.

During the same session a law was made to prevent speculations in gold ; but the disastrous effects of this measure, which caused a prodigious rise in gold, necessitated its almost immediate repeal. Lastly, on some points the customs tariff (law of June 30, 1864) was raised, the banking law (June 3, 1864) was amended, and a retrospective war tax of 25 per cent. was voted on all the incomes of 1863 over $600.

During the following session, the Act of March 3, 1865, authorised the Secretary to borrow $600,000,000, and to issue therefor bonds or Treasury notes of the United States. The interest of these notes, payable within three years, was not to exceed 7·3.

The national debt, which on July 1, 1861, was only $90,000,000, attained during the war to more and more formidable proportions. July 1, 1862, it was $514,000,000 ; at the same date 1863, $1,098,000,000; in 1864, $1,740,000,000; March 31, 1865, it reached $2,366,000,000. The total of the daily increase at one moment exceeded $20,000,000 a day. On July 31, 1865, the debt stood thus :—

DOLLARS.

Debt bearing a gold interest . . 1,108,662,641
Debt bearing interest in paper . . 1,289,156,545
Debt bearing no interest . . . 357,906,968
Interest expired on 1,527,120

Total of the debt 2,757,253,274

The annual interest payable in gold was $64,521,837, the interest in paper $74,740,631. Total, $139,262,468.

The great danger, and I venture to say the great vice of American finances since the adoption of paper money, was the too great difference between the bulk of the circulating medium (on 31st of October, 1865, the paper money of the country amounted to $734,000,000) and the necessities of the country. Add to the State issues those of the old and new banks, and you reach a formidable total that exceeds what is needed for exchange, even in a country where speculation is so active and so widely spread. The difference I have indicated had the necessary effect of considerably augmenting the value of gold, and thus laying constantly increasing burdens on the country; for at the end of every loan, of every transaction on credit, no matter how far the settlement may be pushed into the future, the creditor always looks to a specie payment. After having issued loans, the interest on which was payable in gold, others were prudently issued, on which the interest was payable in paper, but it was not possible to dispose of them without raising the rate of interest and in submitting to harder and harder conditions. The gradual increase in prices, that naturally follows the increase of gold, soon revealed to the

country that the circulation was debased.   The history
of the fluctuation of values during the war is an in-
structive one.   I will give a few figures in respect to
this.

The price of gold rose in 1862, after the issue of
150 millions of paper, from 109 to 120 ; it was 137 in
October 1862.   The following winter, after a new issue
of 100 millions, of which 50 millions in small currency,
gold is quoted at 160, in March at 171.   In October
1863, it is at 156.

The surrender of Vicksburg and the victory of
Gettysburg brought gold down, in 1863, to 122, for
an instant, but it very soon rose again.

In March 1864, it was up to 169; in April, to 187;
in May, to 190 ; in June, to 251 ; in December, to 254 ;
in July, to 286 : it fell in April to 262; in September, to
255; in October, to 229.   In November it is quoted at
260, in December at 244.   The utterly irrational rise of
1864 was due to the issue of the notes at 6 per cent.,
payable in three years, to the draft, and to the discouragement caused by military events.   In the autumn
of 1864 Sherman began his famous march to the Atlantic, Mr. Lincoln was re-elected President.   In four
months gold fell 75 per cent.   Nevertheless gold continued to oscillate in November between 200 and 260.

The successful campaigns of Grant and Sherman, in
the spring of 1865, brought the price of gold down to
150, and the very day of the assassination of Mr.
Lincoln it was quoted at 145.   Since then it has remained almost stationary.   The Government has loudly
proclaimed that it will do its utmost to reduce the

paper currency, and this resolution has largely con-
tributed to maintain the confidence raised by the great
victory of the North.

The unheard of fluctuations in the price of gold
necessarily reacted on the stock-exchange and on railway stock, &c. Some of these stocks particularly
open to speculation have, during the course of the
war, been very nearly as sensitive as gold; merchandise of all kinds was less obedient to the impulse,
but, as the rise was slower, it was more permanent.
The high import duties were a durable cause for the
rise on many articles. Let us quote a few prices: in
December 1861, with gold at par, flour brought
$5·50 a barrel; in December 1862, it was worth
$6·60; in December 1863, from $6·96 to $9·25.
Since then it has followed the price of gold with docility, without however falling as easily as it rose.
American cast iron rose from $23 to $43 a ton;
Rio coffee from $19·50 to $34·75 the hundred
pounds; mahogany from $35 to $110 the ton; Cuba
sugar from $8·75 to $16 the 140 pounds: cotton
tripled in price.

Real estate, as was to be expected, followed the rise
of gold much more slowly. For a long time it kept at the
old nominal prices with gold at 200 and more; in the
most feverish times, speculation throws itself at first on
stocks; it is only when large fortunes have been made
by speculation, that they seek to solidify themselves
in landed property. It was therefore only at the end
of, the war that land began to rise in value, and this
moderate rise has outlived the hostilities. The price of

manual labour, nevertheless, followed closely the price of articles of consumption; these being nothing but a transformation of human industry. Manual labour during the war, when the army called for so many arms, could make its own terms, and they were very hard ones. The average wages of workmen of all kinds rose to four dollars a day.

To borrow is to sacrifice the future to the present. When the civil war broke out, the American people were not able to burden the present with a great part of the sacrifices that the Union called for. The law of July 1, 1862, called the Internal Revenue Act, showed, nevertheless, that the republic was ready to make heavy sacrifices immediately. The citizens called for taxation instead of opposing it; but if expenses can increase to formidable proportions from one day to another, it is not the same with receipts; the mechanism of taxation is not created in a day, and a long enough time is needed for new duties to produce all that can be expected from them.

The two principal sources of revenue of the United States, are the internal revenue and the custom duties. The Internal Revenue Act was only put in force for ten months during the year 1863; the monthly receipts gradually rose from two to nine millions of dollars; the receipts for the ten months were $34,796,257. The receipts rose greatly in 1864, in consequence of the corrections of the original law made by Congress, and to the improvements effected in the modes of collecting the tax. They reached the figure of $102,241,165, an unheard of figure, if it is taken into consideration that it applies to the second collection of the new taxes. The original Internal Revenue Act was amended on certain points June 30, 1864, but the consequences of these modifications were not immediately felt. The financial ideal to which Congress aspired was a receipt of 300 millions from the internal revenue. This sum has not yet been attained; from July 1, 1863, to July 1, 1864, the total amount of the internal revenue was $136,983,422. The next year, from July 1, 1864, to July 1, 1865, it rose to 203 millions. Lastly, from July 1, 1864, to July 1865, it has reached 209 millions. In the quarter ending September 30, 1865, the receipts from internal revenue have been 96,618,885 dollars.

In looking over the Internal Revenue Act and its divers amendments, there is some difficulty in disentangling the chaos of its prescriptions. In its eagerness to obtain receipts, it seems as if Congress had tried to tax everything without exception; it has not been guided by any of the favourite principles of political economy; it has not sought to make taxation weigh heavily on a small number of largely used articles, to put the smallest obstacle possible to production, to only strike at consummation; circulation has been reached through the stamp tax on sales; capital by the income-tax. Contrary to the custom of old countries where taxes were born, if I may be allowed the expression, one after another, at far distant intervals, all American taxes, of whatever nature, are collected by the same hands. There is only one assessor and one collector for each electoral district, and all receipts are paid directly to the latter, whether they come from direct or indirect taxes, from the revenue or from stamps, patents or manufactures, brandy or the revenue. The assessor and collector are amply paid; they are obliged to provide, at their own expense, all the secondary agents required for the service, and are alone responsible to the administration.

The internal revenue is only one of the two great fiscal resources of the Government. The second is the customs. The import duties, as I have said, are paid in gold. They have yielded:—

					DOLLARS.
From June 30, 1860, to June 30,	1861,	39,582,125
,,	,,	1861,	,,	1862,	490,56,397
,,	,,	1862,	,,	1863,	69,059,642
,,	,,	1863,	,,	1864,	102,316,152
,,	,,	1864,	,,	1865,	84,928,260

In the quarter ending September 30, 1865, the receipts from customs have been forty-seven millions of dollars.

I do not speak of the accessory sources of revenue, sales of land, &c., from which the Government could draw, in case of need, a great deal more than it has yet done.

Lastly, if the actual sources of the revenue should become insufficient for the requirements of the Treasury, the United States would still have the right to raise export duties on the cotton, tobacco, and petroleum they supply to Europe.

The interest of the heavy debt, the elements of which I have examined, must henceforth be inscribed on the budget of the United States. In March 1865, this interest was equal to $139,262,468. New loans will be doubtless needed when paper money is withdrawn from circulation, and it cannot be attempted too soon. The interest of this possible loan, that might be called a liquidation loan, cannot be approximatively evaluated at less than 30 millions. With the proceeds of the customs and the internal revenue it will be possible to meet the expenses, and a considerable margin will be left for the liquidation of the debt.* To restrict the circulation should be the first immediate care of the United States financiers. The paper money can be estimated at about one billion of dollars at the present time ; everybody can see that this is too high a figure. One half would be amply sufficient. How will the torrent of circulation be dammed up ? How will a return be made to a specie basis ? How will gold be brought down to par ? There is only one way to bring this about, the annihilation of paper money : all the rest is chimerical. But paper money can be got hold of in only two ways : by taxation, or by loans. If taxation yields a large surplus, the Treasury can either keep or destroy its own notes ; it can also buy up the paper money with the stock of a new loan. By the judicious use of these two means, the finances of

---

* The receipts as estimated for the year ending June, 1867 are :—

		DOLLARS.
From Customs	. . .	100,000,000
„ Internal Revenue .	.	275,000,000
„ Lands	.	1,000,000
„ Miscellaneous Sources	.	20,000,000
		396,000,000

The Expenditures are estimated at $284,317,181.

the country would be very soon brought back to their normal state.

War is always destructive; it in part destroys the capital created by peace. I have often heard it said in the United States, that so far from ruining the nation, the war had enriched it; it is idle to show the fallacy of such a statement. Fleets and armies are not producers, but consumers of frightful appetite. The war has certainly given a prodigious impulse to all sorts of industry, but the same activity would have found elsewhere more fruitful and durable outlets without the war. It cannot, however, be denied that, under shelter of the protective system, the factories and manufacturers of the United States are developing as by enchantment; they wish to ask as little as possible from unjust and rapacious Europe; the American soil ought to furnish all that is needed by America. Political economy, the English science, is held almost in contempt; it will be time enough to think of it when all the slopes of the Alleghanies have been explored and thousands of tall chimneys smoke in their valleys, when Manchester manufacturers shall come to visit model factories in Massachusetts; when all the new industries shall have gone through the period of creation and organisation. Until then the tariffs shall be kept just high enough to hinder any serious foreign competition, just low enough to bring a certain annual sum into the coffers of the State. Such is the feeling of the country, and such the language that interests lend to passions and passions to interests.

I believe I have said enough to show that the

United States can meet the heavy sacrifices laid upon them by the civil war. They will be able without too great an effort to pay the interest of the debt and wipe out a great part of it at the same time ; they will do well to preserve a certain portion as a pledge of union between the states, as a ballast and guaranty against the spirit of secession. Had there been a debt in 1860 the Southern States would not perhaps have thought of separating from the North.

CHAPTER XIV.

AFTER THE WAR.

A COUNTRY should not lightly alter those charters which are the links of successive generations, the columns round which their traditions are entwined and take root; the respect of a people for its constitution should be still deeper, when it is not a mere collection of maxims and political formulæ, but really is the highest, the most fixed and the most durable portion of the law. It is this, let us bear well in mind, which forms the peculiar character of the constitution of the United States; it is an integral part of the *law*. Therefore it is inexact to state, as the greater part of those who have studied and commented on it have done, that the Supreme Court was instituted to interpret it; there is not a judge in the United States, be his legal position what it may, who may not find himself compelled to do so, if it be possible to oppose one of its articles to the State codes and statutes, to the police regulations, or local prescriptions, on which daily sentences are based. The sole difference between an ordinary judge and the judges of the Supreme Court is, that the verdict of the latter is without appeal; but for both, the constitution is essentially the epitome of the law; the supreme court no more makes the laws than any other court. It applies it in particular cases, although in reality its sentences have no other force than the purely moral force of the first. Nothing then is superior to this supreme law, whose name is Constitution. It stands equally above the three powers, who draw from it equal independence and equal security. It is on this account that any change in the fundamental laws have been rendered so difficult; the chance majority of a day cannot change it. All propositions of amendment of the constitution must be supported by a three-quarters vote in the senate as well as in congress; and only then can it come before the legislatures of the different states, and in order that the amendment should be definitively adopted, it must be voted by three-fourths of these legislatures. In the very beginning of the war I ventured to predict that it would not be terminated without an amendment of the constitution, suppressing the three articles relative to slavery. I had the satisfaction, in the early part of 1865, of attending at Washington the great debates brought on by the proposition of a constitutional amendment. I heard nearly all the orators in both chambers; the republicans found no difficulty in showing that the constitutional abolition of slavery was the logical and fatal consequence of the rebellion; the democrats spoke against the amendment, rather not to appear too unfaithful to their post and their party, than to convince their adversaries. So that these verbose debates seemed somewhat cold. Each one felt that the question was settled beforehand, and

x

elsewhere than at the Capitol.   What arguments could
be placed in the balance with so many sacrifices and
sorrows, so much blood and treasure ?   I passed
several days wandering through the beautiful halls of
the Capitol, more occupied, I must confess, with studying the different faces and physiognomies, the parliamentary customs, than in following the monotonous
oscillations of a discussion the result of which was
certain beforehand.   The constitutional amendment
obtained in both chambers the three-fourths majority
of votes, and since then it has already been ratified by
a great many of the legislatures; the only one till now
which has declared against the amendment is that of
New Jersey.   But it is a matter beyond doubt that it
will soon obtain a sufficient majority of votes to become an integral part of the constitution.   Thus, then,
is effaced the only stain which soiled the splendid work
of the great men who founded the American Union !
Henceforth the admiration given to it by all liberal
hearts has no drawback.

The great skill, and perhaps also the great good fortune, of the founders of American democracy consists
in having at once discovered something to oppose to
the simple and brutal domination of numbers.   This
peculiar strength, which counterbalances the tyranny of
the majority, which retains the people in a democracy
without permitting them to slide into a demagogy, which
protects the law against the surprises and temptations
of opinion, is the federal principle.   The friends as well
as the enemies of the United States too often imagine
that their government is a government of numbers;

they do not make sufficient allowance for the proportion
of the influence which has been assigned to the federal
principle. The majority has the chamber of representatives; the federal principle has the senate: it would
never enter the mind of an American democrat, however deeply attached to the idea of popular sovereignty,
that the Government could be carried on with one
chamber. The necessity of an upper chamber is so
universally recognised, that we find one in every state;
each of them taking for the model of its own particular
constitution that of the United States, gives itself a
senate as well as a chamber of representatives. Both
chambers, it is true, emanate directly from popular
elections; the senators are, in many states, re-elected
at intervals, as frequently as the representatives; the
dual principle bears none the less good fruit; it is not
necessary that the senate should be more conservative
than the representatives; it may even happen that the
senate is the more radical of the two, more disposed
for changes. The important thing is to have two chambers, two shades of opinion, two checks; the power of
appealing from Philip drunk to Philip sober.

In the central government, the authority of the
Senate is quite as important as that of Congress, and the
senators are neither chosen by the majority nor yet by
direct suffrage, for they are designated by the legislatures of their states. Quitting the immense hall of Congress, whose hundreds of members speak, gesticulate,
and struggle, how many times have I entered a little
hall, a few steps distant, where fifty persons make and
remake, amend and correct, without ceasing, the laws

which are sent to them. I have shown already how
everywhere the federal or senatorial principle finds its
way through the whole political fabric, in the framing
of parties, in their conventions, and in the presidential
elections. The civil war has not shaken this principle,
which, in my opinion, exercises a most favourable influence over political life in the United States. The
national unity, and with it the central authority, has
been strengthened, but it has not been done at the
expense of this principle. In combating for the Union,
the soldiers of Massachusetts or Maine fought also for
the glory of Massachusetts or Maine. What in the
last analysis is politics, if not a perpetual compromise
between the past and the future? In the American
system, the federal principle represents the past, the
work of time, history; the numerical, or democratic
principle, represents only impatient and still scattered
opinions in search of the future. One thing, in my opinion,
still threatens the federal principle : I allude to the debt.
Before the war, the political equality of the states in
the senate was admitted without a murmur; but is
there not some danger that the senators of a state like
that of New York, which supports the heaviest part of
the public debt, should soon feel themselves more important than those of Kansas or Minnesota? So long as
the differences between state and state bore only upon
the population, the senatorial quality did not appear
unnatural, as it was counterbalanced by the mode of
representation in Congress. But in the event of the
public debt remaining too long a crushing burden, will
not the most heavily taxed states become desirous of

possessing the greatest possible share in the legislative power? These are vague and distant dangers, which may be averted before becoming imminent, like the evening clouds which arise after a summer day, and which fade away without a storm. Every consideration, however, urges the United States to extinguish as promptly as possible a great part of the debt. Let them preserve sufficient for the national unity, but they should not keep enough to force the states to measure and weigh their services to the confederation.

If the federal principle be threatened by the creation of an enormous debt, the democratic principle is in far greater and more imminent and certain peril. I see it in the reorganisation of the rebel states, and in the situation of the enfranchised race. Will it receive, besides what we may call its natural rights, will it receive its political rights, or will it remain a despised caste, without representatives, without influence, and without power? This is the question that has assumed the first place in the United States, and which claims a prompt solution.

The rôle of the abolitionists proper came to an abrupt termination the day when Mr. Lincoln sent forth his emancipation proclamation; the abolitionists claimed for their clients only personal liberty and natural rights. But if the work of the philanthropist and moralist is done, that of the politician begins: the fate of so many men, converted from helots to citizens, cannot remain indifferent to them, whether they obtain their electoral rights or not; henceforward they must be counted as unities (and no longer as two-thirds of a unity, as before the war, and under the rule of slavery) in the figures upon which the national representation is founded. Emancipation will thus give thirty new seats in Congress to the South the day when her representatives can be admitted.

Will not this accession of political power offer serious dangers unless some means be found to reduce and overcome that spirit which armed the South, and which defeat has humiliated without crushing? Those who work for the future, and who are not blinded by the actual protestations of the old leaders of the rebellion, find their real and certain supporters among the freedmen. They seek them in vain among the whites in the South, who do not belong to the aristocracy of the old slave holders; the *poor whites* are still too blinded and ignorant to see that their true interest should bind them, as well as the negroes themselves, to the Union: during four years they have been the courageous soldiers of a cause from whose triumph they had nought to gain. Their low-minded and ignorant sentiments can only be modified slowly by time, by education, by contact with the northern emigrants, by the fecundity of free labour, and by the dying out of all that obtained their first admiration.

But how can the black race obtain political equality when yesterday it was still subjected to the most cruel oppression? President Johnson could have forced it upon the South as one of the conditions of peace; he has not done so; he has not added anything to the conditions offered to the rebels by his predecessor; he has only required of them their return to the Union, and their adhesion to Mr. Lincoln's act of emancipation. He has feared to abuse the advantage of victory and the right of the strongest. He has also feared to overstep his prerogative ; an old democrat and supporter of *state rights*, he has remembered that the Federal Government has always left to each of the Confederates the right to limit or extend at will the electoral rights. The constitution imposes on the states no particular mode of suffrage, universal suffrage no more than any other ; it only exacts a *republican* form of government. This one absolute condition will perhaps furnish to Congress the means of obtaining for the blacks that political equality which Mr. Johnson has not given them. When the new representatives and deputies of the old rebel states arrive at Washington and knock at the door of Congress, the question will be put to them : Who are you ? What state sends you ? Where is your new constitution ? Is it a republican constitution—that is, founded on equality ? You have no longer slaves, but have you no longer privileges ? Do you represent those only who have borne arms against us, and do you come still to continue the war at the Capitol ? What have you done, and what are you doing with those who have always remained faithful to us, who have borne arms and shed their blood for us ?

The representatives of the states who are now re-organising themselves in the South, under the protection of the federal arms, in the confusion of all interests, in the midst of a sort of moral and political anarchy, cannot certainly hope to return as conquerors to those halls of Congress where, during four years, their places have been empty. Congress will verify their powers, and can send them back to their provinces, if they represent rebellion instead of union, privilege instead of justice.

If, however, the states cannot be brought, one by one, to destroy, in their new Constitution, the distinctions founded on colour, there still remains one resource : it is an amendment to the Constitution, resembling that which consecrated the act of emancipation. Without entering into the details of the organic laws of the different states, it would suffice to vote an article conceived in these terms : ' No state can introduce into its laws any article founded upon race or colour.' This would suffice to protect the future of the enfranchised race. This amendment would worthily crown the great work which has been accomplished in the United States during the last five years.

The future of the black race would be too sad if the justice of the United States should not extend to it protection and hope. So long as the negro was a slave, the Southerner despised but did not hate him ; free, he will hate and despise him at the same time. A tardy justice is all the more due to a race which before long is destined to disappear in the South : slavery gave it a monstrous and factitious vitality. The population, in the breeding states, increased with abnormal rapidity. Freely mingled with the white races, the black race, under the influence of natural and fatal laws, will gradually lose its reproductive force, and be lost like a great river flowing into the sea. There will doubtless only remain sufficient traces of the race to prepare for the population of the Southern states another race, better disposed to bear the climate, without losing the habit of labour. Since the days of the black race are numbered, and fatal laws condemn it to die out, or rather to be transformed, it should be spared at least from new outrages and new injustice. Gentle, humble, obedient, and childlike, must it ever leave a dark trace in the history of the civilisation of the new continent? If liberty condemns it to sterility, let her at least give it repose. .The superior races have no need of violence to substitute themselves for the inferior. Everything serves their ambition, and their injustice oftener retards than hastens the slow work of irresistible nature.

LONDON
PRINTED BY SPOTTISWOODE AND CO
NEW STREET SQUARE

Mr. Baillière's Recent Publications.

PAUL JANET.

CONTEMPORANEOUS MATERIALISM:

STUDY OF THE SYSTEM OF DR. BUECHNER.

1 vol. 12mo. cloth, 3s.

HENRI TAINE,

Professor of Æsthetics and the History of Art in the École des Beaux Arts, Paris.

THE PHILOSOPHY OF ART,

Translated from the French, and revised by the Author.

1 vol. 12mo. cloth, 3s.

REVUE DES COURS LITTÉRAIRES

DE LA FRANCE ET DE L'ÉTRANGER.

Publishing the Principal Lectures delivered in Paris and abroad in the State Chairs and Free Classes, by MM. Franck, Alfred Maury, Ernest Havet, Ch. Lévêque, Paulin Pâris, de Loménie, Philarète Chasles, Michel Bréal, Martha, Patin, Janet, Egger, Berger, Saint-René Taillandier, Mézières, Geffroy, Caro, Wallon, l'abbé Gratry, l'abbé Freppel, Taine, Heuzey, Beulé, de Valroger, Guillaume Lejean, Jules Simon, J. J. Weiss, &c., &c.

REVUE DES COURS SCIENTIFIQUES

DE LA FRANCE ET DE L'ÉTRANGER.

Publishing the Lectures delivered before the Faculties by MM. Claude Bernard, Berthelot, Chatin, Riche, Robin, Coste, Becquerel, Vulpian, Serre, Lacaze-Duthiers, Milne Edwards, Boutan, Payen, Pasteur, Troost, Bouchardat, Jamin, Bouchut, Liebig, Moleschott, Palmieri, Remak, de Luca, &c., &c.

These Two Journals are published Weekly, in Numbers containing from 32 to 40 columns 4to.

Price of each Journal:—Six Months, 8s.; a Year, 15s.

The Subscription commenced 1st December and 1st June. The Publication was commenced in Dec. 1863.

Mr. BAILLIÈRE would respectfully inform buyers that the Books on this List are priced at Reduced Rates. To ensure their being supplied at the prices quoted, he suggests that Orders should be sent to him direct.

LIBRARY OF CONTEMPORANEOUS PHILOSOPHY.

12mo. volumes, at 2s. each.

THE FOLLOWING ARE PUBLISHED:—

H. TAINE.—Le POSITIVISME ANGLAIS, étude sur Stuart Mill.

— L'IDÉALISME ANGLAIS.

— PHILOSOPHIE de l'ART.

PAUL JANET.—Le MATÉRIALISME CONTEMPORAIN. Examen du Système du docteur Büchner.

— La CRISE PHILOSOPHIQUE : MM. Taine, Renan, Vacherot, Littré.

ODYSSE-BAROT.—LETTRES sur la PHILOSOPHIE de l'HISTOIRE.

ALAUX.—La PHILOSOPHIE de M. COUSIN.

AD. FRANCK.—PHILOSOPHIE du DROIT PÉNAL.

— PHILOSOPHIE du DROIT ECCLÉSIASTIQUE.

— La PHILOSOPHIE MYSTIQUE en FRANCE à la fin du xviiie Siècle. Saint-Martin et son maître Martinez Pasqualis.

E. SAISSET.—L'AME et la VIE, suivi d'une étude sur l'Esthétique française.

— CRITIQUE et HISTOIRE de la PHILOSOPHIE (fragments et discours).

CHARLES LEVEQUE.—Le SPIRITUALISME dans l'ART.

— La SCIENCE de l'INVISIBLE. Études de psychologie et de théodicée.

AUGUSTE LAUGEL.—Les PROBLÈMES de la NATURE.

CHALLEMEL LACOUR.—La PHILOSOPHIE INDIVIDUALISTE, étude sur Guillaume de Humboldt.

CHARLES DE REMUSAT.—PHILOSOPHIE RELIGIEUSE.

ALBERT LEMOINE.—Le VITALISME et l'ANIMISME de STAHL.

— De la PHYSIONOMIE et de la PAROLE.

MILSAND.—L'ESTHÉTIQUE ANGLAIS, étude sur John Ruskin.

A. VERA.—ESSAI de PHILOSOPHIE HÉGÉLIENNE.

BEAUSSIRE.—ANTÉCÉDENTS de l'HÉGÉLIANISME dans la PHILOSOPHIE FRANÇAISE.

BOST.—Le PROTESTANTISME LIBÉRAL.

FRANCISQUE BOUILLIER.—Du PLAISIR et de la DOULEUR.

ED. AUBER.—PHILOSOPHIE de la MÉDECINE.

LEBLAIS.—MATÉRIALISME et SPIRITUALISME, précédé d'une préface par M. E. LITTRÉ (de l'Institut).

AD. GARNIER.—De la MORALE dans l'ANTIQUITÉ, précédé d'une introduction par M. PRÉVOST-PARADOL (de l'Académie Française).

SCHŒBEL.—PHILOSOPHIE de la RAISON PURE.

BEAUQUIER.—PHILOSOPHIE de la MUSIQUE.

TISSANDIER.—Du SPIRITISME et des SCIENCES OCCULTES.

J. MOLESCHOTT.—La CIRCULATION de la VIE. Lettres sur la physiologie en réponse aux Lettres sur la chimie de Liebig. 2 vol., traduit de l'allemand par M. le docteur Cazelles.

BUCHNER.—SCIENCE et NATURE. 2 vols.

COQUEREL A. FILS.—Des PREMIÈRES TRANSFORMATIONS HISTORIQUES du CHRISTIANISME.

TO BE PUBLISHED :—

AUGUSTE LAUGEL.—Les PROBLÈMES de la VIE.

— Les PROBLÈMES de l'ÂME.

CHALLEMEL-LACOUR.—La PHILOSOPHIE PESSIMISTE.

LOUIS GRANDEAU.—La SCIENCE MODERNE et le SPIRITU-ALISME.

AD. FRANCK.—PHILOSOPHIE du DROIT CIVIL.

S. DE LUCA.—La PHILOSOPHIE CHIMIQUE depuis LAVOISIER.

JULES BARNI.—De la MORALE dans la DÉMOCRATIE.

JOLY.—L'HOMME FOSSILE.

BAUDRILLART.—PHILOSOPHIE de l'ÉCONOMIE POLITIQUE.

CHARLES DE REMUSAT.—La PHILOSOPHIE ÉCOSSAISE.

DE SUCKAU.—ÉTUDE sur SCHOPENHAUER.

FAIVRE.—De la VARIABILITÉ des ESPÈCES.

LIBRARY OF CONTEMPORANEOUS HISTORY.

12mo. volumes, at 3s. each.

THE FOLLOWING ARE PUBLISHED:—

CARLYLE.—HISTOIRE de la RÉVOLUTION FRANÇAISE, traduite de l'anglais par M. Elias Regnault, Tome 1er : LA BASTILLE.

VICTOR MEUNIER.—SCIENCE et DÉMOCRATIE. 2 vols.

JULES BARNI.—HISTOIRE des IDÉES MORALES et POLI-TIQUES en FRANCE au xviiie siècle. Première partie.

AUGUSTE LAUGEL.—Les ÉTATS-UNIS pendant la GUERRE (1861—1865) ; souvenirs personnels. 1 vol.

TO BE PUBLISHED:—

CARLYLE.—HISTOIRE de la RÉVOLUTION FRANÇAISE ; tome II : LA CONSTITUTION ; et tome III : LA GUILLOTINE.

JULES BARNI.—HISTOIRE des IDÉES MORALES et POLI-TIQUES en FRANCE au xviiie siècle. Seconde partie.

ALFRED ASSOLANT.—HISTOIRE de NAPOLÉON Ier. 1 vol.

CHALLEMEL LACOUR.—HISTOIRE de LOUIS-PHILIPPE. 1 vol.

DE ROCHAU.—HISTOIRE de la RESTAURATION, traduite de l'allemand par M. Rosenwald. 1 vol.

DE ROCHAU.—HISTOIRE de LOUIS-PHILIPPE, traduite de l'allemand par M. Rosenwald. 1 vol.

FREDERIC MORIN.—Les HISTORIENS du xixe siècle. 1 vol.

EUGENE DESPOIS.—Le VANDALISME RÉVOLUTIONNAIRE. 1 vol.

EUG. YUNG.—La RÉVOLUTION ITALIENNE. 1 vol.

Cl. BERNARD.—LEÇONS sur les PROPRIÉTÉS des TISSUS VI-
VANTS, faites à la Sorbonne, publiées par M. Émile Alglave. 1866. 1 vol. in-8 avec 92 figures.
6s. 6d.

BOUCHARDAT.—LE TRAVAIL, son influence sur la santé (conférences faites aux ouvriers). 1863. 1 vol. in-18. 2s.

BOUCHARDAT et H. JUNOD.—L'EAU-DE-VIE et ses DANGERS,
conférences populaires. 1 vol. in-8. 1s.

BOURDET (Eug.)—PRINCIPES D'ÉDUCATION POSITIVE. 1863.
1 vol. in-18 de 358 pages. 3s.

BRIERRE DE BOISMONT.—DES HALLUCINATIONS, ou HIS-
TOIRE RAISONNÉE des APPARITIONS, des visions, des songes, de l'extase, du magnétisme et
du somnambulisme. 1862. 3e édition très-augmentée. 6s.

BRIERRE DE BOISMONT.—DU SUICIDE et de la FOLIE SUICIDE.
1865. 2e édition, 1 vol. in-8. 6s.

BROUSSAIS.—EXAMEN des DOCTRINES MÉDICALES. 3e édition.
1829-1834. 4 vol. in-8. 4s.

CUVIER.—DISCOURS sur les RÉVOLUTIONS de la SURFACE du
GLOBE et sur les changements qu'elles ont produits dans le règne animal. 8e édition, 1 vol.
in-18, avec 7 figures. 2s.

DELEUZE.—INSTRUCTION PRATIQUE sur le MAGNÉTISME
ANIMAL, précédée d'une notice sur la vie et les ouvrages de l'auteur, et suivie d'une lettre d'un
médecin étranger. 1853. 1 vol. in-12. 3s.

D'ARCHIAC.—LEÇONS sur la FAUNE QUATERNAIRE professées
au muséum d'histoire naturelle. 1865. 1 vol. in-8. 3s.

DU POTET.—TRAITÉ COMPLET de MAGNÉTISME, cours en
douze leçons. 1856. 3e édit. 1 vol. de 634 pages. 6s.

DU POTET.—MANUEL de L'ÉTUDIANT MAGNÉTISEUR, ou
Nouvelle instruction pratique sur le magnétisme, fondée sur *trente années* d'expérience et d'obser-
vations. 1854. 3e édition. 1 vol. grand in-18, avec 2 figures. 3s.

ELIPHAS LEVI.—DOGME et RITUEL de la HAUTE MAGIE.
1861. 2e édit. 2 vol. in-8, avec 24 figures. 15s.

ELIPHAS LEVI.—HISTOIRE de la MAGIE, avec une exposition
claire et précise de ses procédés, de ses rites et de ses mystères. 1860. 1 vol. in-8, avec 90
figures. 10s.

ELIPHAS LEVI.—La CLEF des GRANDS MYSTÈRES suivant
Hénoch, Abraham, Hermès Trismégiste et Salomon. 1861. 1 vol. in-8, avec 22 planches. 10s.

ELIPHAS LEVI.—PHILOSOPHIE OCCULTE. FABLES et SYM-
BOLES, avec leur explication où sont révélés les grands secrets de la direction du magnétisme
universel et des principes fondamentaux du grand œuvre. 1863. 1 vol. in-8. 6s.

ELIPHAS LEVI.—La SCIENCE des ESPRITS, révélation du dogme
secret des Kabbalistes, esprit occulte de l'Évangile, appréciation des doctrines et des phénomènes
spirites. 1865. 1 vol. in-8. 6s.

GARNIER. — DICTIONNAIRE ANNUEL des PROGRÈS des
SCIENCES et INSTITUTIONS MÉDICALES, suite et complément de tous les Dictionnaires,
précédé d'une introduction par M. le docteur Amédée Latour. 1 vol. 18mo. 500 pages, 4s.
The Volumes for 1864 and 1865 are published.

HÉMENT. — Les CONFÉRENCES du quai MALAQUAIS.—Félix
Hément, les *Mouvements de la mer et de l'atmosphère.*—Louis Jourdan, *Blanche de Castille.*—Ernest
Morin, le *Cardinal de Retz et M. Vincent.* Th. Sauvestre, *De l'éducation des femmes.*—Évariste
Thévenin, *Histoire du théâtre en France.*—P. Vulpian, le *Budget de la famille et le budget de l'État,*
1re année, 1865. 1 vol. in-12 de 172 pages. 1s.

JOLY.—LEÇONS sur la GÉNÉRATION SPONTANÉE, 2 brochures
in-8. 1s.

JEANNEL (J.)—De la PROSTITUTION PUBLIQUE, et parallèle
complet de la prostitution romaine et de la prostitution contemporaine, suivis d'une étude sur le
dispensaire de salubrité de Bordeaux. 2e édit. 1863. 1 vol. in-8. 5s.

LAFONTAINE.—L'ART de MAGNÉTISER, ou le magnétisme animal, considéré sous les points de vue théorique, pratique et thérapeutique. 1860. 3ᵉ édition, 1 vol. in-8, avec figures. 4s.

LONGET.—MOUVEMENT CIRCULAIRE de la MATIÈRE dans les TROIS RÈGNES, tableaux de physiologie, avec figures coloriées. 1866. 6s.

MENIERE.—ÉTUDES MÉDICALES sur les POËTES LATINS. 1858. 1 vol. in-8. 5s.

MENIERE.—CICÉRON MÉDICIN, étude médico-littéraire. 1862. 1 vol. in-18. 4s.

MENIERE.—Les CONSULTATIONS de MADAME de SÉVIGNÉ, étude médico-littéraire. 1 vol. in-8. 1864. 2s. 6d.

MEUNIER (V.)—La SCIENCE et les SAVANTS en 1864. 1 vol. 18mo. 3s.

— La SCIENCE et les SAVANTS en 1865 (premier semestre). 1 vol. 18mo. 3s.

— La SCIENCE et les SAVANTS en 1865 (second semestre). 1 vol. 18mo. 3s.

This work is published every six months, and contains an analysis of the most important publications issued during that time.

MILSAND.—Le CODE CIVIL et la LIBERTÉ. 1865. In-8. 2s.

MOREL.—TRAITÉ des CHAMPIGNONS au point de vue botanique, alimentaire et toxicologique, orné de plus de 100 figures. 1865. 1 vol. in-18 de 300 pages. Prix figures noires, 3s. 6d. Prix figures coloriées, 7s.

MORIN.—Du MAGNÉTISME et des SCIENCES OCCULTES. 1860. 1 vol. in-8. 5s.

MUNARET.—Le MÉDECIN des VILLES et des CAMPAGNES. 4ᵉ édition, 1862. 1 vol. gr. in-18. 4s.

SHRIMPTON.—La GUERRE d'ORIENT, l'armée anglaise et Miss Nightingale. 1 vol. in-8. 2s.

SIÈREBOIS. — AUTOPSIE de l'ÂME : sa nature, ses modes, sa personnalité, sa durée. 12mo. 1865. 2s.

THEVENIN (Evariste).—HYGIÈNE PUBLIQUE, résumé de dix ans de travaux au cons il de salubrité, de 1849 à 1858. 1 vol. in-18. 1863. 2s.

VÉRA.—INTRODUCTION à la PHILOSOPHIE de HÉGEL. 4 vols. 8vo. 1864. 2nd edit. 5s. 6d.

— LOGIQUE de HÉGEL, traduite pour la première fois et accompagnée d'une introduction et d'un commentaire perpétuel. 2 vols. 8vo. 10s.

— PHILOSOPHIE de la NATURE, traduite pour la première fois et accompagnée d'une introduction et d'un commentaire perpétuel. 3 vols. 8vo. 21s. Vols. II. and III. are sold separately, each 7s. 6d.

— L'HÉGÉLIANISME et la PHILOSOPHIE. 1 vol. 12mo. 1861. 3s.

— MÉLANGES PHILOSOPHIQUES. 1 vol. 8vo. 1862. 4s.

— PROBLÈME de la CERTITUDE. 1 vol. 8vo. 1845. 3s.

— PLATONIS, ARISTOTELIS et HEGELII, de medio termino docrina. 1 vol. 8vo. 1845. 1s. 6d.

VIRCHOW.—Des TRICHINES à l'usage des médecins et des gens du monde, traduit de l'allemand par M. Onimus, avec fig. 1864. In-8. 2s.

WOILLEZ (Madame).—Les MÉDECINS MORALISTES, code philosophique et religieux extrait des écrits des médecins anciens et modernes, notamment des docteurs français contemporains, avec un Discours préliminaire de feu le professeur Brachet (de Lyon), et une Notice par le docteur Descuret. 1862. In-8. 5s.

Mr. BAILLIÈRE would respectfully inform buyers that the Books on this List are priced at Reduced Rates. To ensure their being supplied at the prices quoted, he suggests that Orders should be sent to him direct.

LIBRARY OF ILLUSTRATED
STANDARD SCIENTIFIC WORKS.

The following Volumes are now published:—

MÜLLER'S PRINCIPLES of PHYSICS and METEOROLOGY.
With 530 Woodcuts and Two Coloured Engravings. 8vo. 18s.

WEISBACH'S MECHANICS of MACHINERY and ENGINEERING. 2 vols. 8vo. With 900 Woodcuts. £1 19s. Vol. 2, separate, 18s.
Volume I. being nearly out of print cannot be sold separate from complete sets of the 'Library.'

KNAPP, RONALDS, RICHARDSON, and HENRY WATTS'
CHEMICAL TECHNOLOGY; or, Chemistry in its Application to the Arts and Manufactures.

> Vol. I., Parts 1 and 2, 8vo. contains—FUEL and its APPLICATIONS. Profusely Illustrated with 433 Engravings and 4 Plates. £1 16s.
>
> Vol. I., Parts 3 and 4, in 2 vols. 8vo. contain—The ALKALIES and ACIDS. With numerous Illustrations on Wood. 1863. £2 14s.
>
> *These Two Parts are entirely by Messrs. Richardson and Watts.*
>
> Vol. I., Part 5 completing the *Alkalies* and *Acids*, and containing an Appendix to the previous Parts, *in the press.*
>
> Vol. II., 8vo. contains—GLASS, ALUM, POTTERIES, CEMENTS, GYPSUM, &c. With numerous Illustrations. £1 1s.
>
> Vol. III., 8vo. contains—FOOD GENERALLY: BREAD, CHEESE, TEA, COFFEE, TOBACCO, MILK, SUGAR. With numerous Illustrations and Coloured Plates. £1 2s.
>
> ** This volume being nearly out of print cannot be sold separate from complete sets.

QUEKETT'S (JOHN) PRACTICAL TREATISE on the USE of
the MICROSCOPE. Third Edition, with 11 Steel and numerous Wood Engravings. 8vo. £1. 1s. Reduced to 12s. 6d.

FAU'S ANATOMY of the EXTERNAL FORMS of MAN. For Artists. Edited by R. KNOX, M.D. 8vo. and an Atlas of 28 Plates, 4to. Plain, £1 4s.; Coloured, £2 2s.

GRAHAM'S ELEMENTS of CHEMISTRY, including the APPLICATIONS of the SCIENCE in the ARTS. Second Edition, with numerous Woodcuts. 2 vols. 8vo. £2. Vol. II. separately. Edited by H. WATTS, Esq. £1.

NICHOL'S ARCHITECTURE of the HEAVENS. Ninth Edition. 8vo. with 23 Steel Plates and many Woodcuts. 1851. 16s.

MITCHELL'S (J.) MANUAL of PRACTICAL ASSAYING. For the use of Metallurgists, Captains of Mines, and Assayers in General. Second Edition, much enlarged, with Illustrations, &c. 8vo. £1 1s.

BERKELEY'S (Rev. J.) INTRODUCTION to CRYPTOGAMIC BOTANY. Illustrated with numerous Wood Engravings. 8vo. 1857. £1.

ANATOMY of the EXTERNAL FORM of the HORSE. With Explanations by J. I. LUPTON, M.R.C.V.S., and Plates by BAGG and STANTON. This Work will be completed in Three Parts, consisting of 18 to 20 Plates, with Explanations, and One Volume of Octavo Text, giving the Study of the External Form of the Horse and the Physiology of Locomotion. Part I., with Nine Plates and Explanations. Large folio. Price, plain, £1 11s. 6d.; on India Paper, £2 5s. Part II. with Four Plates (Two of which, the *Leg* and *Mouth*, are coloured). Plain, 15s.; Coloured, £1.

> ** The last Part of this important Work will be published in the course of 1866, with the volume (8vo.) of Text.

OLLENDORFF'S GERMAN GRAMMAR. A New Method of Learning to Read, Write, and Speak the German Language in Six Months. Eighth Edition, revised and considerably improved. Post 8vo. 5s. 6d.

GANOT.—ELEMENTARY TREATISE ON PHYSICS, EXPERIMENTAL AND APPLIED.

Second Edition, Translated on the Eleventh Original Edition by Dr. Atkinson, of the Royal Military College, Sandhurst. With 800 Illustrations. Post 8vo. 1866. (Adapted for the use of Colleges and Schools.)

‹ C 310 88

Printed in the United States
79550LV00004B/138

9 781429 004053